Fig. 1 — Handwoven tapestry and pile rugs. Left, top, jute and cotton rug in blue, brown, black, and white; bottom, flax and jute rug in brown, black, and white; right, hanging screen with linen and wool rug woven to match. Colors, browns and black.

From Rug Exhibition, Oregon Ceramic Studio, Portland, Oregon.
Photo by Margaret Murray Gordon. Permission, Handweaver and Craftsman.

OSMA GALLINGER TOD and
JOSEPHINE COUCH DEL DEO

Designing and Making
Handwoven Rugs

TECHNIQUES FOR CREATING EUROPEAN, ORIENTAL

AND AMERICAN RUGS AND HOUSEHOLD FABRICS

Illustrated by
DOROTHY HELEN McCLOUD
and
OSMA GALLINGER TOD

DOVER PUBLICATIONS, INC., NEW YORK

Published in Canada by General Publishing Com-
pany, Ltd., 30 Lesmill Road, Don Mills, Toronto,
Ontario.
Published in the United Kingdom by Constable
and Company, Ltd., 10 Orange Street, London
WC 2.

This Dover edition, first published in 1976, is an
unabridged republication of the work originally
published by Bramhall House, New York, in 1957
under the title *Rug Weaving for Everyone*.

International Standard Book Number: 0-486-23391-X
Library of Congress Catalog Card Number: 76-17665

Manufactured in the United States of America
Dover Publications, Inc.
180 Varick Street
New York, N.Y. 10014

TO COUNTLESS PEOPLE WHO EITHER LOVE RUGS FOR THEIR INHERENT BEAUTY AND INTEREST, OR SEEK TO KNOW MORE OF THEIR MANY DESIGNS AND TEXTURES, BY WEAVING THEM, WE OFFER THIS BOOK OF HAND-WOVEN RUGS AND THEIR FASCINATING TECHNIQUES.

Preface

WITH the increasing interest in handweaving over the past decade, rug weaving has come into its own as a popular American homecraft. A corresponding increase in the amount of instructional material, however, has not been available on this subject. While many books cover the different types of rugs which can be made by hand, up to date no one volume has been devoted solely to rug-weaving methods and designs. Through our experience in teaching hundreds of weavers, both personally and through correspondence, we have been impressed by the many requests for help in the weaving of rugs. Students ask for "different ways to weave rugs," for "new rug designs," or for a book covering the field of rug weaving only. The authors have written this book to fill this need, hoping that it will provide a basic manual of instruction for rug designing and weaving.

Our first aim is to give clear and simple directions for each different rug technique presented. In developing this directional material, we have tried to incorporate the principles of better rug designing, not only in handling traditional forms, but particularly in working with contemporary rug design. A wide range of techniques and patterns to choose from has been described here so that the rug weaver will be better able to work out his or her individual home-decorating problems. It is hoped that this book will also inspire the weaver to achieve and maintain a high level of craftsmanship in the actual making of rugs, for without this high quality no art can long endure. To persons who are not weavers, this book may serve as a cultural guide and a source of useful information on handwoven rugs, and we hope it may even inspire some of these readers to start weaving for themselves.

We feel that this book should be of special help to the home rug weaver who is looking for reliable guidance and good design ideas; to the weaving teacher, both in the field of art and in home economics and occupational therapy, who is seeking to educate her classes in the use of practical and artistic fabrics in the world of today; and to the commercial rug weaver who may find, in the study of handwoven rugs, ideas that may be adapted to the industrial market.

This book covers the methods used in weaving all types of handwoven rugs, their designing and decorative use. It includes only those rugs which are woven with the use of a weft or filler laid in across a warp, or closely related methods. Because this field of weaving is so broad, there is not room here to include the basic principles of weaving itself. We assume that the reader either knows the fundamental processes of weaving or else wishes to learn them from the many books available on the subject. However, this text is not limited to rug weavers only. Weavers seeking to adapt certain rug techniques to other types of weaving will find processes so carefully explained that they may be applied to making related articles such as upholstery, pillows, mats, or heavy fabrics in general.

Rug weaving offers a vital challenge to experienced weavers familiar with textile construction, for to design and make a beautiful floor covering is indeed a great accomplishment. Today, the avenues open in the field of commercial designing have greatly increased since more and more manufacturers have come to realize the benefit of securing rug styles designed by trained artists and craftsmen. There is in fact ample room in our American market for the better grade rug of good design and quality materials. The training and skill of our hundreds of thousands of weavers should be able to meet this need.

Any weaver, whether amateur or expert, is smart to select rug weaving as a specialty. The simplicity of the weaving processes and the small number of materials necessary make economical buying on a large scale possible, and at the same time allow a good margin of profit. From the production standpoint, rugs are woven more quickly than many items. From the sales standpoint, the rug weaver has a great advantage, for rugs have universal and practical appeal.

Let us begin to use our looms more for this highly practical form of craftwork. The field is interesting beyond measure, and we American weavers should lose no time in reclaiming our heritage, the creation of beauty underfoot.

THE AUTHORS

Contents

CHAPTER 1

Rugs and Rug Weaving

THE craft of weaving has had its appeal for homemakers since the beginning of time, and still lures us on to hours of creative pleasure. It has been responsible for the creation of a large proportion of the textiles used in the world. In some bit of handweaving the structure of every new commercially woven fabric has been conceived. From twill to gabardine, from muslin to brocade, every kind of woven cloth once originated in the mind of an individual and probably first appeared across the warp of a hand loom. We therefore owe a debt of gratitude to the loom. As Rodier says, in *The Romance of French Weaving,* "Nothing has ever been invented to take the place of the loom or to rob it of its usefulness."

A loom is a simple device which makes it possible to raise and lower a set of lengthwise warp threads held at a tension and thus form successive openings through which a weaving thread or weft is laid to make a row of cloth. A loom can be either of wood or steel, and has very few parts. It is easy for anyone to learn to manipulate, and it is fun to watch the cloth grow; anyone who has spent an hour or two laying weft threads through the shed, and feeling the rhythmic beat of the batten, will always thereafter treasure the experience. A typical rug loom is shown in Figure 6, and a diagram of a loom and its parts in Figure 7.

Many books have been written explaining the weaving process, and you will find at the end of this book a list of these, any one of which will give you a working background. This book deals only with one phase of weaving, the making of rugs. It is hoped that the rugmaker, after mastering this branch of the art, may later investigate other fields and experience the creative pleasure of weaving various articles of home decoration and personal attire.

HISTORY OF RUG WEAVING

Both from the standpoint of historical importance and decorative significance, there is no type of fabric in the world, unless it be personal clothing,

1

Fig. 2 — Detail from modern interior with handwoven wall-to-wall carpet and upholstery. By Viola Grästen, Nils Nessim Studios, Stockholm. Directions for weaving on page 102.

Courtesy — Swedish-American News Exchange

that has meant more to the comfort and enjoyment of mankind than rugs. It was not only the very first fabric put together but was often the only means of home decoration possessed by men of early civilizations. Rugs offset the bareness of dwellings, whether they were used underfoot as protection on floors of clay, stone, or marble, across openings to form doors, or as partitions to divide halls into rooms. Rugs were used as blankets for warmth and protection or to cover stone benches and tables. A traveler could roll all his possessions into a rug and go forth with his world on his shoulder. Rugs were the one indispensable item of the household and, last but not least, they were the channel through which men could transfer the beauties of the outside world to the home within. It was to make rugs that the first palace industries were formed, and there dozens of weavers sat, knotting, day by day, rug fabrics that were to become famous for all time. We find that these ancient weavers knew as much if not more about weaving than we do, and we are overwhelmed at their ingenuity in designing and their masterful flexibility of method.

The following short passage gives a vital picture of the weaving activities of those days. "Every family had its loom; everybody wove. No craft ever employed so much of the time and energy of a whole nation of people. Such a universal art always has great strength and vitality. The nomads of the desert as well as townsmen, measured their wealth by their weavings."*

Before the days of weaving as we know it, clumps of sheep's wool were

*The Rug and Carpet Book, by Mildred Jackson O'Brien (Second ed., New York: McGraw-Hill Book Company, 1951).

thrown on the earth of a hut to counteract its dampness, and the dwellers just kept walking on the fibers until they held together and formed a feltlike rug. Something more like a woven rug took shape when men laced together soft sections of tree bark or strips from the skins of animals. With the invention of the spinning wheel, men were able to weave continuous wefts over long warps to make actual rugs. From that time until the present day, methods have been devised for intertwining spun fibers of wool, cotton, linen, and silk, as well as synthetic fibers, into rugs of all sizes and descriptions.

Although a lifetime is not long enough to enjoy and become conversant with their many intriguing varieties, the rugs of the world may be listed under a few simple heads. The most important and universally made, grouped from an international viewpoint, are the types presented in this book, pile, tapestry, needlework, and woven. Many of these rugs can be woven on two-harness as well as four-harness looms, and the texture of all of them consists simply in the repetition of a knot, stitch, or weaving unit first devised by a human hand.

PILE RUGS

To Persia are attributed the very earliest and loveliest pile rugs as well as the responsibiliy for spreading the art of rugmaking throughout the world. The invention of one little rug knot, known as the "Sehna" or Persian knot, made with a tiny tuft of wool or silk, is at the root of the art of pile rugmaking. This knot and the related Ghiordes, Spanish, and Rya knots eventually covered the floors of almost all the countries of the

Fig. 3 — Floor coverings and hangings in rug techniques. On wall, left, multi-level rug of linen, jute, and wool in yellows, chartreuse, and orange. Right, mohair and wool rug. Left, on chair, rug in brilliant colors of wild cotton.

From Rug Exhibition — Oregon Ceramic Studio, Portland, Oregon. Photo by Margaret Murray Gordon. Permission, Handweaver and Craftsman.

3

world, and were repeated in thousands of different ways. Whether or not the idea came from the warm pile of animal fur which had been used since ancient days to provide bodily warmth, the pile rug certainly utilizes the same principle of insulation from the cold and is the warmest type of rug made. The Turks, defying their cold climate, sewed tufts of wool all along their warps to make their rugs warmer. The Scandinavians, too, learned from experience the wonderful insulating properties of a tufted Flossa rug, and we find the Rya knot universally employed in cold northern climates. The early colonists must have used the same reasoning, for the hooked rug was very popular in early days, both warm and comfortable to the foot and simply a variation of the tufted rug. It happens, too, that its character of many repeated knots is such that designs are easy to introduce, and the changes of color can be gradual and occur at any point. Pile rugs, therefore, prove a perennial medium of comfort and beauty.

The first pile rugs probably belonged to Persian royalty and brought the purity and brilliance of outdoor gardens to cold indoor rooms where floors were stone or marble. These rugs were huge in size and knotted by hand. Through devious trade channels, the little rug knot worked its way into other countries; but no matter where it is found, it is still called Oriental today.

The history of the transfer and growth of the art of pile-rug weaving takes us to Europe where Spain first acquired the art from the invading Moors. From there it permeated the Continent, where developed those exquisite Savonneries of France, the deep pile rugs of Austria, the beautifully dyed rugs of Germany, and the Rya and Flossa rugs of the Scandinavian countries. The

4

Crusaders brought the art to England, and there we find its careful adaptation to now famous rug types, the Wilton, Axminster, Scotch ingrain, and the Brussels carpet. In all rugmaking countries the love of flowers and gardens seems more dominant than any other note, and the strong influence of Persian designers can be clearly traced in many of the most modern pile rugs of today.

TAPESTRY RUGS

The very first tapestries were rugs, not to be hung on the wall for decoration, but to cover a palace floor, and the ancient word for carpet was *tapis*. Our later word, "tapestry," therefore, really suggests a carpet, and although wall hangings eventually received the name, a tapestry was initially a *tapis* or floor covering. It is interesting to note that the wall *tapis* was used to hang between rooms or spaces, making partitions in houses, partly to prevent sound from traveling and partly for appearance and a feeling of warmth. Hence, the texture was often heavy and thick, and tapestries and rugs were interchangeable. Only later do we find more decorative and less weighty wall hangings covering the wall itself. Among the earliest of tapestry weavers were the Egyptians, and ever since their time the art of tapestry has given rise to breathtaking examples from various parts of the world. The first tapestries, however, were quite simple in design and had very few colors. Shading was done by crosshatching at right angles to the weaving.

Like pile-rug weaving, the path of the tapestry weave spread northward into Europe where it was developed to perfection by the French weavers in their Aubusson rugs and wall hangings. No designs were too complicated for those gifted weavers to attempt, and the many alluring pastel shades of these rugs are the wonder of all who have seen them. Tapestries of extraordinary loveliness were also produced in mid-European countries — Bessarabia, Yugoslavia, Poland, and Italy — while in Norway and Sweden tapestry rugs adhere to the national characteristics of simplicity and functional beauty.

Navajo rugs should be mentioned here as a truly representative type of the American tapestry rug. They are also the oldest type of rug made in this country and are regarded by some as much a part of our heritage as old Colonial rugs. The Navajos became a relatively peace-loving people, traveling in small tribes but always weaving and raising sheep on the mountains to provide their meat and wool. Navajo rugs are in a category by themselves as they are not duplicated anywhere else in the world, and we should be proud that they originated on American soil. Genuine Navajo rugs are simple and beautiful, and some lovely ones are to be found in many of our museums, especially in the far West. They are still being woven today by Navajo craftsmen who use much the same primitive methods their ancestors used to create the first original designs, and we trust that production methods will not entirely ruin their genuine quality and beauty of coloring.

NEEDLEWORK RUGS

Several of the rug techniques in this book, although basically handwoven, owe their origin to needlework processes. Throughout the many centuries when pile and tapestry rugs were in full flower, embroidered rugs were being made on a smaller scale, mostly by unpretentious needleworkers at home. Their art, universally employed in Europe and Asia, seems to have been bypassed by production methods. Cross-stitch and chain-stitch rugs are the most familiar types. There are some lovely examples in museums, among them the famous Caswell carpet, product of a New Englander and worthy of mention because in the design of this lovely carpet are wrought much the same lovely galaxy of floral forms that the Persians used so successfully in their rugs. Its stitch, the "chain stitch," is to all intents and purposes a modern "Soumak." Our laid-in and embroidered Flossa rugs are also essentially needlework rugs.

WOVEN RUGS IN AMERICA

In the early days of our country's history, rugs of any kind were a hard-earned and welcome luxury protecting the foot from the dampness of crudely built houses. The very poorest homes had dirt floors with sand scattered over them for cleanliness, or animal hair and rushes for added warmth, a custom still continued in Norwegian farmhouses. In the better homes of the early settlers, long before wood floors were used, it was the custom to take large sails, paint them heavily on both sides to make them lie flat, and use them as a firm, protective floor covering. Tilelike figures were even painted on their surfaces, forming a design similar to our modern linoleum. Those who could not afford complete sailcloth coverage, painted smaller cloth squares to use where most needed.

Then came the rag carpet, woven on its strong flax or cotton warp and making use of discarded scraps of clothing. A sturdy type was the warp-face rug with a weft of any material whatever concealed by a brilliantly striped wool or linen warp. Later came the ingenious handwoven Colonial pattern rugs with their beautiful symmetrical designs. Little distinction was made in those days between coverlets and rugs. They were often interchangeable. It was the custom where home furnishings were meager to take the night-time coverlet for a daytime rug, or a soft warm rug for a nighttime blanket, a custom also typical of Oriental lands and just another proof of the universal similarity of our fabric needs.

The early colonists also developed to perfection a reversible-rug technique known as Summer and Winter, with design spaces predominantly dark on one side and light on the other. This idea was considered practical for rugs and coverlets, the dark side used for rough family wear especially in winter when clothes and footwear presented the problem of greater soil, and the light side saved for summer or days of entertaining. Because of its firm structure, Summer and Winter has remained one of our most useful rug methods.

The Log Cabin, too, a simple textural rug of alternating warp colors, proved practical because it offered attractive design easily achieved, and did not show soil readily. It was used a great deal in both New England and the South.

With the revival of handweaving some seventy-five years ago, there came a great interest in these and other rug techniques, some of them brought to us by citizens from overseas, such as the Mattor, Crackle, bound-weave, and variations of pile and tapestry.

The looms of America are capable of weaving any size, shape, and kind of rug that has ever been known, and the onetime dependence upon foreign imports for a high-quality product is a thing of the past, although we still do import a great many types of rug fabrics. In our factories, we now produce the traditional Brussels, Wilton, ingrain, and Axminster carpets plus the Oriental, hooked, chenille, needlework, and many others.

There is a new trend toward a plain but more textured carpet that has added greatly to the growth of the rug industry and provided opportunity for the acceptance of new rug designs by our handweavers, the more skillful of whom find their field in the creation of textures to be produced by others. The strict simplicity of modern decoration demands a departure from the standard, though beautiful and familiar forms, and so a variety of new ideas in rug textures are needed each year. We handweavers can be justly proud of our fine heritage in this important art of rugmaking and aid in continuing its creative growth.

Fig. 5 — Handwoven
tapestry and pile rug
in modern interior.

Courtesy — Clem H. Smith

Fig. 6 — A rug loom and its products. The loom is a 4-harness jack type.

CLASSIFICATION OF RUGS

The relationship of warp and weft is the factor that determines the character and kind of rugs we make. We must ask: What does the weft do as regards the warp? Does it pass through it evoking a flat rug, or is it tied to it in vertical knots making a pile rug? Moreover, if the weft passes through, does it do so from selvage to selvage making clean-cut rows; or does it connect with other wefts making tapestry?

And, if it is woven completely through, how are the warps set; close enough so that they hide the wefts, or so far apart that the weft sinks down into them; or again, at just the distance to make warp and weft show evenly?

8

These factors guide the rug weaver in an understanding of the classification of rug types according to their inherent structure.

There are two main groups of rugs:

1. *Pile Rugs* — those with tufts or loops above the flat surface:
   a) *Cut pile,* such as velvet, clipped rugs, etc.
   b) *Looped pile,* such as boutoné

2. *Flat-Surfaced* — those with warp and weft crossing at right angles, forming smooth-faced weaves:
   a) *Tapestry*
   b) *Woven:* (1) warp face; (2) weft face; (3) warp and weft evenly distributed

The succession of chapters in this book follows this simple and logical progression, which is given by Nancy Reath in her book, *Weaves and Their Classification.* We therefore start with pile rugs, the first type made by man, a simple type requiring merely the repetition of a single knot on a planned design. Yet this primitive knot, like so many little drops of water or tiny grains of sand, has given rise to some of the most impressive rugs in the world, of intricate design but simple workmanship. Next follows, as it did in history, the tapestry type, slightly more difficult to execute but quite rewarding in its provision for beauty of design and texture. It is interesting to note that both of these types offer a greater range of free design than any other types and may open avenues of creative artistry to the modern weaver.

Coming now to the rugs called "woven," possibly the best known among our American weavers are those with warp and weft more or less evenly distributed. But before we study these, there is a large group of rugs with either warp or weft, but not both, showing, known as "warp face" and "weft face." The warp-face fabric is a very ancient one coming from a time when there were no modern reeds to keep warps apart, so that they were left to gravitate together to a width of cloth governed by their size and closeness. With the filler entirely covered, all the design is in the changing colors of the warp stripes. As for weft-face rugs, the opposite is true, and the warps are so far apart that the filler sinks down covering them entirely, and all the design is in the changing weft colors, with certain rhythms and textures achieved by the threading and weft successions.

Of those rugs woven with warp and weft more evenly distributed, there is much to be said and a large part of this book is devoted to them. Beginning with the simplest two- and four-harness rag rugs and continuing through twill and pattern rugs, we shall describe many practical techniques as well as some interesting multiharness rug weaves and unusual rug textures. The chapters conclude with information applicable to all types — the designing of borders and timely suggestions to rug weavers.

9

The detailed classification given in the following chart explains the relation-ships between these types of handwoven rugs. They have been divided into two columns, one for those rugs that can be woven either on two- or four-harness looms; the other for those rugs that require looms of more than two harnesses. The weaver can thus see at a glance which types are possible to weave on his or her kind of loom. Note that many types can be woven on both two- and four-harness looms. The column at the left indicates the location in the book where each type of weave will be found.

Location in Book	Looms of Two or Four Harnesses Using Plain Weave	Looms of Three, Four, or More Harnesses
Part I	*Introduction*	
Chapter 1	Rugs and Rug Weaving	
2	Rug Design	
Part II	*Pile Rugs*	
Chapter 3	Oriental Pile or Knotted Rugs	
4	Scandinavian Pile or "Flossa" Rugs	
5	Embroidered Flossa Rug Technique	
6	Fluff Rugs and Chenille Rugs	
7	Boutoné Loop Rugs	
Part III	*Smooth-Faced Weaves: Tapestry*	
Chapter 8	Tapestry Rugs	
9	Navajo Rugs	
10	Soumak Rugs	
11	Laid-In and Imitation Tapestry Rugs	
Part IV	*Warp- and Weft-Face Rugs*	
Chapter 12	Warp-Face Rugs	
13	Log-Cabin and Basket-Weave Rugs	

EQUIPMENT AND MATERIALS FOR WEAVING RUGS (Figs. 6, 7, 8, 8a)

ESSENTIAL EQUIPMENT

A Sturdy Loom or Frame with a wide shed, Figure 6. Any strong floor loom can become a rug loom, but the shed must be wide to make room for a shuttle full of rather heavy material to be put through.

Table Looms are usually not strong enough for rug weaving, but there are some sturdy types on which it is possible to weave such objects as bath mats, as well as narrow strips of rugs which are sewed together to make larger, more serviceable rugs.

The Beater should be strong and fairly heavy. A flatiron rod may be added below the shuttle race to aid in the heavy beat.

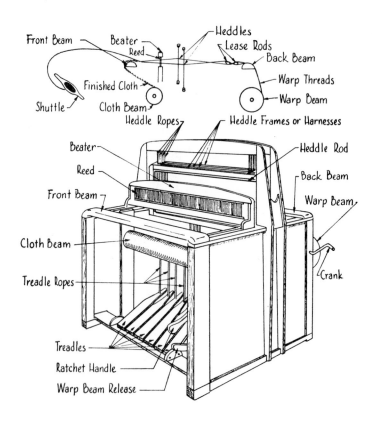

Fig. 7 — Diagram of a loom and its parts.

12

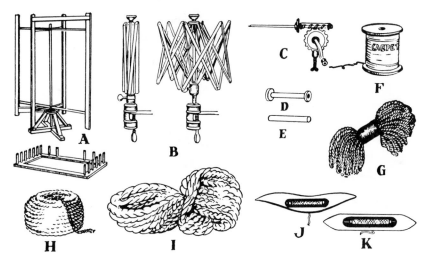

Fig. 8 — Equipment and yarn for weaving rugs.

Fly-Shuttle Looms are used by rug weavers desiring production. They are made like heavy floor looms, but have a wider reinforced shuttle race. This catches a shuttle thrown rapidly across the warp by the weaver who pulls on a cord which releases the shuttle. This is sent flying from one shuttle box to another on the opposite side of the shuttle race.

A **Warping Board or Warping Creel** (*A*, Fig. 8), from which to wind warp thread efficiently and quickly on the loom, so that the weaver will not be held up by tangles, a poor uneven warp, too long a time in warping, etc. For sectional warping, a warping creel; for chain warping, a large four-sided creel, or warping board.

A **Swift or Skein Winder** (*B*, Fig. 8), on which to place skeins of rug material for winding off on shuttles, or on which to make skeins of strips of rags such as sheeting, preparatory to dyeing. Other types of skein winders are shown in supply catalogs, and one can also wind skeins between two large extension pegs or between two chair backs.

A **Bobbin Winder** (*C*, Fig. 8), to wind thread for the binder or for the plain weave or tabby that must be woven as a heading at the ends of most rugs.

Bobbins or Cops (*D* and *E*, Fig. 8), which slip over the steel pin of the bobbin winder to have the binder thread wound around them. They are later inserted into a throw shuttle, *J* or *K*. The wooden bobbin, *D*, with its phalanges at the ends is the safer type; the stiff paper bobbin, *E*, is more economical, and can be made and glued together at home. Any cop should have its opening of such a size as to slip over the steel pin of the bobbin winder and be held firmly.

Shuttles on which to wind the various types of fillers. The type depends upon the size and kind of filler.

13

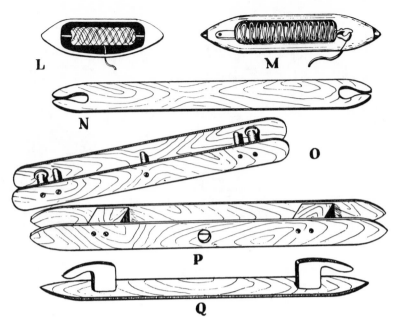

Fig. 8a — Equipment and yarns for weaving rugs.

Throw Shuttle (*J, K, L,* Figs. 8 and 8a). This is necessary to carry the bobbins of thread for the binder or plain weave. Three types are shown: closed bottom, *J;* open bottom, *K;* and a heavy boat shuttle, *L,* large enough to hold a half spool of carpet warp without rewinding it on bobbins. Larger shuttles of these types are also used for winding narrow rags and lightweight filler.

Commercial Fly Shuttle (*M,* Fig. 8a). This heavy wood shuttle reinforced with steel at the tips and sides is used to pack filler within its recess, which readily slips out of the opening at the side when the shuttle is thrown from selvage to selvage by the action of the pull rope of a fly-shuttle loom. This type shuttle is used by rag-rug weavers seeking good production.

Stick Shuttle (*N,* Fig. 8a) is the most reasonable kind of shuttle for holding rug filler. It is made of wood with a mouth at each end through which the weft can be wound and held. Stick shuttles range in length from 1 to 3 ft., depending upon the width of the warp. They are used for both carpet-warp binder and heavy filler on table looms where the shed is narrow and will not take the thicker models, *O, P, Q.*

Large Rug Shuttles (*O, P, Q,* Fig. 8a). The most commonly used rug shuttle is made of two thin sidepieces of wood, joined at a distance of 1½ to 2 in. by bars of wood or dowels. This type shuttle holds a great deal of filler and enables the weaver to go through a half or whole rug without piecing. In the shuttle at *O,* the spools at the ends revolve, making it easy to unreel the filler without twisting the shuttle back and forth. The shuttles at *P* and *Q* are excellent for holding heavy filler or rags.

14

RUG MATERIALS

The warp yarns or basic foundation threads stretched on the loom for weaving offer considerable range in size and kind, but the one requirement is that they be strong. The government has adopted the size 8/3-ply as its minimum size for strong acceptable rug warp. This is one size smaller than 8/4-ply which is the warp most used by home weavers.

The filler or weft with which rugs are woven ranges from the simplest strips of rags prepared at home to expensive wool rug yarns, some of them imported. In between we find a variety of good rug materials manufactured by our reliable thread companies — cotton, wool, and today some synthetics such as rayon and nylon.

DESCRIPTION OF WARPS

Common practice among rug firms engaged in the weaving of rugs has been to employ the following sizes: 4/4, 4/3, 5/3, 8/4, 8/3, and 9/3 ply. Handweavers have added a few more: the very strong cottons 10/3 and 3/2; and linens 10/5 and 10/2. These threads are more expensive than the cotton warps first listed, but serve to produce rugs of more beautiful finish and quality. Following is a complete list of warps, both cotton and linen, arranged according to size with the heaviest at the top, and approximate yardages. This will enable the rug weaver to estimate the cost of his rug, and he may be able to reduce this considerably without sacrificing quality too greatly. For instance, it is a perfectly possible and accepted practice to employ an 8/3-ply warp rather than an 8/4-ply, with the same setting, F, Figure 8.

In addition to cotton and linen rug warps, the weaver can use 2-ply wool yarn if quite closely twisted in its spinning. The Navajo rug weavers employ hand-spun yarns for the basis of their all-wool rugs.

Warp Sizes

Cotton		Linen	
Size: Ply	Yds. per lb.	Size: Ply	Yds. per lb.
4/4	840	10/5	600
4/3	1120	20/6	1000
3/2	1260	10/2	1500
5/3	1400	16/2	2400
8/4	1680		
8/3	2240	*Wool*	
9/3	2520	2 ply	approximately
		home-spun	1200
10/3	2800		
	(Bath mats only)		
		3 ply	800
		closely spun	

Various Rug Weights

For heavy, medium, and lightweight rugs, use the following warps:

Heavyweight Rugs: Cotton 4/4, 4/3, 3/2, 5/3, or 8/4 or 8/3 doubled
                     Linen 10/5, 20/6, or 10/2 doubled

Medium-Weight Rugs: Cotton 8/4, 8/3
                     Linen 10/2

Lightweight Rugs (or Bath Mats): Cotton 9/3, 10/3
                     Linen 16/2

RUG FILLERS

The main kinds of filler are: cotton rug yarns, 3- or 4-ply; lighter weight cotton rug-weave yarn; wool rug yarns, domestic or imported; chenille; nylon strips; silk stocking or nylon loops; thrums; and cotton, silk or wool rags. The following commercial rug fillers also are sold by our weaving supply houses: tufting yarns, mottled rug yarns, rayon fillers, hosiery loops, and other novelty items suitable for weaving rugs and bath mats.

Cotton Rug Yarn is a soft, thick filler coming in 3- or 4-ply weights, known as "Rug Yarn" or "Rugro," *G,* Figure 8, and for a lighter-weight filler for bath mats or two-weft rugs, rug-weave yarn. Cotton rug yarns range all the way from plain popular colors to mottled fillers made by the twisting of two or more colors together.

Mop Yarn, H, Figure 8, is a cheap undyed cotton filler costing half the price of regular rug yarn, but available only in natural colors.

Wool Rug Yarn is the best material for weaving rugs that will prove lastingly beautiful. It comes in 2- or 3-ply weights, *I,* Figure 8. There are some good domestic varieties and very fine imported Persian wool rug yarns.

Chenille. The rug weaver will find in cotton chenille an excellent rug material. It makes beautiful rugs and is suitable for bath mats, because it has a pleasing fluffy texture and is quite absorbent. Although it costs a bit more than cotton rug yarn, it makes a far superior rug. In fact chenille rugs in Summer and Winter or Crackle weave are good sellers. Any of the two-block patterns are excellent woven with this material. One occasionally finds a wool chenille filler, and this is recognized as superior to cotton because of its soft quality, warmth, and durability.

Attractive rugs can be woven using chenille filler with twill, herringbone, and Indian Saddle Blanket weaves; and equally effective are rugs planned in three-harness weave. The texture of chenille softens the colors which is another point in its favor.

For two-harness rug weavers, chenille makes a beautiful even mat surface when woven as plain weave only. Stripes always can be added for design to take the place of the set patterns of four-harness looms. Chenille is adaptable to both laid-in and imitation tapestry rugs.

Nylon Strips. A glossy silky rug filler now furnished by weaving supply houses and some mail-order houses that makes soft, attractive, and fairly durable rugs. This material can be used as a substitute for more expensive wool and cotton fillers in the making of both two- and four-harness rugs.

Silk Stocking and Nylon Loops are waste sections from stockings or underwear sold by knit-goods manufacturers. The material is reasonable in price and makes an attractive filler. Stocking loops can also be made at home from discarded stockings.

Rags consisting of strips cut from cotton, silk, rayon, or wool are used as the filler for rag rugs. These are usually prepared at home, although there are textile mills that sell rags by the pound.

Mill Ends. The "mill ends," such as selvages and cuttings that come from fabrics woven in textile mills, make useful economical rug filler. They are of cotton, wool, silk, and synthetics.

Woolen "mill ends" make splendid weaving filler for rugs. If the weaver lives near a woolen textile mill, it is possible to acquire the cut selvages or remnants at low cost. These soft wool cuttings from blankets, suitings, and wool yardage can be adapted by the ingenious person to take the place of more expensive wool yarn, to make a wool rug, regarded as the best rug material for warmth and comfort. This material, if all of the same color, can very well be used as pattern filler.

Cotton mill ends or selvages are excellent for rag rugs, coming as they do in gay assorted colors. Silk and rayon strips make rugs in soft attractive textures.

Thrums. The waste ends of warps can be saved for use as filler, splicing the groups as one weaves. Since warp threads are hard and closely spun, the resulting rug texture is matlike and firm.

Modern Wool Substitutes. It is generally recognized that wool makes the best possible filler for woven rugs. It is soft, warm, and durable. It is unfortunate that its cost makes it prohibitive for some. However, we are fortunate to be living in an age of creative manufacture, and in the past century we have developed new carpet materials to replace wool. There is a new rug and carpet material which may break into the handweaving field, called "carpet rayon" which is blended with wool. This is quite resistant to moths and very much stronger than the rayon found in underwear and dresses.

17

CHAPTER 2

Rug Design

RELATIVITY must always be the basis for a serious discussion of design. The basic elements of design — space, color, pattern, and texture — are each one so completely dependent upon the other that, in separating them for analysis, we must constantly keep in mind that meaningful and original design can only be brought about by the thoughtful recombination of these elements within the artist himself.

SPACE

If the floors of your home were the canvas of a painting, then every rug might be said to occupy a definite space in that painting. Actually, if an aerial photograph were taken, the average room would look very much like a two-dimensional abstract, and the location, size, and color of each object in the room would show up in a clarified and objective manner. For this reason, many floor plans of rooms are drawn for use by architects and decorators. They enable designers to see more accurately the *exact relationships of the objects and areas* with which they are working. Any one of us, therefore, as an amateur designer in his own home, might well start by working out a simple floor plan for those rooms in which he intends to place a handmade rug. Floor plans are not new to anyone who has seen the average homemaker's magazine or looked at an architect's blueprint. For our purpose here, however, we will use the simplest layout possible to illustrate the point.

Any rug that the weaver designs for a particular room might be placed, as at Figure 9, after first making a number of rough trial and error sketches. Once this is done, the imaginary rug can be brought to life by a more accurate measure of floor space and a *determination of size and shape* (such as 4 by 6 ft., oval or rectangle), by cutting out a paper pattern and reshaping it until you *feel* that the shape and size is correct. I emphasize "feel" because it is really the individual's sense of proportion more than a predetermined standard which should govern artistic judgments.

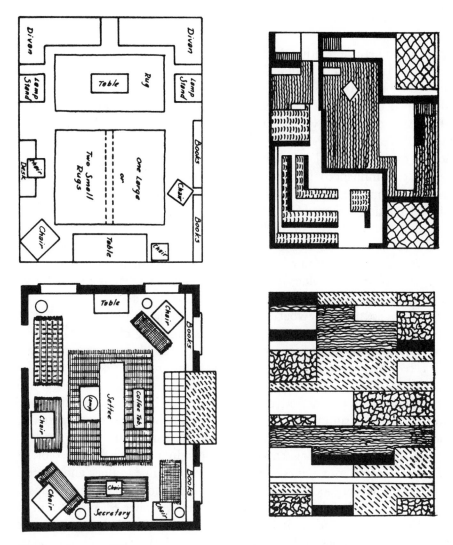

Fig. 9 — Design forms, texture types, and rug arrangement.

COLOR

The next step is to determine color. This is facilitated by the same method we used in determining size and shape. Add colored pencil to the rough sketches and you will have some idea of the color relationships in your room and what color your rug should be.

Because weaving is an art and not just a craft, the use of color is as involved as it would be for the art of painting; therefore, any complete discussion of the utilization of color in weaving is precluded. It can be briefly noted, however, that color is composed of *three important factors:* hue (i.e., green, blue, red), value (i.e., light or dark), and intensity (i.e., bright or dull).

Hue is something with which we are all familiar. It is the element of color that is most often described as "color" itself. Hue, in weaving, is achieved by the juxtaposition of one hue or color upon another. For instance, red warp over red weft produces red cloth. If it is the exact same hue of red in each case, then we say we have a "pure" color. Colors that are not "pure" in weaving are produced by combining colors of varying hues, values, and intensities (i.e., red warp over blue weft results in a purple hue). The exact hue is influenced in turn by the setting of the warp and the size of thread used in the weft. You can plainly see that we have begun a long chain of contingencies which can be solved successfully only by the experimentation of the weaver himself.

Value is easy to understand. We simply say a color is light or dark and we have the whole definition. Ordering blue, we usually state whether it is to be baby blue, royal blue, navy blue, etc. This is what is meant by value, and it is equally as important to the artist as is hue itself.

Intensity depends somewhat upon hue and value. A pink hue of low value does not have intensity or brightness. An orange hue of medium value may be said to be brilliant if it strikes the eye and holds its interest as against, say, a red hue of darker value. Perhaps the most striking examples of intensity are the fluorescent colors that we now see so often in some articles of clothing and in outdoor advertising. The color intensities used in weaving, however, are less simple to identify at first but become very apparent with practice and study. A warp and weft of the same hue make for greater intensity than is the case when one is of a lighter or a different color.

The size of the rug will determine its color (hue, value, and intensity). That is why it is a good idea to figure out size and shape first. For instance, a small rug may be bright; no brilliant color, however, is good in large quantities unless the room is big enough to allow it. A large rug is better woven in modest hues and values. The color of the rug will also be determined by what object or group of objects in the room you wish to be the center of attention. If it is the rug, make it stand out by contrast. If it is an antique cherry table, blend the rug as a complementary factor.

It would be well to state here that simplicity is the most successful rule to follow in the beginning. If the color on your paper sketch and in the skein of yarn looks different when it is woven into the finished rug, don't be alarmed. Subtle color changes offer the most thrilling possibilities in the world of the weaver.

PATTERN VERSUS DESIGN

Pattern may be divided into two parts for the sake of easy definition. It may be a *free form* or a *stylized form* which has a definite repeated motif.

Both are patterns, and the distinction between the two is not always easy to determine. For the sake of clarity, let us designate free forms as *design* and stylized forms as *pattern*. We cite characteristic examples of each.

Free forms are often used by the rugmaker in hooking, crocheting, or knitting a rug, for these techniques easily allow the inclusion of abstract shapes or the realistic portrayal of objects. In the field of weaving, the techniques available for achieving this same type of design are: tapestry, pile, boutoné, Soumak, laid-in, two-warp rugs, and shag rugs. Examples of free tapestry design forms with which we are familiar are the Navajo rugs of the North American Indian and the tapestry rugs of the South American Indian. A contemporary rug of free design by a modern weaver is shown in Figure 10.

Although the thread groupings in pattern weaving are countless, it ought to be remembered that they are also *planned groupings,* and must be thought

Fig. 10 — Pile rug in free unconventional design.

Courtesy — Robert Sailors

out to be effective. Only constant thought and experimentation with both warp and weft combinations will reveal correct settings.

Pattern is neither traditional nor modern; it is the grouping of threads in relation to spacing, color, and texture to produce the desired effect. The tendency to simplify elaborate thread groupings or patterns in modern weaving, in order to allow texture and color to predominate, is a current trend. This trend should not be mistaken as a criterion for evaluating original design.

TEXTURE

Today, if we see a rug that has a nubby or rough surface, we say it has a "nice texture." We would never think of applying the word "texture" to a finely grained Oriental rug, for instance, and yet this too has texture. By this I mean that it has a *surface quality* or *finish* all its own. The particular texture of an Oriental rug may be smooth as a mirror so that the intricate pattern and subtle colors are perfectly reflected to the beholder. If this surface were broken here and there by varying texture, or the whole surface texture were uneven, the beauty of design would be interrupted by confusing re-fractions of light. In contrast to the Oriental is the modern sisal and hemp rug or the uncut loop carpet which appeals to the observer primarily through its rough texture which refracts the light in a satisfying display of light and dark.

Texture should be the first and last consideration of the rugmaker. If the rug is to be in a playroom or log-cabin-style living room, the weaver will want a corresponding quality to be reflected in his rug. He will doubtless choose a rough texture, a simple pattern, and a practical color. An elaborately figured rug, although beautiful, would be strictly out of place in this setting.

It will begin to be seen now what is meant by "rug quality," and why we prefer to use the word *texture* in a much broader context than is generally applied. Texture is the incorporating factor of all the elements of design, shape, color, and pattern. The size and the twist of threads to be used in achieving the texture desired in your rug will be much easier determined once it has been decided what kind of "rug quality" you are working for.

If the relative aspect of original design is constantly kept in mind, it will be readily seen that any one of its elements may be used as a point of departure: a beautiful color, a special kind of yarn, or an interesting pattern. Each of these ideas can be the central theme of an effective and original design as long as the other elements are related carefully. Always remember that, in designing and weaving a rug, it is just as important to be aware of these basic concepts of design as it is to become familiar with the specific skills required to carry out the project.

CHAPTER 3

Oriental Pile or Knotted Rugs

THE soft pile rugs we walk on with such unconcern are made in a most interesting way. The word "pile" comes from the Latin *pilus,* which means "hair." In fabrics, it refers to the downy nap of a cut surface such as velvet pile, pile rugs, etc. The effect of the smooth, velvety surface is produced by clipping across the ends of many loops tied closely together over a foundation of warp. Each separate knot is tied around one or more warp threads. The manner of tying these knots distinguishes certain types of

Fig. 13 —
Group of girls
working on a
large Flossa
rug.

Courtesy — Swedish-
American News
Exchange

Fig. 14 — Example of a cut pile rug. Designed and woven by Sara Mattson Anliot.

pile fabrics. There are, in general, four types: the Ghiordes or Turkish knot, the Sehna or Persian knot, the Spanish knot, and the Rya or Scandinavian knot.

There is no reason whatever why the modern handweaver cannot learn the art of making pile rugs well enough at least to make himself a lovely rug by one of these four methods, shown in Figure 15. The technique is delightful to learn. You will find yourself always wanting to make just one more rug knot or finish another row.

TEXTURE AND DECORATIVE USE

Most handwoven pile rugs have a clipped surface with a pile of greater or less depth. They impart a feeling of warmth wherever used, both from their appearance and actual foot comfort. Examples are found in Figures 14, 16, 17, and 18. Use them in living rooms, music rooms, and bedrooms. However, it is sometimes desirable to leave the pile knots uncut to achieve a rougher, more textural, surface. This is known as uncut pile. Examples are shown in Figures 22 and 23.

COLOR AND DESIGN

In pile rugs we find possibly a greater variety of color and design than in any other type. A change of color alters the design, since the texture is always uniform. Each knot can be tied in its own color or color shade.

24

This gives the weaver an unlimited range of design. It can be free or conventional, realistic or symbolic; but the handweaver should seek just one thing, simplicity. Just a few figures and color changes give pleasing results.

Here are a few of the symbols pictured by the Oriental pile-rug weavers: the knot, the wheel, the fan, canopy and urn, the basket, book and coin, the bird, lotus flower, leaf and pomegranate, the rosette and cypress tree. They used a beautiful range of color, from sky blue to mulberry and wine, from oyster to apricot, or peach, orange, flame, and red, gorgeous greens and golds, brown and sienna, white and ebony, with dozens of shades between.

A rug weaver can study the many beautiful pile rugs in museums and plan a simpler one, either realistic or keyed to modern color blends or contrasts in space proportions. For a color palette, the yarn companies have provided an extensive range of beautiful tones and shades.

MATERIALS

Warp: Use 8/4 or 8/3 cotton set at 6 to 8 pairs per inch; or 10/5 or 4/4 cotton set at 6 to 8 single threads per inch. For very heavy rug knots, set the warp at 4 pairs per inch.

Weft: Choice of weft depends upon the thickness of the texture desired. Wool rug yarn forms a rich soft fullness. Persian rug yarn is silky and

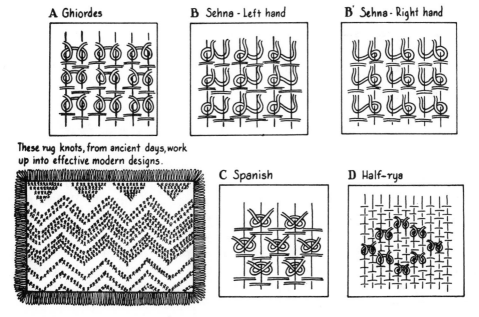

A Ghiordes   B Sehna - Left hand   B' Sehna - Right hand

These rug knots, from ancient days, work up into effective modern designs.

C Spanish   D Half-rya

Fig. 15 — The four types of pile rug knots.

25

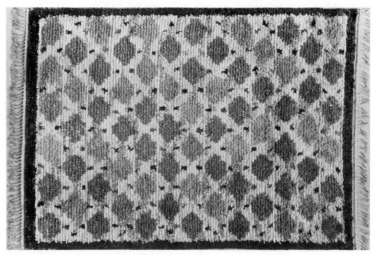

Courtesy — Swedish-American News Exchange

Fig. 16 — Carpet, "The Golden Coin," designed by Els Gullberg.

beautiful. Germantown can be used double, triple, or quadruple. Cotton rug-weave yarn can be used for a cotton texture, single for bath mats, double or triple for heavier rugs.

EQUIPMENT

Use a strong floor loom. A heavy beater is desirable.

METHOD (Fig. 15)

The four kinds of knots shown here produce slightly different textural appearances. The surface may be clipped or unclipped, the former being the usual procedure.

1. The Ghiordes or Turkish Knot (A, Fig. 15). Each knot is tied around two adjacent warp threads or pairs of threads. Weave two or more rows of plain weave after each row of knots, the number depending upon how thick the final texture should be. Make knots over the entire surface.

2. The Sehna or Persian knot (B, Fig. 15). In this knot a double looping is made around two adjacent warp threads or pairs of threads. Weave two or more tabby rows after each row of knots. Cover the entire surface with knots. The knot can be left-hand, B, or right-hand, B'.

3. The Spanish Knot (C, Fig. 15). This type is different from all the other kinds in that each knot is formed over a single warp or pair of warps instead of two adjacent warp threads, as shown at C. Weave several rows of tabby after each row of knots. Cover the entire surface with knots.

4. Rya or Scandinavian-Type Knot (D, Fig. 15). This type of knot is

26

Courtesy — Swedish-American News Exchange

Fig. 17 — Modern rug designed by Sigvard Bernadotte at Nils Nessim Studios.

similar to the Turkish knot, *A*, Figure 15, but there are more tabby rows between rows of knots, so that the pile lies flat, instead of standing up vertically, as is the case when the horizontal rows are closer. A Rya rug is shown in Figure 25. Scandinavian rugs made with fewer tabby rows between, and therefore with closer and more vertical knots, are known as "Flossa" rugs, Figures 13, 14, and 19.

"Half-Flossa" rugs are those in which sections of erect close pile form a design which shows in relief against sections of plain weave, Figure 22; and "Half-Rya" rugs are those in which sections of pile lying flat form a design set off by sections of plain weave, *D*, Figure 15 and Figure 25.

Rya Versus Flossa. The terms "Rya" and "Flossa" are not interchangeable, although both types of rugs are made with the same knot. Flossa rugs, with their closer rows of knots, are much firmer and thicker than Rya, take longer to make, and cost more, using more yarn for their knots. The ends of the knots are held up vertically by closely adjacent knots, and form a deep, full nap which, when clipped, offers a beautiful velvety-looking surface enhancing any color change planned in the design. Flossa has the advantage of the rich tones which seem to appear when one clips straight across ends of yarn, one of the pleasing characteristics of cut-pile rugs.

In Rya rugs, on the other hand, the greater number of tabby rows between rows of knots causes the knots to lie flat, forming a more flexible texture. Charming color effects are, of course, possible, with more of the thread lengths visible. Rya rugs take less material than Flossa and are more economical to make. Their soft pliability makes them desirable for bedrooms

27

and informal living rooms and, made with cotton, they make wonderful bath mats.

In Scandinavia, we are told, there seems to be a further distinction as to use. The Flossa rugs are preferred in the more sophisticated-type home of the city, and the Rya goes well in peasant households.

The next chapter will describe in detail the making of the Flossa knot and its use in Flossa and Rya rugs, giving the weaver basic and authentic information on how this simple knot is built up into successive rows to make rugs of one's own color choice and design. The same directions can be applied to both types of rug, since the weaver simply adds more rows of plain weave between rows of knots to produce a Rya rug.

There is also a type of rug which uses the same knot but, instead of spacing out complete rows of knots, the rows themselves are interrupted, and knots are made in design groups, with plain weave in a heavy tabby material. This shows up as a definite design background leaving the knots in relief patterns called "Half-Flossa." See Figures 22 and 23.

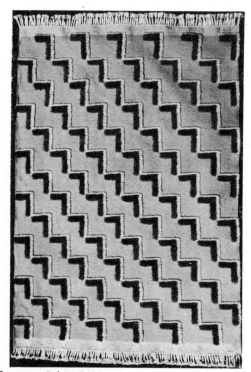

Courtesy — Robert Sailors

Fig. 18 — Pile rug with simple repeated motif. Warp, 10 ply cotton twine, 6 threads per inch. Weft, wool rug yarn.

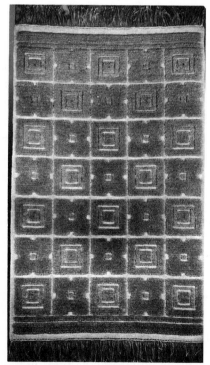

Courtesy — Viola Anderson

Fig. 19 — Flossa rug with clipped pile made of Persian rug yarn.

Fig. 20 — Circular Flossa rug of unusual design depicting the story of cotton.

Courtesy —
Kamma Zethraus
and Handweaver
and Craftsman

CIRCULAR FLOSSA RUG OF UNUSUAL DESIGN

It is very rare that one finds a circular handwoven rug. This rug of unusual conception and design was woven by Kamma Zethraus, an associate of Dorothy Liebes. It will be welcome to the handweaver who desires a beautiful round rug for a certain space. The rug, 54 in. in diameter, is woven with a deep wool pile, and a detail of the knotting is shown in Figure 21, the finished rug in Figure 20.

In this rug the designer depicts the beauty of growing cotton. Three bolls of cotton are shown spilling cotton toward the center of the rug. The wide dark portions represent the outer shell of the bolls and are the brown background showing without knots covering it. The fine dark lines represent the outlines of the cotton tufts. The Swedish Flossa technique was used; see Chapter 4.

The white portions of the rug were knotted with bleached worsted and all of the darker portions in mohair. The warp is heavy linen, about as

Fig 21 —
Close-up of
process of
making Flossa
rug knots.

Courtesy —
Kamma Zethraus

heavy as carpet warp, threaded to diagonal twill set at 10 per inch, and the weft dark brown oxhair. There are five rows of white knots per inch with two twill rows of brown oxhair between all rows.

When this rug was taken from the loom its beauty was further enhanced by shearing and shaping it with scissors. The curving outlines of natural mohair acted as margins toward which to round and trim the white bolls and the mohair outline tufts were trimmed off closely, nearly to the brown background. The excess corners of weft background were trimmed off following the round outline of the Flossa. The sheared edges were stitched on a sewing machine. A tape facing stitched to the back of the rug provides a firm finished edge.

RUG SETTING

Warp: Heavy linen set at 10 per inch
Filler: Thick white wool, dark brown oxhair and mohair
Knots: Each knot tied over two warp threads
  Five knots per inch, horizontal
  Five rows of knots per inch vertical
  Depth of pile about 1½ in. Use 1½-in. Flossa bar.

30

CHAPTER 4

Scandinavian Pile or "Flossa" Rugs

TECHNIQUE

THE Flossa rug technique employs the same method as the Ghiordes Oriental rug knot. It is used in Scandinavian countries for rugs, seat cushions, footstools, mats, and pillow covers. The knots are tied on the warp threads and clipped after the weaving has been finished to form a pile surface, the strands of clipped yarn standing at right angles to the fabric. The word "pile" refers to a nap surface made up of erect hairs or fibers on the surface of the cloth, like velvet, Oriental rugs, etc. After a design has been formed by tying knots or loops across the warp according to a plan, the ends are clipped to form tufts; and these, when sheared still closer, form a smooth nap for the rug surface. In making pile rugs, every knot is tied separately over a pair of warp threads, a longer process than weaving with rug yarn across many warps at the same time. The method described below is an authentic Scandinavian technique and should be followed as closely as possible. An actual rug in process of weaving is shown in Figure 13.

The Flossa rug technique is simple enough to be easily mastered, yet interesting enough to hold the weaver fascinated as he acquires the rhythm of making the knots, and of finishing row after row of the fluffy wool or cotton pile surface. It is a technique in which the weaver may strive for a quality product dependent only upon his care in weaving and the acquisition of skill resulting from practice. It challenges him to conscientious effort, for in this type rug only firm careful knot-tying gives satisfactory results. Although these rugs take longer to make than any other kind, the result is considered worth the effort, and a well-made Flossa rug will last much longer than the person who weaves it.

TEXTURE

In Flossa rugs, the knots may cover the entire surface of the fabric (see Figs. 16 and 17) or they may be used only as raised parts where the design occurs (see Figs. 22 and 24). The background parts are plain or tabby weave using a heavy yarn. In this case the rugs are known as "Half-Flossa."

The type of Flossa rug described in this chapter is formed of solid rows of knots with several rows of tabby between the rows, this being concealed by the tufts. The following definitions describe variations of this standard form.

For *Half-Flossa,* make close knots over that part of the surface which is designated by the design, and weave heavy tabby rows between to show as background.

For *Rya* rugs, make complete rows of knots but between each row weave from two to four times as many rows of plain weave as described for Flossa rugs.

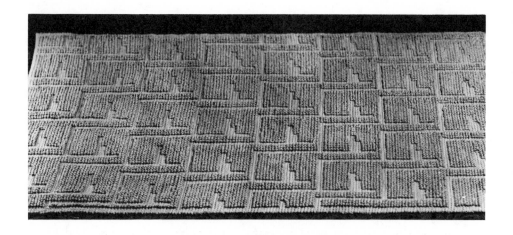

Fig. 22 — Half-Flossa living room rug with uncut pile.

Fig. 23 — Close-up of texture of rug in Fig. 22.

Courtesy — Helen Druley Eeles

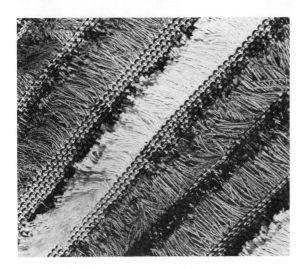

Fig. 24 — Modern Half-Flossa
rug with wool added to
warp ends for
braided fringe.

Fig. 25 — Detail of Rya
rug with intermittent
stripes.

Courtesy — Robert Sailors

For *Half-Rya* rugs, make the knots only at those places designated by the design, so they appear as groups or part rows with plain weave showing as background. But in Rya, no matter whether we have complete rows or part rows, the rule of more tabby between rows always holds, so that the finished knots and their ends lie flat.

DESIGN AND COLOR

While the surface is uniform, the color of the knots may vary. A design worked out on graph paper is followed. Each square represents a complete knot made over two heavy warp threads, as shown in *D,* Figure 27. A new color may be started at any knot by cutting off the end of the old color and changing colors at the next knot. One horizontal row of squares becomes one row of tufted weaving, with each square transformed into its own colorful tuft. This makes it possible to obtain very beautiful color effects, using small bits of colored wool. The paper design should be colored for ease of copying. Since each knot is independent, a new color can be started anywhere. See the colored rug design hung above a Flossa rug in process in Figure 13.

The weaver has a wide range of possible motifs from which to choose, with varied and subtle effects due not only to choice of color and design, but to the unexpected shadings produced by the clipped yarn surfaces. Motifs range from birds, flowers, trees, and traditional emblems to modernistic forms of every conception. The blends of color possible can only be discovered by studying pile rugs in museums, especially Persian pile rugs, noted for their beautiful color blendings.

To test both design and colors of a planned Flossa rug, first make a colored design on graph paper, then weave a small section of it only on your loom, employing all of the chosen colors. Clip the loops and discover the effect of resulting surface colors, for they are often quite different from the color of the yarn in its skein. You can then be sure of your results in the large rug on which you will spend so much time and which should justify its creation by its final successful color blends.

PREPARATION OF MATERIALS (Fig. 26)

The material most often used for the knots is, of course, woolen yarn; yet these rugs are sometimes made of heavy cotton rug yarn, or of a multiple-strand material, such as tufting cotton. Rags, too, may be used for both the knots and the background, but they should be most carefully cut and of good quality. The amount of work does not justify using rags, however. On Half-Flossa rugs, a rag weft can be used for background tabby between wool knots.

Warp: Use 8/4 or 8/3 carpet warp set at 16 threads per inch (8 pairs); or 4/4 cotton or 10/5 linen warp set at 8 single threads per inch.

Weft: Soft, heavy, well-twisted wool, such as weavers' rug wool, Persian rug yarn, etc.; or Germantown used double; or rug-weave cotton, a light-weight cotton rug yarn.

Binding Tabby: Double carpet warp or thrifty-knit cotton, homespun wool, or 4-strand cotton. Heavy 10/5 linen also may be used for binder.

Preparation (Fig. 26). Assemble all colors on a table. The easiest way to work when knotting a rug is to have ready a small skein of each wool color. Hang a goodly number of skeins from the top of the loom as shown in Figure 13 and *G,* Figure 26, or place the skeins in a basket beside the loom.

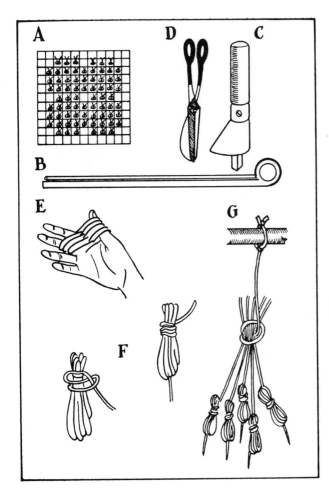

Fig. 26 — Preparation and equipment for Flossa rugs.

A skein is made by wrapping the rug yarn in and out between the thumb and first pair of fingers, as in *E*, Figure 26. Leave 1 ft. of the first end hanging when starting, and wrap the last end around the skein in a collar as in *F*. Make a slipknot to fasten the end as shown. To use, attach the end of the skein to the rug, and it will keep pulling out, as much as necessary. Arrange a group of these skeins, and fasten them together with a cord attached to the top of the loom, as in *G*.

EQUIPMENT (Fig. 26)

Kind of Loom. Use either a two-harness or a four-harness loom. A floor loom with heavy beater will give the best results, for this type of rug must be firmly beaten to "pack" the rows of knots.

In addition to the loom, the following appliances are needed in weaving Flossa rugs.

A Gauge Bar or Flossa Bar (*B,* Fig. 26), over which the knots are tied. This consists of two flat rods of iron, held together at one end by a clamp or welded handle. The other end is also closed by welding. This bar should be long enough to reach across the warp, and its width determines the length of the final cut tufts, as the wool goes around the bar between the knots. The usual width is ½ to ⅝ in. If two metal rods are not available, use a single bar of wood of such width and thickness that the tufts will have the right depth. Flossa bars are available at some suppliers.

A Sharp Knife (*C,* Fig. 26), also called a cutting knife. This cuts the knots of wool by passing quickly along over them, with its blade sinking between the two flat rods, or if a wooden rod is used, with the blade passing straight down the middle of the rod, and sinking down into the wood when cutting. Any good sharp knife may be used.

Sharp Shearing Scissors (*D,* Fig. 26), for trimming surface of tufts when rug is finished.

METHOD (Fig. 27)

Threading. The Flossa knots are made on a tabby or plain-weave background. Any threading that will give tabby or plain weave can be used.

The total numbers of warp threads across the loom should be even. Call shed 1 the shed made by raising the odd-numbered warp threads 1, 3, 5, 7, etc.; and shed 2 the shed made by raising the even-numbered warp threads 2, 4, 6, 8, etc.

Weaving a Tabby or Heading. For the tabby binder, use carpet warp double, its equivalent, or a heavier cotton such as 4-strand. Homespun wool is effective. Weave a heading of 1-in. plain weave to make a firm end. Start weaving left to right, *A,* Figure 27, tucking the end into the second row. Weave about 1 in., ending at the left and passing *under* the last two pairs of warp as at *B.*

The authentic heading of the experts is made of alternate rows of black and either white or gray tabby. In adopting this tradition, start the black at the left and the white from the opposite side. Cut the black off next to the last row, bringing the white from the right and passing under the last two pairs of warp, *B.* From now on weave only with white.

Weaving First Row of Knots. The Flossa knots are made on a closed shed, all warps on the same level.

For the very first knot, insert the end of the wool skein up and under the second pair of warps, as at *C.* Carry to the right over the third pair, down to the left, and out between the second and third pairs as at *D.* Pull taut.

Lay a gauge bar or wood rod over this knot as at *E,* with the handle or longest end at the right. For the next knot and for all knots hereafter, carry the wool *over* the bar, *E* to *F,* then up under the next pair of warps,

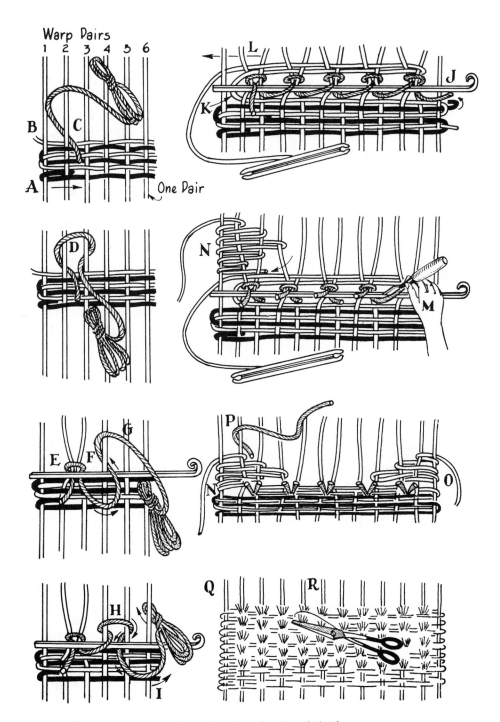

Fig. 27 — Method of making Rya knot for Swedish Flossa rugs.

F, to the right over the next pair, *G,* then out between *F* and *G* and *under* the bar at the same time as at *H,* curving arrows. Repeat this process for each knot, always going over the bar at the beginning of the stitch, *I,* and under it at the end of the stitch, *H.* Leave the last warp thread, *J,* empty and clip off the yarn after the last knot at the right, leaving an end of 1 in. The detailed sketch shows only a few warp threads. A photograph of the process of knotting over a gauge bar is shown in Figure 21.

It takes two pairs of warp threads for each knot, *D,* or two heavy single threads if 10/5 linen is used. Since there are 8 pairs per inch, the rug will have 4 knots or tufts per inch. A rug 30 in. wide will have 240 pairs of carpet warp or equivalent in 240 heavy single warps, and 120 knots in each row, less two knots, or a total of 118, as a pair of warps is not used for knots at each side.

Binding First Row of Knots. Two rows of plain weave follow each row of knots and are woven in at once before cutting the loops or pulling out the bar. The last row of plain weave ended at the left, *B.* Make the next shed for left-to-right weaving. Carry the binder thread under the bar, omitting the last warp thread as at *K;* weave to the right; change sheds, and weave to the left, *omitting* the last warp at the right, *J;* and passing under the last two warps at the left on the last row back, as shown at the arrow, *L.* If the wool used for the pile is heavy four rows of plain weave may be woven here instead of two. The object is to make a firm background and to hold the knotted rows apart to prevent too thick a pile. For a Rya rug, weave from six to ten rows of plain weave between rows of knots; see Figure 25.

Clipping First Row of Knots. The plain weave now holds the knots firm enough so that they can be clipped. Run a very sharp knife rapidly left to right through the center of the metal bar groove or between the two wood bars as at *M.* If the knife does not sever the loops, run it through again. Pull out the bar and beat the tabby against the cut pile row with several firm beats.

Extra Selvage Fill-In. A fine point in the art of Flossa rugmaking is filling in the selvages left open by skipping the last warp. There are two reasons for the extra fill-in: first, to make a firm edge; second, to blend the selvage color with the rest of the rug. The tabby is white or neutral, and would form a harsh contrasting line if brought to the edge. For the fill-in triangles, *N,* use a strand of wool similar to the main color of the tufted design. Make a skein of this wool. Start it back in selvage as at arrow *N,* then weave back and forth, in and out two pairs of warp; for the next row, take in three pairs, then four; reduce to three and two and finish at the left. Let the skein drop until ready for the next triangle at the end of the next row of knots. Make another skein, filling in the right side as at *O;* leave the end hanging. Beat again to squeeze down both triangles.

Second Row of Knots. Start with the desired color of rug yarn with the end, *P,* exactly the same as at *C.* Continue the steps as follows:

NOTE: If your warp is composed of heavy single threads, substitute these for warp pairs in the wording.

1. Make a row of knots, omitting outside warp pairs.
2. Weave two or four rows of plain weave, omitting outside warp pairs.
3. End shuttle under last two warp pairs at left.
4. Fill in with rug yarn at left and right sides; beat all up firmly.

If the rows of fill-in build up too rapidly to maintain level weft rows, make fewer rows of fill-in.

A wise precaution on the part of the weaver — if he wishes a truly successful rug — is to weave a small sample. This serves several purposes: in addition to giving him the general effect of the rug and the color tones which will appear when the rug is clipped, it discloses the number of rows of fill-in necessary. The materials themselves — warp, filler, and binder — determine this, as well as the number of tabby rows between tufts and the most desirable length of tufts.

Shearing Rug Surface Smooth. The rug has been completed. All rows have been cut at the same height with a knife, and the finished appearance resembles *Q.* Give the rug an extra shearing with a sharp scissors, *R,* to make the pile surface as level as possible. There are special shearing scissors available with handles curving higher than the blades. You will be more than pleased with the lovely tones of the clipped rug yarn and the matching edges effected by the fill-ins. The underside of the rug will have a firm durable base because of the binding plain-weave rows between rows of knots. The rug will be beautiful in texture if the knots have been carefully and snugly tied, and the successive rows of knots and plain weave firmly beaten into position.

PILE RUG WITH SMOOTH BASE

Instead of tying the knots over pairs of warp on a neutral shed, tie them on the upper warp threads only of one of the sheds, but always the same one. For instance, raise shed 1 of a plain-weave shed. Tie in a row of knots with any of those shown in Figure 15, using two adjacent warps or two pairs of adjacent warps (four warps) in the upper shed only. In the same shed 1, weave a row of tabby and a second row on shed 2.

For the next row of knots, raise shed 1 and tie in a row of knots. Follow with two rows of tabby, one on the same shed 1, the other on shed 2.

This technique produces a fabric with a very flat smooth base or undersurface. The warp should be set somewhat closer, such as at 10 or 12 pairs per inch. Free designs on graph paper guide the worker, with one square for each pair of threads in the upper shed.

CHAPTER 5

Embroidered Flossa Rug Technique

THE embroidered Flossa rug weave is an interesting rug technique which resembles Flossa rug weave but is executed with a needle threaded with rug yarn on a fabric which has been prewoven. The worker can weave his own background fabric and attach the Flossa loops with the needle. This technique will be welcome to those weavers who do not have a strong floor loom on which to make firm rugs, for they can weave the background cloth, even on a table loom in narrow strips to sew together, and make the rug later as a living-room project. The loops are made over a bar just as in Flossa, and the results are much the same. In fact, the technique was created in Scandinavia (see Fig. 28).

TEXTURE AND DECORATIVE USE

The texture is a clipped pile with fluffy ends made by cutting the embroidered loops. The loops can cover either the entire surface, making a solid pile ground, or only part of it, producing a half-tufted texture. The worker has great liberty in controlling the thickness of the pile surface by the distance he allows between loops.

Like all pile rugs, embroidered Flossa rugs are welcome wherever warmth is desired or where absorbent surfaces are practical. This places them in the den, bedroom, or bath. If a coarse material is used for the loops, such as heavy rags or jute, door mats can be made by this method.

COLOR AND DESIGN

The weaver can make extensive design and color plans, for the method permits the addition of designs at any point, free or conventional. Rugs may be made with a modern allocation of design spaces using well-balanced blends of shades or color contrasts. Traditional backgrounds also can be used to set off design figures — flowers and trees, rug motifs of all kinds, such designs as the ancient rug weavers planned so carefully for their rugs.

Designs are made like cross-stitch patterns, worked out on graph paper, each square covering ¼ in. space of the finished rug. Knots at every ¼ in. make a well-filled fluffy surface.

The weaver should assemble the selected colors, prepare them in skeins as described for Flossa rugs, Figure 26, and hang them over the loom or nearby.

MATERIALS

Instead of a warp to weave on, this technique starts with a fabric already woven with a wool weft on a linen or cotton warp. The loops are made on this woven background.

For the sewed loops, use wool rug yarn for the softest texture, or make heavy rug yarn by threading two strands of Germantown or 2-ply yarn through the needle, folding it back on itself, making four strands in all with which to sew.

Cotton rug-weave yarn is a substitute for wool and costs much less, although the finished rug will not be as satisfactory as one made of wool.

EQUIPMENT

To weave the background fabric, use a strong two- or four-harness loom wide enough to make the size rug desired, or sew narrower strips together.

For making loops, one large needle, either a candlewick needle or a large upholstery needle, is required.

A stick measuring ¾ in. wide, ⅜ in. thick, should be tapered at one edge to ⅛ in., and the other edge should have a groove running down its length, K, Figure 28.

METHOD OF WEAVING THE BACKGROUND MATERIAL

Warp Plan

Warp: Linen 10/5, 20/6, or 10/2
   Cotton 4/4 may also be used

Weft: Wool yarn the same weight as the warp or a bit heavier

Flossa Weft: Rug yarn used singly and doubled back from the needle, making two strands; or Germantown or Norwegian 2-ply yarn used double, and doubled back, making four strands

Threads per Inch of Background Fabric: 15 threads, arranged in 5 groups of 3 threads each

41

Loops per Inch of Embroidered Flossa: 4

Threading Plan. Harnesses 1, 2, 1; 4, 3, 4. Repeat all.

   Sleying: Sley in a 10-dent reed, 3 threads (1, 2, 1) in a dent; skip a dent; 3 threads (4, 3, 4) in a dent; skip a dent. Continue this. Or, if the warp is not too heavy, use a 15-dent reed, 3 in a dent, skip 2 dents, and repeat.

Weaving Plan. One shuttle only of wool-yarn weft.

   Mat texture: One row each: harnesses 1–2, 3–4, 1–2, 3–4, 1–2, 3–4, then 1–3, 2–4. Repeat all. At points where tabby harnesses 1–3 and 2–4 occur, there will be openings like holes in which to sew the Flossa loops.

   Entire plan: Plan the size of the rug. Weave this as a heavy finished mat to size plus the fringe, using a heavy yarn for the first and last 2 in. of the rug. The rest of the mat will be covered; weave this so as to produce openings, *I*. These form marked points for attaching the loops.

End of Mat to Show, A–G.

   A. Leave 4 in. of fringe.

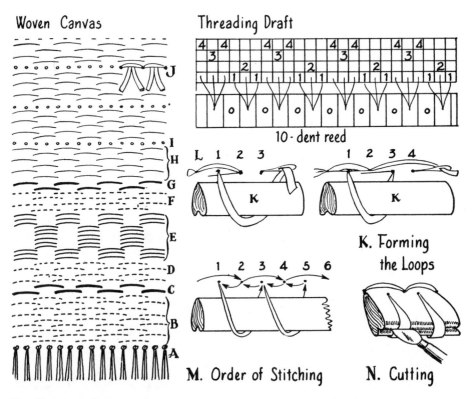

Woven Canvas

Threading Draft

10-dent reed

L. Forming the Loops

M. Order of Stitching

N. Cutting

Fig. 28 — Needlework Rya rug method.

B. Weave with light-colored wool, harnesses 1–2, 3–4, 1–2, 3–4; repeat for a width of about 1 in.

C. Weave with dark wool, harnesses 1–2, then 3–4, two rows, forming a thin stripe across.

D. Light, 4 rows: harnesses 1–2, 3–4, 1–2, 3–4, about ½ in.

E. Harnesses 1–2 light; 3–4 dark. Repeat three times, 6 rows. Change to harnesses 1–2 dark; 3–4 light; repeat six times, 12 rows. Change to harnesses 1–2 light, 3–4 dark; repeat three times, 6 rows.

F. Same as D.

G. Same as C.

Main Texture. This consists of woven sections, *H,* interrupted by rows of holes, *I.*

H. Between holes: Light, harnesses 1–2, then 3–4. Repeat three times, 6 rows or about ½ in.

I. Row of holes: Light, harnesses 1–3, 2–4, 2 rows only. Keep repeating the main texture; then reverse to the other end, following *H* with *G,* etc.

METHOD OF MAKING LOOPS

Form regular Flossa knots over a bar and attach them to spaced openings in the mat fabric which is constructed along the same principle as cross-stitch material with regular spaces for sewing. See two finished loops, *J,* Figure 28, after bar has been removed.

Sewing: Start the needle of wool as at *L.* Take one backstitch to fasten the end; then enter at a point beyond the first opening, i.e., at point *2,* and out at point *1,* ready to start a loop. From now on there are two stitches only to make all the way across each row of openings, *I.*

First Stitch: Place stick *K* below the openings. Carry the yarn down over the stick, up under the stick, skip opening *2;* enter the needle at the next opening *3,* out at *2.* This produces a loop.

Second Stitch: From opening *2,* carry the needle and yarn to the right, skip the next opening, *3,* enter at *4,* out at *3,* forming the top or fastening of the loop. The needle at *3* is now ready to pass over the stick for the next stitch.

Continuous Order of Stitching, M: Go around the stick, skip opening *4,* enter at opening *5,* back and out at *4;* then fasten, sewing from *6* to *5,* etc. Always progress two points forward to the right and one point back to the left.

Cutting, N: Use a sharp sturdy knife. Turn the stick up so that the groove is in a good position to cut. Pull the loops taut. Run a knife along the groove, cutting the loops as at *N.* Make the loops as far as the length of the stick, then cut; remove the stick, insert it again, continue to the right, etc.

CHAPTER 6

Fluff Rugs and Chenille Rugs

FLUFF RUGS

Among the most interesting and valuable textures for the home weaver are those in which a looped warp or weft produces a shag-surface effect, or those in which these loops may be clipped to form a pile surface. The method given here proves a rapid way of obtaining a pile rug. The threading is easy and results in a soft rug that is a pleasure to step on, excellent for bedside rugs and bath mats.

While in Flossa-rug weaving the weft is looped around a bar and the loops are clipped, in the method shown here the loops are produced by simple weft overshots across a wide block, *B–C,* Figure 29. These overshot loops are clipped later with scissors and fluffed up by brushing, *E.* The threading is so arranged that there is a tie-down at intervals of every 2 in., *A–B.* The overshot loop thus produced is cut in half to form a shag 1 in. high, *B–C.* For a shorter shag, plan overshot loops 1½ in. wide, making loops ¾ in. high. The tie-down sections consist of from 6 to 8 threads in twill or its reverse. This same technique may be used for heavy seat mats and pillows.

TEXTURE AND DECORATIVE USE

While the "fluff" of these rugs is not as full or closely set as the looped and cut weft of a pile rug, the surface has just enough shag to make it a soft pleasing texture. The method is best employed for bath mats and soft bedroom rugs.

DESIGN AND COLOR

Designs are in horizontal stripes since, in order to be woven easily, the weft must be continuous. A new weft color can be introduced at the selvages. Two alternating wefts can also be used since their strands go along continuously; and with two well-planned colors this gives a delightful effect. However, just one color makes an attractive mat, especially in pastel shades.

The pattern weft is what makes the "shag." Each row is followed by a row of tabby which binds it down and forms a permanent background

44

surface to show between the loops after they have been clipped. For this reason the tabby weft should be fairly heavy, such as carpet warp doubled or 4-strand cotton, or any weft which will fill in well. The pattern weft or fluff material may be rug-weave cotton yarn or tufting cotton used double, soft-wool rug yarn which fluffs up nicely or several strands of Germantown wool used together — in other words, a filler lighter in weight than regulation rug filler, since the ends combine to make tufts.

WARP PLAN FOR FLUFF RUG

Warp: Carpet warp 8/4, 8/3, or 5/3; or 10/2 linen.
Weft: Pattern: Wool or cotton rug yarn or rug-weave yarn
   Tabby: Carpet warp doubled, or weft heavy enough to produce a firm
      matlike surface
Threads per Inch: 12 to 15
Width: As desired

THREADING PLAN

The threading plan of Figure 29 gives a twill tie-down, *A* to *B,* which alternates with the overshot section for the loops, *B* to *C.* Note that the tie-down section has double threads at start and finish for strength to hold the loops. To thread this section, thread in succession two separate threads on harness 1; a single thread on each of harnesses 2 and 3; then two threads in succession on harness 4. Do not put through one heddle as a pair, but place side by side without doubling, one thread each through successive heddles on harnesses 1 and 4, which form flat pairs when woven. Although through separate heddles, they are sleyed together through the same dent.

	Threads
Selvage	4
Pattern, A–B, 6 threads	6
B–C, 30 threads	30
Repeat *A–B,* then *B–C,* a total of 36 threads, as desired.	
End with *A–B*	6
Selvage	4

WEAVING PLAN

Tie-up Counterbalanced Harnesses	*Tie-up* Jack Harnesses	For Weaving	Use Treadle
2–3	4–1	Pattern	1
1–3	2–4	First Tabby	2
2–4	1–3	Second Tabby	3

45

Start the rug with a section of plain weave. Then weave in the following order:

Harnesses 2–3, pattern yarn; harnesses 1–3, tabby thread; then harnesses 2–4, tabby. Repeat these three rows. If you wish more tufting to show, weave: harnesses 2–3, pattern yarn; harnesses 1–3, tabby; harnesses 2–3, pattern; harnesses 2–4 tabby. Repeat these four rows.

METHODS OF WEAVING (Fig. 29)

A rug can be woven entirely of the overshot loops with tabby after each row, thus making a complete fluff surface, *F;* or sections of overshot with

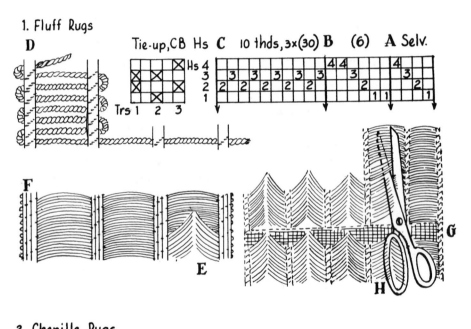

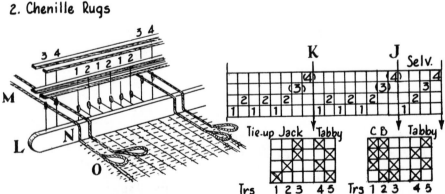

Fig. 29 — Methods of making fluff rugs and chenille rugs.

sections of plain weave between, as at *G,* can be woven; shag borders at the ends with plain weave for a center section may be preferred. In this case make end borders 5 or 6 in. wide by weaving across the entire width of the rug for this distance. Then weave fluffs at the edges only to form vertical side borders, reversing the fluff weft back and forth for 2 or 3 in. at the sides, as at *D.* This gives fluffs across a wide margin at the base, and across the width desired for vertical side borders.

A very narrow edge border of tufts can also be woven, then a wide border of tabby, followed by a center of tufts. One row of tufts for a narrow 2-in. border is made by reversing the pattern weft around the first section, as shown in the sketch, *D.*

CLIPPING TUFTS

Use long sharp scissors, and be careful not to cut into the plain weave under the overshot loops. Cut at the center of each loop section as shown at *E* and *H.* After clipping, fluff up the tufts by brushing with a stiff brush.

CHENILLE RUGS WITH WARP LOOPS

There is a type of rug in which loops of warp make a shag surface at intervals. This technique is called chenille by some, but is not to be confused with the rough-surfaced texture, "chenille," of twice-woven rugs.

TEXTURE AND DECORATIVE USE

This technique is also used effectively in drapes and seat mats. Clusters of loops can be set off against plain backgrounds to form designs in both drapes and rugs.

Chenille rugs with warp take-up can form most beautiful floor coverings, such as that shown in Figure 30. The design can be planned for texture contrasts between the background surface and the clusters of warp loops. As such, rugs in self-tone are especially effective.

Chenille rugs are suitable for studio interiors, living rooms, libraries, and music rooms. They offer opportunities for subtle rug designs. If woven with warp and weft and chenille loops, all in the same color, lovely shades and shadows bring out the contrasting textures.

EQUIPMENT

Two warp beams are necessary for this type of rug, one to carry the yarn for the chenille loops, the other the plain background warp. Incidentally, the method is similar to that used for making velvet. The loom must be strong, the warp beams strong; the chenille roller can be weighted. The method of adding an extra warp roller is detailed in Chapter 27, Figure 110.

Courtesy — Thurman Hewitt

Fig. 30 — Studio rug woven with warp loops, chenille fashion, an ideal rug for the outdoor living room.

A bar for drawing up warp loops is also needed. Its width is usally 1 to 2 in., but it should be the size necessary to make loops the desired length, N, Figure 29.

MATERIALS

The warp and tabby weft should be carpet warp 8/4 or 8/3 doubled or 10/5 linen or 4/4 cotton warp used singly. The warp on the second or added beam for the chenille loops can be of cotton or wool, and should measure at least ⅛-in. in diameter, M, Figure 29.

48

WARP PLAN

Regular Warp: Use carpet warp double and plan 6 pairs for each inch.

Chenille Warp: Plan 2 strands for each inch and choose from the following kinds:

4-strand cotton; thrifty-knit tufting cotton; rug wool; rug-weave yarn or equivalent.

Tabby Weft: Carpet warp double or 4-strand cotton.

THREADING PLAN

Thread as in the draft of *J–K*, Figure 29. The warps of warp beam No. 2, chenille loops, are shown in parentheses. Sley eight warps per inch — two chenille on harnesses 3 and 4, and six regular warp pairs on harnesses 1 and 2. Keep repeating *J–K;* add selvage at both sides.

WEAVING PLAN

One shuttle only, see Figure 29.

Weave alternate tabby and chenille sections as follows:

Section 1, Tabby: The sections between the drawn-up loops are tabby which acts as a binder. Weave four rows, alternating harnesses 1–3, then 2–4 (treadles 4 then 5); or for a texture not including the heavy yarns which fall below: treadles 1 then 2 (jack: harness 1 then 2; counterbalanced: harnesses 2, 3, 4 then 1, 3, 4).

Section 2, Chenille Loops: Treadle 3 (jack: harnesses 3–4; counterbalanced: harnesses 1–2).

Slip stick *N* through the shed as shown. Draw up the chenille warp only as at *N*. Do not weave. This section is simply to draw up the warp in loops. Leave the stick in until the loops are bound down by Section 1 again.

Now weave Section 1, which forms four rows of binding tabby to hold down the loops just formed. See the finished loops, *O,* Figure 29, already bound down, new loops forming at *N*.

After weaving the four rows of Section 1, make the shed for Section 2. Pull the stick out of the last row of loops and insert it into the row being formed. Keep repeating Sections 1 and 2 as far as you wish the chenille surface. Then weave plain weave for the space desired. In the floor rug of Figure 30, notice that the sections of plain weave are quite wide, from 8 to 10 in., and that the sections of chenille loops, bound down with the four rows of tabby after each row of loops, measure almost the same.

CHAPTER 7

Boutoné Loop Rugs

Rugs, soft to the feet, serviceable in texture, and in attractive geometric or tile-like designs are made in a looped or tufted technique known as "boutoné." They have been developed to a fine measure of perfection by the Canadians. The semitufted example shown in Figure 31 can be woven in pleasing color tones of wool or cotton yarn, with the design parts raised in loops against a plain-weave or tabby background. Thread the loom to any pattern that will produce tabby. Designs suitable for this technique are shown in Figures 31, 32, and 33.

DECORATIVE USE

Mats made with loops or tufts fit well into rooms where soft-textured surfaces are needed. Their texture is pleasing to the foot and their structure is thick yet flexible. They make wonderful bedside rugs or bath mats, comfortable cushion tops, or seat covers for hard chairs.

TYPES OF DESIGN

Since designs are transferred to the rug surface from a graph-paper pattern, almost any type of figure can be adapted, provided it is adjusted to rug proportions. However, the technique seems most suitable for smart tile-like designs with their outlines showing in looped relief against a lower background surface. In the design of Figure 33, the light unshaded portions form the background or untufted portions, and against these, in clear relief, the shaded or design portions stand out. In Figure 33 these are marked with X's that fill in the squares. The loops are in heavy colored yarn.

In Figure 31 are shown both the graph-paper design and the finished rug in looped technique from a conventional design planned for an allover effect. The loops may be all of one color, or a second color may be used

50

as an accent in the rosette forms at the center. Symmetrical designs like those shown are intriguing, and hundreds of variations are possible. The rugmaker can also create original motifs in free design, lay these out on a piece of smooth wrapping paper the shape and size of the final rug, and plan to use suitable color harmonies for the looped parts against a neutral background. It is best to start with simple figures. The design described in Figure 33, *A,* represents one motif only of the rug in Figure 32, in which this same motif is repeated many times.

MATERIALS TO USE AND WARP SETTINGS

The foundation or untufted parts are made of very heavy cotton warp or, as a substitute, carpet warp doubled. Loops are of wool, nylon, silk, or cotton rug yarn.

Warp: Cotton 4/4 or linen 10/5 at 8 singles per inch, or carpet warp 8/4 or 8/3 doubled and set at 8 pairs per inch. If you have a rug warp already set at 15 or 16 per inch, it can be rethreaded in pairs, and

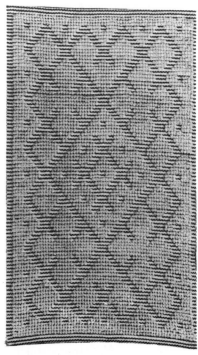

Courtesy — David Brown

Fig. 31 — Design and finished bath mat in looped boutoné technique.

51

Fig. 32 — Two good tile designs for boutoné bath mats.

sleyed one pair of ends per dent in every other dent of a 15- or 16-dent reed. For the best results when using pairs of warp, thread successive strands on the same harness, such as two warps on harness 1, two on harness 2, etc. They appear as flat pairs when woven.

Weft: Tabby: Carpet warp doubled or a single strand of 4-strand filler, or tufting cotton.

Tufts: Wool rug yarn or cotton rug-weave yarn. Both of these have a wide range of beautiful color tones.

METHOD: ADAPTING GRAPH-PAPER PATTERN TO RUG LOOPS

In working the pattern out on graph paper, make an outline of the final rug in good proportions, such as 2 parts wide to 3 long. Shade in all design parts or mark with X's for ease of following. See the design, Figure 33, marked parts, *A,* for looping; unmarked parts, *B,* without loops. To estimate the final size of the rug, figure that each square will measure ¼ in., or that there will be four squares per inch.

In the following directions, the word "warp" refers to the heavy single cotton or linen warp, or to the carpet warp doubled and used in pairs. Thus "two warps" can mean either two heavy single warps or two pairs of lighter-weight warp.

Let each two heavy warps (or pairs of doubled carpet warp), *C–D* in Figure 33, equal one square of the graph-paper pattern. In weaving, notice that one of these warps (or pairs of warp), *C,* is in the upper shed row, regular heavy lines, and that the other warp, *D,* is in the lower level, dotted vertical lines. Each square of the design equals one woven loop and occurs between each two warps in the upper level, right over the warp in the lower level. At the background places of the design, i.e., blank squares with no X's, there will be no loops, but just plain weaving.

HOW TO PUT IN A ROW OF LOOPS (Fig. 33)

First of all, at the starting end of the rug, *E,* for the hem, weave 1 or 2 in. of tabby using tufting or 4-strand cotton or carpet warp doubled to give the necessary filling-in quality. If fringe is desired, leave enough warp to tie — approximately 4 inches.

Name the shed in which odd warps are up (i.e., warps 1, 3, 5, 7, etc.) shed 1, and that in which even warps are up (warps 2, 4, 6, 8, etc.) shed 2. Finish the last row of tabby, *F,* before beginning to weave a row of loops, with shed 1, odd warps (dotted) up, and even warps (solid) down. This binds down the even warps before they become the framework of the loops. The tufting is always done on shed 2, even warps up, *G.*

After finishing the last tabby row, shown in detail at *F,* drop the tabby weft on shuttle *H.* Now take up the tufting weft on shuttle *J.* Weave through, carrying the heavy tufting weft from side to side, on shed 2, even warps up.

Next, take a pickup stick, *K,* either a flat stick about ½ in. wide or a ⅜-in. dowel, and, following the direction of the tufting weft, from right to left in this case, pick up loops of weft, as at *K,* wherever there is a shaded

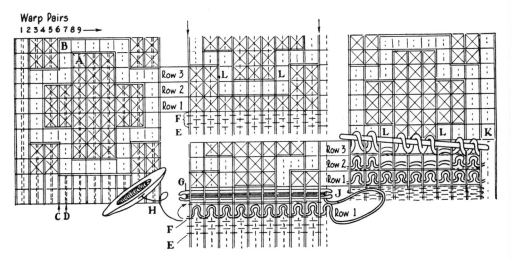

Fig. 33 — Directions for boutoné or looped rugs.

53

square of design. Where there are no X's, skip over with the pickup rod as at *L*.

If the rug is wide, use two sticks one after the other. After the row has been completed, leave the sticks in, drop shuttle *J* with the tufting weft, and weave three rows of tabby on sheds 1, 2, 1. After the tabby is in, draw out the sticks, beat the tabby up again firmly. This finishes one complete round of loops on shed 2, and tabby on sheds 1, 2, 1.

You are now ready for the next row of the design. Proceed as just described, and weave through with a heavy weft, pick up the loops, leave the stick in, and follow with three rows of tabby. Draw out the stick. Keep repeating.

In Figure 33, the center diagram, row 1 (solid squares) is shown put in with continuous loops just above the tabby at *F*. After this row of loops, the tabby thread on the shuttle weaves three rows above the row of loops on sheds 1, 2, 1; see the curved arrow.

Row 2 is shown being put in with a stick shuttle of heavy yarn; see *G*. Note that five empty squares occur at the center of this row and these will have no loops, tabby only showing, as in row 2 in diagram at right.

Row 3 is shown being picked up with rod, *K*, empty squares marked *L*, in the diagram at the right.

FINISHING THE RUG

When all loops of the design have been completed, the rug will have its design surfaces raised in fluffy relief texture against a flat background of plain weave. You need not clip the loops; they are soft in texture and all of the same height. In choosing a pickup rod, you can estimate how deep a "pile" or loop you wish. The deeper the pile to be made, the thicker the stick must be.

At both ends of the rug or mat, weave at least 1 in. of plain weave against which to tie the fringe or, if a hem is desired, weave 2 in. of plain weave.

CHAPTER **8**

Tapestry Rugs

RUGS in tapestry weave are generally found and used in warm climates, and the heavier pile weave rug is found in colder climates where it can provide welcome foot warmth. The tapestry weave is a flat weave with no pile loops either cut or uncut, and the design is formed by the interlocking at desired intervals by different-colored wefts. If these are of heavy texture, the resulting tapestry is a rug; if they are lighter in weight, the technique produces a more flexible wall hanging. Tapestries are woven by laying the colors in through the warps with the fingers, and the weaver often sits at an upright loom, as in Figure 36. Making a tapestry is not difficult, but it is more detailed than other types of weaves. It is a good project to plan for the winter months.

An interesting fact about tapestry weaving is that it was and still is worked from the wrong side. The pattern is hung above the weaver, and his yarns are made up into small skeins, in some such manner as shown in Figure 13. This method of working has given rise to many poetic similes regarding life and its challenge to keep on weaving with the strands one holds even though the pattern is not visible until complete.

While the basic weave of tapestry fabrics is plain weave in which the weft threads pass under and over successive warps, it differs from this in that the warp threads are sleyed so far apart that the weft threads are packed down closely between them, thus covering up the warp entirely. It is a "weft-face" technique with only the weft showing.

It can be readily seen that, since the weft covers the warp, the warp underlies it as a framework, so to speak, and the successive weft rows form vertical ridges over the covered warp threads. In rows where the color does not change, the weft carries through from selvage to selvage; but in those places where designs occur, a weft thread meets another weft thread of a different color, and this thread now takes over and proceeds with the in-and-out texture, at the same time lending a change of color and design to

55

Fig. 36 — Polish
craftsman weaving
Gobelin technique.

Courtesy — Nova Scotia
Bureau of Information

Fig. 37 — Tapestry
rug in
contemporary
design woven by
the interlocked
tapestry method.

Courtesy — Clem Smith

the total effect. The design thread does not lie over a background tabby, as in laid-in, but alternates with another single weft of about the same size in another color when the design shows such a change. Tapestry weaving may take a bit longer to do than laid-in, but is made worthwhile by the result achieved (see Figs. 37, 39, and 115).

KINDS OF TAPESTRY

There are several different kinds of tapestry: slit, diagonal, dovetailed, and interlocked. Each derives its name from the method used in joining adjacent weft threads when the design and colors change. There are also vertical stripes as compared to lines running at angles of varying degrees with interwoven or interlocked wefts. All of these are shown in Figure 40, and described in the following. Through his choice of methods the tapestry-rug weaver can secure the angle of design and the texture he desires.

TEXTURE AND DECORATIVE USE

Tapestry rugs have a thick, padded texture, the same on both sides. Their soft weft surface, worked in wool, silk, or cotton, has a smooth comfortable appearance. While not as warm as pile rugs, they can be made in a heavy, warm texture by using a yarn of considerable weight. Use tapestry rugs wherever a rug of carefully wrought design is an asset, for the tapestry technique gives a beautiful texture and shows its in-woven figures to advantage. Tapestry rugs are good in living rooms, music rooms, and libraries. When woven of medium-weight yarns, they can be used as wall hangings and throw rugs interchangeably.

DESIGN AND COLOR

Tapestry rugs depend for their beauty and interest on their design. A very plain tapestry rug is hard to find. However, because of the nature of the tapestry method, with the interlocking weft strands, a beginner in this type of weaving should use designs bordered by straight lines, that is, vertical, horizontal, or slanting. After the weaver has mastered the interlocking method, he can execute designs in curved lines with finer gradations of ascending steps. The design colors should be in sufficient contrast

Fig. 38 — Detail of slit and interlocking tapestry. Red and orange geometric motif designed by Lili Blumeneau.

Courtesy — Juta Cord

57

Fig. 39 — Handwoven fabrics in a Florida weaving studio.

to show up against the background. Good designs for tapestry rugs are shown in Figures 37, 39, 41.

MATERIALS

The setting chosen for the warp should be tested on a trial section to be sure that the weft, no matter what its weight, sinks down between warps and completely covers them.

Warp: 8/4 or 8/5 cotton set at 4 to 10 pairs per inch, depending on the thickness of the weft used. For a heavier warp, use 4/4 cotton or 10/5 linen at 4 to 6 pairs per inch.

Weft: Wool rug yarn and Persian rug yarn are preferred for their soft quality. For a substitute, make the wool weft by doubling or tripling Germantown yarn. If cotton is used, rug-weave yarn is about the right weight, or lightweight 3-ply rug yarn, or two or three strands of four-strand cotton.

EQUIPMENT

There are regular tapestry looms used vertically, Figure 36. However, a two-harness or a four-harness loom is satisfactory. The interlocking is done

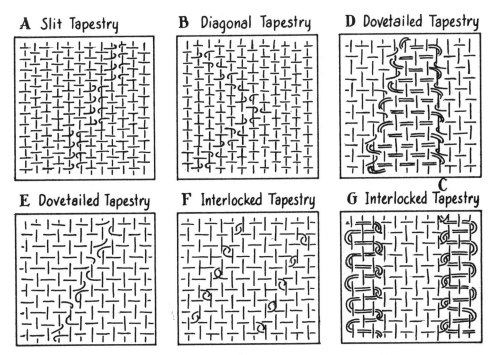

A Slit Tapestry   **B** Diagonal Tapestry   **D** Dovetailed Tapestry

E Dovetailed Tapestry   **F** Interlocked Tapestry   **G** Interlocked Tapestry

Fig. 40 — Methods used in weaving tapestry.

with the fingers. A wide shed stick, to keep parts of the shed open when weaving, is helpful.

TAPESTRY METHODS

Slit Tapestry. This is the most familiar type, Figures 38 and *A,* 40. The best examples are the Kilim rugs with short slits between sections, some ancient Peruvian textiles, and a certain Chinese type called *K'ossu* or cut cloth. A kind of slit tapestry also is made in Scandinavia, in which the design is woven in wherever desired, but the background is not woven. This forms a beautiful soft wall hanging, in which vertical warps show in sections, setting off the tapestry designs. Slit tapestries, dating from medieval times, are on display in most museums.

Diagonal Tapestry. In this type of tapestry, a slanting trend is given to the design by weaving over an additional warp in every weft row, *B,* Figure 40, and Figure 42. It resembles the slit tapestry to some extent, but for shorter vertical distances. The wefts reverse around adjacent warp threads and do not touch each other. An angle of about 45 degrees is formed. The technique shown in Figure 42 might be described as: "slit tapestry with weft diagonally locked with warp according to intended design."

The weaver may make a more gradual slant in the diagonal design by

59

progressing to the right or left two warp threads at a time instead of one. He may also make a sharper upward angle by having the wefts reverse around the same warp twice before progressing to the next warp thread. In either case the slits are very small and hardly noticed in the finished fabric. The method is practical and useful for tapestry rugs.

Dovetailed Tapestry. In this type of weaving, instead of leaving slits between adjacent warps, one reverses around the same warps, as in *C, D,* and *E,* Figure 40. A vertical column with several rows repeated before changing is shown at *C.* This forms a secure enough texture to keep repeating vertically for a border. An abrupt upward angle is shown at *D.* Here two weft rows are repeated before progressing one warp to the right or left. A 45-degree angle is shown at *E.* Here only one weft row is woven and then reversed around the warp before progressing one warp to the right or left.

Interlocked Tapestry. Here we have the interlocking of adjacent weft threads around each other at their reverse points. This occurs *between* the warp threads instead of *around* them, *F* and *G,* Figure 40. This method is characteristic of Norwegian tapestries as well as of some very ancient Peruvian textiles. An angle of progression, adding one warp at a time, is shown at *F;* and a vertical progression upward is shown at *G.* Both this type and that at *C* are excellent for borders at the sides of a rug, as shown in Figure 39, lower left, and Figure 121.

For detailed instructions of a simple design, taken row by row, see Chapter 9, "Navajo Rugs."

Navajo Rugs

Weaving a Navajo rug is both an educational and an entertaining project. The Indians evolved their tapestry rugs from stark beginnings. They spun and carded sheep's wool into warp and weft, dyed it with juices from roots and berries, planned their designs from tribal motifs, and wove them on their own handmade looms. The technique is not difficult to master. It is a form of tapestry adapted to the use of coarse wools in the making of rugs and blankets. Weaving to the Navajos was a ritual. We can benefit by learning their thoroughness and care. For individuals or groups, Navajo rug weaving opens an interesting field of tribal design.

DESIGN AND COLOR

Designs for Navajo rug weaving are characterized by borders and simple tribal motifs, as shown in the two floor rugs, Figure 39. Contrasting colors in stripes or angular motifs are woven against backgrounds of plain color. Three methods are used in making these motifs:

1. Horizontal stripes of contrasting colors
2. Vertical stripes
3. Tapestry methods for tribal-motif designs

The colors most often used are rather bright and bold. Gray is the favorite background color for stripes or designs in red, white, and black — strong colors which the Indian loved. In recent years commercialized Navajo rugs have introduced orange, blue, and green but one should use these colors sparingly to reproduce the authentic type.

The simplest Navajo rugs are of a neutral tone with bright bands in good proportions at intervals. Their arrow-weave borders are delightful, formed by two contrasting weft colors twisted together. Bright borders placed at the ends of rugs may have their colors repeated in diamonds forming central motifs. Small spots of color add charm and color on plain grounds. All of these are shown in Figure 41.

When the rug weaver has mastered these simple designs, he may launch out on the weaving of tapestry rugs of more varied design, Figures 5 and 39. The three methods at the weaver's disposal are described later.

TEXTURE AND DECORATIVE USE

Genuine Navajo rugs have a firm beautiful all-wool texture. They are heavy, thick, and firm. The rows are firmly beaten and cover the warp completely. Their homespun wool yarn imparts a textural appearance to the surface.

Large Navajo rugs are suitable in living rooms and halls. Their most usual background colors of black and white and gray make them blend well with daily living tones. They also make splendid rugs for cottages or ranch houses. Their durability makes them a welcome addition to boys' rooms and game rooms. Color accents can be added in the designs used to match bright accessories.

MATERIALS

The warp used by the Indians was usually strong, well-twisted, homespun wool, and the filler was wool of a softer, thicker texture. The following materials may be used instead:

Warp: Carpet warp 8/4, 8/3, or 5/3 used double, set at 6 to 8 pairs per inch; or 4/4 cotton warp, or 10/5 linen warp set at 6 to 8 singles per inch; or firmly twisted homespun, 6 to 8 ends per inch.

Weft: Wool is preferable, homespun yarn, medium weight; Germantown doubled or tripled. Substitutes: commercial cotton yarns, such as rug-weave yarn or 3-ply rug yarn.

EQUIPMENT

The Indians used two-shed vertical looms which they constructed themselves. Today, we most often use strong, wide floor looms, either two- or four-harness, threaded for plain weave. A firm, heavy beater is necessary.

DESIGN SUGGESTIONS FOR NAVAJO RUGS

Horizontal Stripes of Contrasting Colors (Fig. 41). Horizontal stripes may be used for the entire design of a Navajo rug or just for borders. Plain wide bands may be used for backgrounds for such motifs as diamonds, birds, stars, etc. In planning designs, it is a good idea to work with crayons and graph paper. In Figure 41 some characteristic Navajo stripe proportions are given. To enlarge them, multiply the dimensions of each part by 2, 3, 4, as desired. Weave the white parts white; the vertically shaded parts, black; the dotted parts, red; the arrows red with white or gray; the horizontal lines, dark gray; the hatched parts, light gray.

Arrow-Weave Border (A to G, Fig. 41). Weave plain weft for the background. Plan the width and color of the border carefully. Choose two

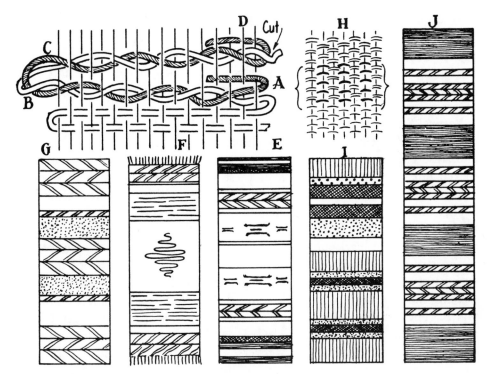

Fig. 41 — Design suggestions for Navajo rugs.

contrasting colors, as at *A*. One of these may be the former background color, or choose a light and dark for the arrow against a medium-tone background. Thread the new ends back into the warp. Open the next shed and, with the hands, slip the two weft strands through. When in the shed, twist them as shown, holding them at the opposite end, *B*. Beat up the cloth, change sheds, and then twist the strands again and lay them through the next shed, as at *C*. Pass one end of the two arrow colors around the last warp, and thread back into the same shed, as at *D*. Cut off the other end flush against the selvage. If strands are twisted in the opposite direction, they form an arrow, as in borders at *E;* if in the same direction, they form diagonal twill lines, as at *F*.

Two rows form one complete arrow; but one or more may be added to give the zigzag effects, as at *G*. Borders are made by repeating either the *E* or *F* methods.

Two-Color Transition Border (*H,* Fig. 41). For a subtle border, often used to act as a transition or softening border line between two colors, simply alternate two different colored wefts as follows.

Weave the first color only for a space.

Add the second color and alternate with the first for transition (see brackets).

Weave the second color only for a space.

Accenting Horizontal Stripes (*I* and *J*, Fig. 41). The same proportions given at *E, F,* and *G,* for the arrow rows may be used for simple stripes across the rug warp in accenting colors. Plan such stripes as *I* and *J* on graph paper. Simple stripes, repeated continuously, are most effective. Rows. of arrow may be laid in at intervals between these.

Vertical Stripes and Side Borders (C and G, Fig. 40). To design a Navajo rug with plain center and borders all around, at sides as well as across the ends, use either the dovetailed tapestry method, *C,* Figure 40, or the interlocked tapestry method, *G.* Both of these make it possible to add a border color in vertical columns around the sides. A rug with such a clearly outlined framework may have a simple diamond woven at the center. Borders may be designed with simple repeating motifs as in the rug, Figure 39, lower left, where a beautiful black and white side border adds charm to the entire rug.

Tapestry Design Methods for Tribal Motifs. By the methods of Figure 40, designs of one color can be woven against a background of another color, passing the varying colors back and forth between a certain number of warps. The line of division between the colors is a single warp thread, around which each color weaves, *C, D,* and *E,* Figure 40, or two adjacent warp threads around which they reverse, *A* and *B,* Figure 40. The result is that the colors overlap each other slightly, giving a fringed effect, or just touch each other at points of change giving a smoother surface.

PLANNING DESIGNS

Plan these on graph paper, letting each warp equal one square. Work without too definite a design after learning the angles of your motifs, starting a triangle, and letting it grow. But make the plan of the entire rug definite before starting. See the center diamond in *F,* Figure 41.

Arrange all the colors of yarn to be used on a table, and make them up into small skeins as for Flossa rugs.

METHODS

Any of the methods shown in Figure 40 are useful for Navajo tapestry rugs. The dovetailed and interlocked types are most common although diagonal tapestry may be used for slanting lines.

Dovetailed Method (C, D, and E, Fig. 40):

First row: Make shed 1 with the odd threads up, threads 1, 3, 5, etc. Weave from left to right, and insert colors where planned. Weave all ends in the same direction, starting with the end at the extreme left, and move right.

Second row: Make shed 2 with the even threads up, such as 2, 4, 6, etc. Reverse the wefts around the thread counted out on your plan. Take the threads in the same order, weave from right to left, stopping at the warp planned, where the design color ends.

Weft threads pass around warps only and do not interlock with each other. Third row: Make shed 1. Weave threads in order, following method of first row.

Interlocking Weft Threads (F and G, Fig. 40). In this method, two adjacent weft threads interlock each other in between the same two warp threads. Otherwise the process is the same as the method above. Follow the same tabby succession in and out of warp threads as if weaving with one color only.

Diagonal Tapestry:

1. *Weaving a Moderate Angle* (*B,* Fig. 40). In this method, one of two adjacent weft threads gets wider in each successive row as it crosses over one more warp thread, while the weft thread next to it gets narrower as it crosses over one less warp thread. Overlapping is not necessary as the warp additions between rows hold the fabric together.

2. *Weaving a More Abrupt Angle, at About 52 Degrees* (*D,* Fig. 40). In this method, each weft color goes over the same number of warp threads twice before it adds or subtracts another warp thread. Start weaving on the first shed, with odd threads up. Weave four rows with the adjacent weft colors lapping over the warp thread that is common to both. On the fifth row, add a warp thread to one of the wefts, such as the weft on the left side. Follow this in the next row by subtracting a warp thread for the weft on the right side. Now weave around the two newly established warp threads for four rows. Continue weaving thus. Adjacent colors do not interlock.

Fig. 42 — Diagonal design combining slit and interlocking tapestry.

Courtesy — Lili Blumeneau

A SAMPLE NAVAJO RUG

A small Navajo rug makes a wonderful mat for a table or a colorful hanging on the wall. For the first project, make a bright-red mat for a boy's room or a library. This will measure 18 by 24 in. Just to give an original touch, reverse the colors of large rugs and use a bright red for a background with borders white and two shades of gray, black accents, and a touch of soft earth brown at the center.

Here are the directions. Follow exactly for an attractive border effect. Colors are marked: Red (R), White (W), Black (B), Light Gray (LG), Dark Gray (DG), and Brown (Br). (See Figure 60 on page 110.)

WARP PLAN

Warp: Medium homespun yarn set at 8 threads per inch; or carpet warp 8/4, 8/3, or 5/3 set at 8 pairs per inch
Weft: Germantown, doubled or tripled; or wool rug yarn
Threading: Plain weave

WEAVING PLAN

Rug measures 20 by 30 in.

Rug End: Leave 4 in. of warp for fringe; then weave 2½ in. red, plain weave.

Entire Border: 5 to 7 in.

Transition band: 1W, 1R, 1W, 1R, 2W, 2R. An arrow with a heavy black and light gray twisted (*A,* Figure 41)

Border proper: 8W, 8LG, 8DG, 8B, 8Br, 4W, 2R, 2W, 2R, 2W, 2R, 4W, 8Br, 8B, 8DG, 8LG, 8W. An arrow, same as first arrow

Transition band: 2R, 2W, 1R, 1W, 1R, 1W

Rug Center: 12-in. plain red. At the middle of the red center, measuring 12 in. long, weave a diamond motif as in the preceding directions, diagonal tapestry, *F,* Figure 41.

Border: Same as the first border, 5 to 7 in.

Rug End: 2½ in. plain red. Leave 4 in. of warp for the fringe. Remove from loom. Tie the fringe at the ends.

CHAPTER **10**

Soumak Rugs

SOUMAK rugs come from the Far East and are not generally known to Western weavers, but the technique is a new and interesting one to attempt. It is applicable to either two- or four-harness looms when making rugs. It is to all intents and purposes a "chain" embroidery stitch, the very same that is used for outlining fancy work patterns. In Soumak, however, the outlining or chaining is done across the warp threads of a loom in successive rows to form a solid texture. Although it takes longer to make this kind of rug than plain-weave rugs, the weaver is rewarded by a surprisingly durable and satisfying product.

TEXTURE

The texture of Soumak forms a flat, smooth, and thick surface, the same on both sides; and the woven or embroidered weft strands, firmly packed against each other row on row, hug closely to a strong warp, completely covering it. The heavy matlike surface of the finished rug sticks fast to the floor and protects its polished surface. When made of wool, the rugs give a feeling of warmth and comfort.

DECORATIVE USE

Soumak rugs are useful wherever a durable matlike surface is needed. They fit well into the decorative scheme of a living room or hallway with their restful, even texture wrought in low, subdued tones. They can be used where there is considerable wear on a floor; being reversible, they are doubly practical.

COLOR AND DESIGN

Given the basic "chain" stitch of Soumak, shown in Figure 44, it is an easy matter to introduce color where desired. The yarn being used can be changed to another color by fastening the new end on the underside, running

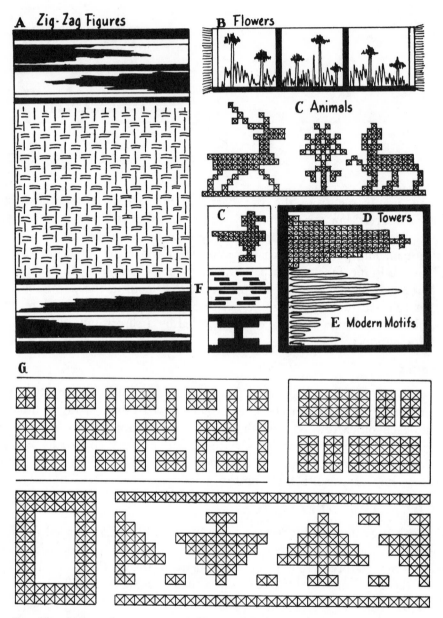

Fig. 43 — Free and conventional designs for Soumak, laid-in, and imitation tapestry.

the old end a short distance along the new, and fastening it on the back of the rug. Designs in stripes, diamonds, squares, oblongs, triangles, and other simple figures may be used (see Fig. 43).

EQUIPMENT

Use any strong loom thread for plain weave. The "chain stitching" is made easier by the use of a long, pointed throw shuttle or a flat stick shuttle.

MATERIALS AND WARP SETTING

Warp: Use a strong warp, linen 10/5, cotton 4/4, or pairs of carpet warp, 8/4 or 8/3. *Setting* — set the heavy warps or pairs at 8 to 10 per inch. If you are using a loom already threaded at 12 to 16 singles per inch, rethread in pairs for Soumak, and set 6 to 8 pairs per inch.

Weft: For the pattern filler, use real wool rug yarn, if possible, as this is flexible and soft in its feel and appearance. The weft material should be of good quality, soft and easy to work with, and this should be used on a pointed throw shuttle or a stick shuttle in order to reach readily within the warp threads. A good substitute is lightweight cotton rug yarn, although it makes rugs less warm and durable. For tabby weft, use the warp double or a cotton double the weight of the warp.

METHOD: PLANNING A HEAVY HALL RUG
(Figs. 43 and 44)

Plan a practical hall rug or a fireplace rug for the living room. If its design is successful, make several rugs of different sizes in the same colors to group in a rug ensemble as shown in Figure 72.

The tones used for halls and living rooms are fairly low in value, so plan to weave a rug background that will act as a foundation to your color

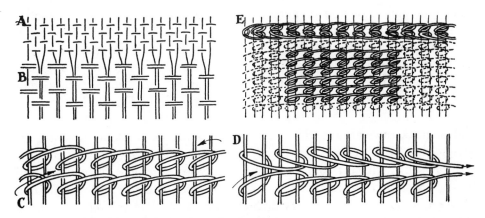

Fig. 44 — Methods used for making Soumak rugs.

scheme in mahogany, rich brown or green, henna, old blue or rose. Add borders or designs with a dash of brighter color at the ends.

DIRECTIONS FOR MAKING (Fig. 44)

1. Make a heading at the ends of the rug, *A,* by weaving the tabby with carpet warp. If the loom is threaded as singles, this will be a closely woven heading as shown.

2. Weave four rows of plain weave, *B,* over pairs of warp with the regular rug yarn to be used for the Soumak stitch. This gives a solid background to weave against. To be able to weave tabby both as singles and as pairs, thread the loom to twill. For singles in tabby, weave harnesses 1–3, 2–4; but for pairs of warp in tabby, weave on any two opposite pairs, such as harnesses 1–2 against 3–4, or harnesses 2–3 against 4–1.

3. Do not raise shed. Soumak is woven across a neutral shed. For the first row of Soumak, carry the weft left to right over four warps and back under two. Weave all across to the right selvage, as at *C.*

4. For the second row of Soumak, carry the weft right to left over the same four warp threads of each unit and under two. Note the sketch at *C,* arrows, and the same direction of weft to form a slanting trend. Either weave back and forth, or fasten the yarn at the end of each row and weave only from left to right.

TWILL AND ARROW MOTIFS (Fig. 44)

At *C,* the stitches all run in the same direction, twill fashion. At *D,* the stitches of successive rows run in opposite directions forming arrows. The arrow stitch, or two rows running at opposite angles, also may be executed, both rows at the same time, in the manner of chain stitch in embroidery, by looping a double weft forward over the warps, and pulling their ends through in the center of the stitch; see small arrows.

Use colors in series for successive arrow bands, or weave a background texture of one color and occasionally insert an accenting arrow in another color. When desired, a new color may take the place of the old over a certain number of warps and, as these color changes are made in successive rows, figures are formed. *E,* Figure 44, shows a rectangular figure in a second color at the center, and an arrow-chain border at the top, again in accenting color. See good designs for Soumak in Figures 37 and 57, in *F* and *G,* Figure 43, and *3,* Figure 48.

If Soumak rows are used in succession, all going in the same direction and giving the "twill" effect mentioned, *C,* Figure 44, over a large space, the resulting rug will curl somewhat. To avoid this, alternate sections of twill Soumak with sections of arrow Soumak. However, if the texture is to remain constant, keep repeating the twill Soumak, but at intervals of 2 in. or so run one row of arrow across. This will keep the surface from curling.

70

The arrow Soumak, if repeated continuously, never curls, for this consists of alternate rows of Soumak going each way.

DIRECTIONS FOR MAKING EVEN SELVAGE (Fig. 44)

Skip the first four or six warp threads before starting the wrap-around stitch with pattern threads from left to right; and stop wrapping short of last four or six threads at the right. Bring the pattern yarn up to the surface at the left of the skipped warps. Treat tabby as in Flossa, taking two extra stitches at the left under and over these omitted threads of selvage before going across the entire warp left to right. Here is a complete unit and its return:

1. Start the pattern rug yarn at the left side (neutral warps, no shed), skipping the first four or six threads; loop across entire surface to the right, stopping short of the same number of threads. Draw the filler up to the surface.

2. Filling in at Selvages. Make shed 1. With carpet warp used double or equivalent, weave across the selvage threads on the left side, left to right, as far as these skipper selvage warps go. Make shed 2. Return to the left edge with the same. Make shed 1. Weave across the warp from the left selvage to the right selvage.

Make shed 2. Weave across the selvage threads on the right side, right to left, as far as the empty selvage warps go. Make shed 1. Return to the edge with the same. You have now filled in on the left side, woven across to the right side, and filled in on the right side. Drop the fill-in thread at the right selvage to wait for a second row of Soumak.

3. Bring the shed back to neutral. Weave the second row of Soumak with pattern rug yarn right to left on neutral shed, reversing the direction of loops. Stop short of the selvage warps. Draw the filler up to the surface.

4. Make shed 2. With the fill-in weft, weave across the selvage threads on the right side, right to left, as far as these skipped warps go. Make shed 1. Return to the right edge with the same. Make shed 2. Weave across the warp from the right selvage to left selvage.

Make shed 1. Weave across the selvage threads on the left side, left to right, as far as the skipped selvage warps go. Make shed 2. Return to the edge with the same.

You have now filled in on the right side, woven across to the left side, and filled in on the left side. Drop the fill-in thread at the left selvage to wait for the next row of Soumak. Then repeat the four steps above.

The complete repeat consists of:
1. Row of Soumak, left to right.
2. Fill in on left, travel to right, fill in on right.
3. Second row of Soumak, right to left.
4. Fill in on right, travel to left, fill in on left.

71

DIRECTIONS FOR A SOUMAK RUG
WITH SMOOTH BACK

For a Soumak rug with plain smooth back rather than one with both surfaces showing overlapped yarn, make stitches on one shed only, and after each complete Soumak row add two rows of tabby instead of one, and fill in at the selvages. The warp for this type should be set closer, at 10 to 12 pairs per inch.

1. Shed 1. Soumak, left to right around the desired number of upper warp threads only.

2. Keep shed 1 for tabby: fill in on left; shed 2, back to left selvage; shed 1, travel across from left to right selvage; shed 2, right to left across right selvage threads; shed 1, back to right selvage; shed 2, travel across from right to left selvage.

3. Shed 1. Soumak right to left.

4. Same as 2.

Repeat all.

CHAPTER 11

Laid-In and Imitation-Tapestry Rugs

LAID-IN RUG WEAVING (Fig. 45)

IT IS possible to add designs to rugs over the regular background texture, a technique commonly known as "inlay" or "laid-in" weaving. This proves desirable from the standpoint of interest, but the inlay material should not be too heavy or it will form a raised surface which is impractical for a rug. For that reason, certain types of laid-in are more practical than others. The laid-in figures cover the warp which is set far apart to make possible a weft-face texture. The following are practical methods:

1. Regular inlay, called also "in-and-out laid-in," with design threads passing through the same shed as the tabby and in addition to it.

2. Entwined laid-in with design threads twisted with the regular weft.

3. Brickwork inlay, using a pickup stick to secure the effect of brickwork for the design threads.

4. Laid-in on Summer and Winter or twill in which every fourth warp thread acts as a tie-down to bind the added design thread, a laid-in method called "Dukagäng."

DECORATIVE USE

Rugs with added figures are intriguing to the weaver. It enables him to select design types suitable to certain rooms. If he weaves commercially, he can add interesting motifs which have an appealing sales value. Since the designs can be so variable, these rugs can be adapted to all rooms, even those decorated by modern color spacings and texture contrasts.

DESIGN AND COLOR

Use very simple figures for rug inlay, and do not mix either colors or design forms, but rather plan one or two simple forms against the background in one or two colors only. The person who makes laid-in rugs should plan for

73

added designs when creating the initial rug. Designs suitable for in-and-out laid-in are shown at *B, C, D, E, F,* and *G,* Figure 43. The best laid-in figures have connected parts throughout, making it possible to carry the added design thread right along. See the design in *B,* Figure 45. Note arrows to designated places where a new design thread must start and end because of a break in the design. At *C,* the laid-in thread is continuous, a unique but pleasing type of free rug design.

MATERIALS

Laid-in motifs may be added to any rug with a plain-weave or twill background. Great care should be used in selecting the right size of laid-in yarn, such as will add new color effect but will not add too much bulk to the texture. In rugs with wool or cotton filler, the filler can be divided in half for the laid-in strand. In rag rugs, the background rags can be cut a bit narrower at this point; but if warp is set far enough apart, such as 8 to 10 per inch, there is room for both strands. The important thing is so to gauge the background and added laid-in strand that together they do not form too much additional bulk.

EQUIPMENT

Inlay methods 1, 2, and 3 are suitable for two-harness looms. Method 4 is planned for four-harness looms but may be imitated on a two-harness loom by picking up every fourth thread on a stick and holding it as a third harness to bring forward when needed for the laid-in design.

A long pickup stick is needed for doing rug inlay.

INLAY METHODS

1. Regular Inlay or In-and-Out Laid-In (A, Fig. 45). In this type of laid-in weaving, the added design thread or rug filler passes under and over every other strand of warp, and is followed by a binding tabby thread through the same shed. At *A,* Figure 45, the heavy rug yarn, 1, is the design thread shown weaving under and over alternate warps; and the finer thread or binder 2 is shown following directly through the same shed.

Method. Plan your design on graph paper. Let each square of your graph-paper design equal four warp threads. As the shed is made, two threads on the upper level represent one square of design.

Make your shed for the regular tabby row; lay the design or added thread in through this shed as far as desired, or as far as the graph-paper pattern designates; then weave across the entire warp with regular tabby thread. Beat all close together.

A UNIQUE BEDSIDE RUG OF SILK RAGS, *C* and *D* (FIG. 45)

A hit-or-miss bedside rug made of finely cut silk rags makes a welcome gift. It may prove colorful if made of discarded silk or rayon dresses

74

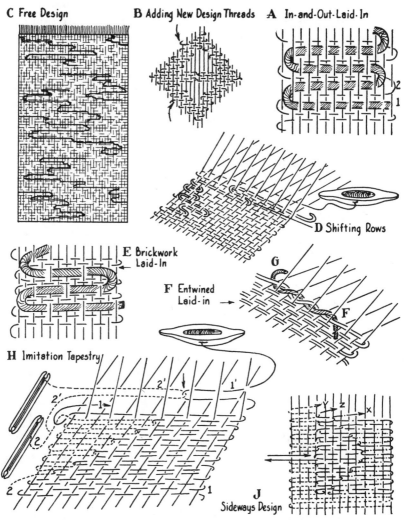

Fig. 45 — Methods used for rug inlay, imitation tapestry, and entwined laid-in.

cut into strips for the weft. The runner or rug is woven as plain weave with the rags in any sequence of coloring whatever. The laid-in parts may be of especially bright bits of silk. The laid-in yarn travels from row to row, followed after each by a row of tabby through the same shed. The weaver may pass the laid-in yarn back and forth at will. Note the character of this design, *C*. To get to another point of warp do not skip over more than two or three warps, but pass to the next row and then travel horizontally to the next point, as shown in detail at *D,* arrow. Try to start the next row at the warp thread that is closest to the reverse point of the last row.

75

This unusual laid-in rug gives one an immediate impression of beauty, both in color and design. It was made to simulate the appearance of pebbles and sand on the beach, and lovely tones of wool were intermixed with scattered laid-in figures of gold, copper, and silver threads.

The chenille was hand-dyed in the color of actual sand. The "pebbles" and "stones" were made of knitted tubing combined with assorted yarns of the same natural colors of stones. When some of them particularly gleamed or sparkled, the proper silver, gold, or copper thread was added to the combination of threads to be knitted together for that particular stone of the rug. No two stones of the same color are side by side in the rug. When a pattern treadle was depressed, the openings in the section of the shed to be used for the tubing were measured, each opening or space being measured separately. Then the colored threads for the pebbles were measured separately according to the requirements of each opening; they were then joined together and knitted to make a piece of tubing which was finally "laid in" the shed, thus placing the "pebbles in the sand" of chenille and rug yarn.

There was no pattern to follow for making this rug, just the imagination and feeling of the weaver who provided the place where the stones would

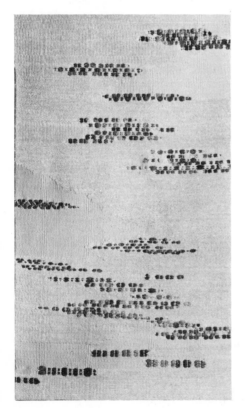

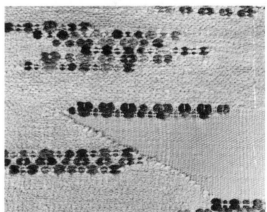

Fig. 47 — Detail of rug in Figure 46.

Fig. 46 — Rug, "Pebbles and Sand," showing free laid-in design in colorful wools and synthetics.

Courtesy — Elvira R. Ponkey

fall and where the sand would be smoothed by rolling water, and also where it would be scuffed up by people walking on the sandy beach. Needless to say, the finished product had to have a feeling of rhythm and motion, a beginning and an end to coincide with the meaning of the title. The close-up in Figure 47 shows the beauty of the textures, both the background texture and that produced by the knitted tubing, but one must see the colors of the rug to realize what an exquisite thing a laid-in rug can be.

RUG SETTING

Warp: Black carpet warp

Weft: Chenille and cotton filler, and several weights of cotton and metallics combined for pebbles

Threads per Inch: Three ends per dent in every fourth dent of a 10-dent reed

Threading: Standard twill or tabby woven as plain weave

2. Entwined Laid-In (F and G, Fig. 45). Adding an extra weft strand to the regular background weft yarn or rag, and twisting the added strand with the regular strand results in a technique called "Entwined Laid-In." This method is employed in Scandinavia to give softly blended color sections to the centers of rugs or their borders. The method is shown in *F*, Figure 45, and resembles the regular laid-in at *A* and *B* of the same figure except that the added strands are twisted with the background strands instead of being laid beside them. For an example of this method, see No. 3, Figure 48.

Method. Determine at which warp thread you wish the laid-in to start. When you reach the point of change, add the new colored weft, *F*, run it along in the same shed as the regular weft but twist them together. Bring added thread out at the desired point, and let it hang as at *G,* ready to be picked up at the return of the regular weft in the next row. Returning thus from left to right, either twist in the same direction for a twill texture or in the opposite direction to make arrows. The method is the same as that used for making the twisted arrow, *AB,* Figure 41. The twisted strands do not cover the warps but go between them. Rectangles, triangles, diamonds, etc., may be laid in very effectively in this manner, and the laid-in parts blend well with the rest of the rug because they contain the background yarn.

3. Brickwork Inlay Using a Pickup Stick (E, Fig. 45). The brickwork type of laid-in makes a pretty texture. It also is serviceable, for the laid-in yarn is bound down by every fourth warp thread, and the rows are staggered so that they hold each other in place, as shown in the detail, *E*. The designs should be simple and worked out on graph paper. Because of the brickwork texture, it is possible to progress diagonally upward adding a half brick each row. Therefore, diamonds and zigzag figures are good.

77

Method. Let each square of your graph-paper design equal four warp threads. As the shed is made, each two threads on the upper level represent one square of the design.

First Row of Bricks—

Step 1. Make the first shed, No. 1. Half of the warp threads are raised, and each two warps cover the space of one square. With a pickup stick, pick up every other warp in raised level, thus bringing every fourth thread on top of the stick; see *E,* Figure 45.

Step 2. Turn stick on edge, run the design thread under as far as the squares of the design indicate.

Step 3. Pull out the stick, and run the finer tabby binder through the same shed.

Step 4. Change the shed to shed 2, and weave the tabby through alone.

Second Row of Bricks—

Step 1. Make shed 1. Insert the pickup stick as before, but this time out of each two warps representing a square pick up the one not picked up before. This will come in the middle of the last pickup or "brick."

Step 2. Turn the stick on edge, and run the design thread through.

Step 3. Pull out the stick, and weave the tabby through the same shed.

Step 4. Change to shed 2. Weave the tabby through alone.

Repeat the first and second rows of bricks throughout.

When there is a skip in the design and there are blank squares on the paper pattern before coming to the next filled-in squares, turn the first design thread around, use no laid-in across the blank space, but start another design thread where needed, as shown in *B,* Figure 45. If the weaver wishes the bricks to show still more, he should repeat the first row of bricks twice before progressing to the second row; repeat this also. The bricks will be heavier.

4. Laid-In on Twill and Summer and Winter (E, Fig. 45). The process and results are much the same as for brickwork inlay, the difference being that the shed is more easily made and no pickup stick is necessary. Although this method belongs to four-harness weaves, we will add it here, as it is a true inlay method. Use either a counterbalanced or jack loom. In the directions, the treadling for the former is given first.

A. Twill Laid-In: One starts with a rug loom threaded to twill in carpet warp at from 12 to 16 threads per inch.

First Row of Inlay—

Step 1. Treadle harnesses 2, 3, 4 together (on jack loom harness 1). All threads on harness 1 will rise, i.e., every fourth warp. Run the design thread through.

Step 2. Weave tabby on harnesses 1–3.

Step 3. Weave tabby on harnesses 2–4.

Second Row of Inlay—

Step 1. Treadle harnesses 1, 2, 4 together (on jack loom harness 3). All threads on harness 3 will rise, i.e., every fourth warp between the first inlays. Run the design thread through.

Step 2. Weave tabby on harnesses 1–3.

Step 3. Weave tabby on harnesses 2–4.

Repeat the first and second rows of inlay throughout the space desired for the design.

In twill, a regular slanting twill-texture trend can be developed by weaving inlay as follows:

First Row of Inlay—Treadle harnesses 2, 3, 4, lifting the warps on harness 1 (on jack loom, treadle harness 1). Weave the design, and follow with tabby, harnesses 1–3, then 2–4.

Second Row of Inlay—Treadle harnesses 1, 3, 4, lifting the warps on harness 2 (on jack loom, treadle harness 2). Weave the design, and follow with tabby, harnesses 1–3, then 2–4.

Third Row of Inlay—Treadle harnesses 1, 2, 4, lifting the warps on harness 3 (on jack loom, treadle harness 3). Weave the design, and follow with tabby, harnesses 1–3, then 2–4.

Fourth Row of Inlay—Treadle harnesses 1, 2, 3, lifting the warps on harness 4 (on jack loom, treadle harness 4). Weave the design, and follow with tabby, harnesses 1–3, then 2–4.

B. Summer and Winter Laid-In:

First Row of Inlay—

Step 1. Treadle harnesses 2, 3, 4 together, lifting the warps on harness 1 (jack, harness 1). Run the design thread through.

Step 2. Weave the tabby on harnesses 1–2.

Step 3. Weave the tabby on harnesses 3–4.

Second Row of Inlay—

Step 1. Treadle harnesses 1, 3, 4 together, lifting the warps on harness 2 (jack, harness 2). Run the design thread through.

Step 2. Weave the tabby on harnesses 1–2.

Step 3. Weave the tabby on harnesses 3–4.

Repeat the first and second rows of inlay throughout the space of added design.

IMITATION TAPESTRY

Tapestry and inlay are closely related in that each produces an added design to the fabric, but in laid-in an added design thread is necessary, while in tapestry the design or color change is part of the regular weft row. A method of interlocking wefts to produce the design results in what is appropriately called "imitation tapestry." In this, too, the interlocking wefts form the design changes without an extra added design thread.

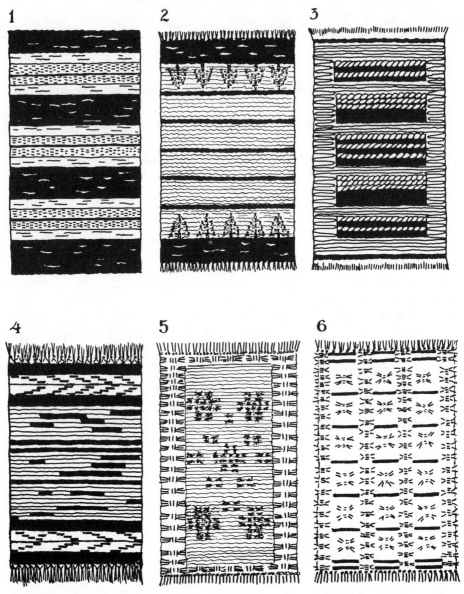

Fig. 48 — Six variations for two-harness rugs. No. 1 is a design with stripes in "Pepper and Salt" weave, alternating with light and dark bands. No. 2 is a rug with borders of small trees made of short laid-in rag ends. No. 3 illustrates the use of entwined borders shown at F and G, Figure 45. No. 4 shows arrow weave made by twisting rags of two colors around each other as at A, B, C, Figure 41. In No. 5 both center design and borders are made of laid-in rag ends. No. 6 has design with vertical stripes and small motifs made of laid-in rags on picked up sheds.

COMPARISON TO REGULAR TAPESTRY

The imitation-tapestry technique produces an effect similar to regular tapestry but is easier to execute. However, it is limited as to design possibilities. The figures in C, Figure 45, and A, B, D, and E, Figure 43, show its character. The method is shown in H, Figure 45. It employs two weft threads at the same time and through the same shed, interlocking with each other and reversing somewhere in the shed. For this reason it is sometimes called "Clasped Weave."

The technique differs from regular tapestry in that each color weaves, interlocks, and returns in the same row instead of waiting for another row. This makes two wefts in each row, as shown in the sketch in H, Figure 45. Since the rows are double, a lighter-weight rug yarn than usual can be used. In fact, this technique is a "find" if various belt-weave yarns, heavy wools, etc., are on hand. By doubling them up in this way, a filler about as heavy as a regular rug yarn can be acquired. Weavers usually like imitation tapestry as it proves interesting to make the design changes and the work is creative. The technique was first brought to the author's attention by the gift of some rugs from Sicily, woven in this way.

TEXTURE AND DECORATIVE USE

The texture is similar to tapestry but the wefts are double, and it is, therefore, a comparatively heavier texture. Since there is a nubby projection where the wefts interlock, a series of nubs outlines the design, a rather unique and interesting effect. Imitation tapestry rugs are excellent for modern interiors stressing texture change. The technique can also be applied to heavy runners, rug-weave pillows, to chair-back sets, etc.

DESIGN AND COLOR

Designs are simple, developing from two forms placed side by side and increasing or decreasing in size. Two-color effects are characteristic. The choice of colors is most important. There should be enough contrast to set off the design, one lively and one dull; or two complementary colors, or two shades of the same color if far enough apart in value.

Creating the designs is fascinating and the weaving is fast. It is fun to interlock the colors and see them flow back and forth freely, as in the rug in A, Figure 43. Fabrics also can be woven sideways as shown in the skyline design, E, Figure 43, or the cross, D. Flowers, too, may be woven as in B, Figure 43. Here, however, a third weft must be introduced. Since this is more difficult, it should not be attempted until after the two wefts have been mastered. Imitation tapestry, using a third weft, is especially useful for making borders at the sides of rugs.

81

MATERIALS

Since the weft rows become double, consisting of two rows of weft through the same shed, a yarn about half as heavy as the usual rug yarns should be used. Wool rug yarn is excellent, since it is not so heavy as cotton rug yarn. Cotton rug-weave yarn or smooth narrow rags are good to use. Germantown yarn doubled also can be used for lightweight mats.

EQUIPMENT

Any floor loom producing plain weave is satisfactory. The technique employs two shuttles used at the same time. Since one of these remains fairly stationary, while the other does the actual weaving, some weavers use a ball of thread in place of the second shuttle and allow its end to travel out from a wire hook which keeps it at a comfortable level at the left side. This takes the place of shuttle No. 2 in *H,* Figure 45.

METHOD EMPLOYED (H and J, Fig. 45)

For plain weave, before starting the tapestry, or between two sections of the same, use the same yarn as planned for the tapestry but double it, so that the texture of the background or the ends of the rug will be as heavy as the tapestry parts. Next, take a shuttle of each color, numbered 1 and 2 in the sketch. Start No. 1, a straight line, on the right side; No. 2, a dotted line, on the left side. See base of sketch *H.* Weft No. 2 does not weave at all. It simply receives the shuttle of No. 1. Thread No. 2, therefore, can be either loose on a ball in your lap, or on a stick shuttle. However, it is convenient also to have threads Nos. 1 and 2 on the same kind of throw shuttle, especially in drawing up the wefts after the interlocking, which is done with a shuttle in each hand. Weave several rows of plain weave with thread No. 1 before beginning tapestry. Several rows are shown finished; for directions below, follow numbers at upper part of diagram *H.*

Step 1. Make Shed 1. Weave with weft No. 1 from right to left. At the left selvage, pass it around weft No. 2, the dotted line, as shown. Do not change sheds, but carry weft No. 1 back toward the right through the same shed, as shown by arrow. Let weft No. 2 be very loose so that No. 1 can pull it toward the right. Stop motion at any point, where you wish to show the change of color, as shown by the vertical arrow. Now pull gently on each weft from side to side; leave each weft slightly on a slant, and beat with the beater.

Step 2. For the next row make shed No. 2, and again weave from right to left with weft No. 1; interlock with weft No. 2, and return in the same shed, placing point of reverse a little further to either side as the design shows. A little practice will enable you to get the reverse point exactly where desired.

Continue repeating steps 1 and 2. Step 2 is the same as step 1, but is made on shed 2.

This method takes care of two colors, and will cover all designs where in any row there is only one change. However, for putting in flower blossoms, or an area where the design shows two design changes, as in *B,* Figure 43 and *J,* Figure 45, make the first change and return to the right side with thread, *X.* Then, from the left through the same shed, bring the second thread, *Y,* to meet the third thread, *Z,* which remains in the center, and interlock with it, returning to the left side. With three threads the process takes nearly as long as real tapestry. Nevertheless, it is good to know this method, for most of the design can be woven quickly if you use two threads and simply add a unit or two of the three-thread type for accent or interest.

Fig. 49 — Colorful rug in dark and light squares of mixed cretonnes made of tufts of rags laid in by the method shown at 5, Fig. 48.
The heavy cotton fringe of rug filler matches the predominating pink tone. The Embroidered Swedish Flossa Rug Method of Chapter 5 can be used for the same effect.

PART IV

Warp- and Weft-Face Rugs

CHAPTER 12

Warp-Face Rugs

THE texture, thickness, and firmness of a rug depend first on the warp setting, second on the kinds of warp and weft used, and third on firmness in beating. In experimenting with effects, it is necessary only to vary the placing of the warps and their threading, or the weft colors and their textures, to get entirely different products.

In a practical weaving texture and one which is used a great deal, equal amounts of warp and weft show. The home weaver will find this a good choice for many rugs. Usually warp set at 10 to 12 or even 15 threads per inch and crossed with a medium-weight rug filler results in this texture. With warp and weft bearing equal amounts of wear and tear, a rug will last longer than when either element is exposed more. This is known as a balanced setting with a fairly even distribution of warp and weft; it is recommended for most rag rugs and for many of the four-harness techniques described.

However, on either side of this setting are two extremes, known as "warp face" and "weft face." In the former, the warp is set so closely that the weft does not show, and the warp, often striped, stands out boldly and provides the design. In the weft face, the warp is set so far apart that the filler sinks down between its threads and forms a thick weft surface. Any design or change of colors must be provided for in the weft, since this covers the warp. The three textures just described might be called evenly balanced, warp face, and weft face. Textures in between these definite types are sometimes desired by the weaver for unusual effects. For instance, if a ridged rug is desired, a pattern rug or a rag rug can be set at 16 warps per inch. The warp will show more than the weft but it will be modulated by it. Such a texture might be preferred for a certain purpose, such as a door mat, but the 12-per-inch setting should be used for softer household rugs. The same warp set at 20 to 24 per inch would produce a completely warp-face rug.

Most primitive rugs were warp-face woven in plain weave, but with only the warp showing and the weft concealed. The reason for this was that there were no reeds to keep the warp threads apart; they gravitated toward each other until they almost touched, covering the weft. Attractive striped designs could be arranged in the warp and, in fact, this was about the only way to achieve design. Some beautiful examples among primitive textiles can be seen in our museums.

The modern weaver uses a reed to get the warp-face effect in rugs, setting the warp as close as 20 to 30 per inch. The warp must be strong to withstand the wear on a rug. The best rag carpets of the early days were of this type, with linen or closely spun wool warp set at 20 to 24 per inch. These were practical for several reasons. They could be woven rapidly, for the design was in the warp and could be woven with a continuous weft, without interruptions for piecing. This weft could be anything at all, such as old rags or jute, since it does not show. The fine examples in Figure 51 are typical of a certain period.

TEXTURE AND DECORATIVE USE

Warp-surface rugs are firm and like a mat. If the warp is coarse, the rug takes on its character of stiff unyielding texture. If it is a ply yarn of more smoothly spun fibers, the rug structure allows these to show, making a softer surface. In either case, the stripe designs planned for decorative purposes are always vertical, and can be just as bright and gay as the warps themselves. Use these rugs to lengthen short, dark hall ways, to add cheer to stairways and landings, and to add length to small rooms.

DESIGN AND COLOR

A favorite type of Colonial rug was made of gay woolen warp stripes throughout, with wefts of discarded household cottons, such as sheets, towels, or dresses. The rags were all carefully cut the same size so that the texture was uniform. Rugs of this kind were made with very brilliant rainbow stripes, a charming floor accent which would be suitable in many a modern interior. The weft shows only slightly at the selvages where it reverses, but this can be hidden by making the edge threads of warp the same tone as the weft filler planned, or of a natural color which is hard to detect.

The following are several desirable types of warp-face or warp-surface rugs for the modern weaver to make:

1. Striped warps similar to those just described
2. Pepper-and-Salt design
3. Log-Cabin rugs
4. Mattor rugs

Nos. 1, 2, and 3 require only two harnesses; No. 4 requires a four-harness loom.

MATERIAL

Choice of Warp. In warp-surface rugs, since the wear comes only on the warp, the very best yarn must be used, such as heavy woolen yarn, 10/5 linen which comes in many colors, carpet warp 8/4 or 5/3, or heavy warp 4/4. Be sure to use fast colors and strong thread from standard thread companies.

Choice of Weft. Since the weft does not show, it may be any color or kind of thread, but always the same kind in the same piece. Old sheets, towels, rayon underwear, etc., can be used. Rugs also can be made heavy or light in weight by varying the size of the filler. Wool from suits can be used for the heaviest wefts, cutting these carefully to form even strips. Lighter-weight rags should be used for thin textured rugs.

Do *not* use the slot-and-hole method of piecing because a smooth weft must be made so that the rug surface will be flat and even. Piece rather as shown in *D* or *E,* Figure 64. If the rags used for filler are firm and smooth, the flat piecing at *D* is best; if they are lighter in weight and not so strong, the piecing at *E* is more practical.

EQUIPMENT

In addition to a sturdy floor loom, be sure that the reed and beater are strong and will accommodate a close setting. Two threads per dent in a coarse reed generally are better than one thread per dent in a closer reed. For instance, if you want 24 threads per in., a 24-dent reed is entirely too fine to take carpet warp, but two threads per dent in a 12-dent reed will give a close setting.

METHOD FOR MAKING SIMPLE WARP-FACE RUGS

Stripes for Warp-Face Rugs. If a hand-warping board is used, count off the desired number of threads for the first color. Change colors at the beginning or end of the warp length, tie on the next color, and proceed. Another method is to wind enough colored threads for a group, and chain off separately. Then follow with an entire fresh chain for the next color. On a sectional beam loom, buy or wind small spools for each color and arrange each 2-in. section of warp by drawing the desired colors from the spool rack and then through the threading guide in the order desired.

Thread Accents. For stunning vertical stripes, interrupt long repeats of a light warp color with two or three sharply contrasting threads; or alternate a long repeat of a dark with very bright or light threads. Use black against white or gray, red against gray or pale blue, brown against yellow, flame against aqua, etc.

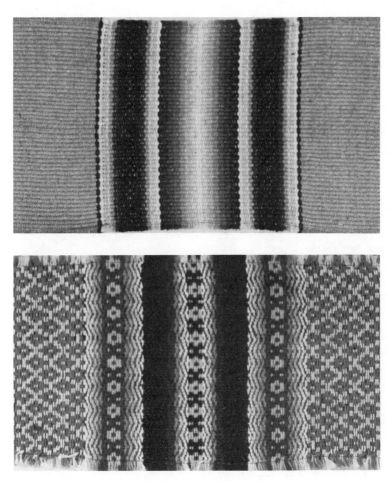

Fig. 51 — Two examples of traditional warp-face American carpets.

CONTRASTS AND BLENDS

Blend any series of colors rainbow fashion. Warp-surface threads show their color much more purely than when modified by the weft, which is one of the advantages of this kind of rug.

For actual warps and many other suggestions, see Chapter 18 on rag rugs.

WARP-SURFACE RUG IN STRIPE DESIGN
(Figs. 51 and 52)

The rug or carpet section shown at the top in Figure 51 is a typical warp design with brilliant colored stripes characteristic of the early nineteenth century in Pennsylvania. The background is a soft tan, and the stripes tend toward reds and yellows with a touch of green. The actual parts of the stripe are shown in detail at the bottom in Figure 52.

87

This rug was used in a home in Philadelphia in 1840. The warp is 4/4 wool, the best quality that could be bought to render the warp-face texture durable, and the weft is natural linen combined with jute to add strength to its quality. In early days every effort was made to give durability to hard-earned necessities. The rug at the bottom in Figure 51 is also a durable warp-face rug threaded to a diamond pattern, with more harnesses required to make the design possible.

WARP PLAN

Figure 51, upper rug
Warp: Tightly spun wool, 4-ply
Weft: Jute or finely cut rags (half the size of a pencil when twisted tightly)
Threads per Inch: 20
Width: 36 in., if two vertical stripe motifs are used
   18 in., if one vertical stripe motif is used
Total Threads: 734 for two stripes, 367 for one stripe

THREADING PLAN

See the shaded plan of one complete warp stripe, No. 2, Figure 52; also consult Figure 51.

Complete Warp Stripe (No. 2, Fig. 52)
X: Outside margin or background:
5-inch neutral tan warp. Number of threads   100
YZY: Complete right side colored border:
Y: First color blend, in chartreuse, black, and white:
   3 black threads, 3 white, 3 orange, 3 yellow, 3 chartreuse, 3 light green, 3 dark green, 3 blue-green, 3
   black, reverse to 3 blue-green, 3 dark green, 3
   light green, 3 chartreuse, 3 yellow, 3 orange, 3
   white, 3 black
      Total number of threads   51

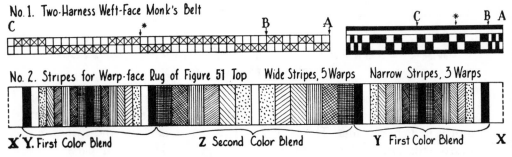

No. 1. Two-Harness Weft-Face Monk's Belt

No. 2. Stripes for Warp-face Rug of Figure 51 Top   Wide Stripes, 5 Warps   Narrow Stripes, 3 Warps

X' Y. First Color Blend   Z Second Color Blend   Y First Color Blend   X

Fig. 52 — Threading arrangements for warp-face and weft-face rugs.

Z: second color blend in pink, flame, dark red: 5
deep mahogany, 5 maroon, 5 dark red, 5 light red,

5 flame, 5 pink, 5 white, reverse to 5 pink, 5 flame,
5 light red, 5 dark red, 5 maroon, 5 deep mahogany
    Total number of threads 65
Y: Repeat first color blend. Number of threads 51
    Total number of threads complete stripe 167
X': Center of a wide rug or selvage of narrow rug of one motif:
    10-in. neutral tan warp. Number of threads 200
    (5-in. neutral, 100 threads, if for narrow rug)
YZY: Complete left side colored border:
    Same as Y, Z, Y above. Number of threads 167
X: Outside margin:
    5-in. neutral background tan warp. Number of threads . . . 100
    Total threads of rug warp 734
Note: If threading only one stripe, omit last two items.

WEAVING PLAN

Weave as plain weave with neutral-colored jute or rags; or any weft half the size of a pencil when twisted slightly.

"PEPPER-AND-SALT" STITCH

One of the most interesting and all-purpose warp designs known is the simple alternation of two contrasting colors. Black and white are excellent and form a warp almost neutral in its effect. Brown and white, deep blue or green and ivory, dark red and cream, dark gray and yellow are all good. Simply thread one dark and one light, and repeat all the way across the warp. If this speckled warp, known as "Pepper and Salt," is set very closely in the reed and woven with either a one-color weft or two alternate weft colors, the texture is mottled in appearance. If a heavy weft is used, alternating with a lightweight weft, the result is delightful in its ridged quality.

The principle of "Pepper and Salt," with interruptions in its sequence at intervals, gave rise to the Log-Cabin weave, described in the next chapter.

CHAPTER 13

Log-Cabin and Basket-Weave Rugs

THE Log-Cabin technique has come down to us from Colonial days. It is a quaint pattern for rugs, always popular and appealing because of the smart simplicity of its small squares of alternating color tones. The traditional form consists of a plain-weave threading of two contrasting colors as in "Pepper and Salt," but so arranged that the first color is predominant in one square, the second in the other. This breaking up of the regular speckled rhythm is achieved by threading in an extra warp wherever the change is desired. The change throws the dark colors that before were on shed 1 (warps numbered 1, 3, 5, 7, etc.) to shed 2 (warps numbered 2, 4, 6, 8, etc.), which means that in weaving light colors will now appear on the upper level of the shed, where it had shown dark colors before, and where light colors had previously come up, dark colors will now appear. The tone of the whole block changes at the warp change, which also forms a dividing line in the design.

TEXTURE AND DECORATIVE USE

In Log Cabin, the warp is set closely enough to make it a warp-surface technique, but the weft shows slightly and aids in the color effect. It is a splendid technique for rugs, its charm depending on the color blends and texture changes between blocks, not on a large spreading design. We usually find it woven in blocks or squares of the same size, as in the little rug sketch, No. 1, Figure 53. However, its square or oblong design blocks may be any size, making it suitable for modern interiors. It is also an authentic period rug of the past century, and excellent to use as a quaint note in restored rooms.

DESIGN AND COLOR

The striped warp of Log Cabin that weaves up into columns or blocks is quite different from the usual striped warp that weaves up in plaids of clear color contrast. Here, although we have plaids, each color carries some of the other color with it.

Log-Cabin effects are made possible by adding an extra light or dark thread to change stripe shadings. The dividing line between blocks made by adding an extra warp may be placed at any point whatever. This makes it possible to plan borders at the sides of Log-Cabin rugs, or large spaces across the center, as suggested in the sketch, No. 2, Figure 53. Delightful variations are possible by changing the size of the blocks and grouping them within these border bands.

If the same colored weft is used in weaving, the result is a series of vertical stripes or columns in an all-over tone influenced by the weft color. However, if alternate weft colors are used, the result is a series of columns in speckled texture, No. 1, *a, b, c,* Figure 53. If the color succession is changed, and an extra weft of either color used at a point, the tonal effect changes, and at this point dark-toned columns become light, and light-toned columns dark. If changes are made at regular intervals, the effect is of alternating squares of color tones. This effect of small squares is what gave rise to the name "Log Cabin" from its resemblance to logs laid together. Its final weave resembles the texture of a basket; hence, it is sometimes called "basket weave," although it is not the regular technical basket weave of two successive warps alternating with two successive wefts.

MATERIALS AND SETTING FOR LOG CABIN

Set carpet warp 8/4 or 5/3 at 12 to 16 threads per inch, or 10/5 linen warp or 4/4 cotton at 8 to 10 per inch. For very heavy weft, set pairs of cotton warp 8/4 at 8 to 10 pairs per inch; this will show up the warp color more and give a more pronounced difference between the colors of the squares. In place of pairs of 8/4 cotton warp a strong, heavy 3/2 cotton warp can be used by itself.

For the weft, use evenly cut rags in two colors, or commercial rug yarn either 3- or 4-ply. Since the weft is more or less covered, it is not necessary to purchase expensive wool weft.

However, if a rug of better quality with a pleasing sheen on the warp surface which shows most is to be made, purchase heavy linen or wool warp which comes in many beautiful colors, and weave with wool rug yarn.

A COLONIAL LOG-CABIN DESIGN — TWO COLORS (Fig. 53)

The Log-Cabin threading is plain weave on a two-harness or twill on a four-harness loom. The two contrasting warp colors alternate in such a way that all the darker threads show on the up-shed at intervals, causing a dark woven square, and the light threads show up in between, causing a light square.

In the draft, the dark threads (see X's) are used for the border, *A–B.* This may be as wide as desired, appearing when woven as in (*a*) of sketch

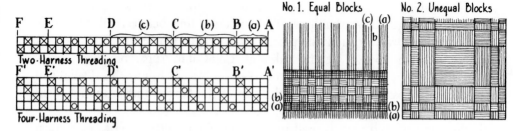

Fig. 53 — Threading arrangement for two- and four-harness Log Cabin rugs.

No. 1. From *B–C*, dark threads (*x*) are threaded on the first harness and light threads (*o*) on the second harness, shown woven at (*b*). From *C–D*, light threads are threaded on the first harness and dark threads on the second harness as at (*c*). The pattern keeps repeating *B–C* then *C–D*, forming alternating blocks, (*b*) and (*c*).

To obtain wider spaces of either block, as shown in sketch No. 2, repeat either block such as *B–C* or *C–D* more times in the threading, in contrast to fewer repeats of a narrower block.

To thread this pattern on a four-harness loom, run the alternating colors through the four harnesses as shown in sketch *A′–F′*, using in succession harnesses 1, 2, 3, 4, and the same order of colors as given for the two harnesses.

WARP PLAN FOR A RUG 28 IN. WIDE

Warp: 8/4 carpet warp
Weft: Two colors Rugro
Threads per Inch: 12
Width: 29 in. (weaves to 28 in.)
Total Threads: 352

THREADING PLAN

Choose two contrasting colors. In warping two colors, be sure that each color goes through a separate space of lease reed or a distributor to prevent twisting.

Threads

A–B, border (warp two dark threads in succession). Repeat *A–B*,
    4 threads, 8 times. 32
B–C, first block (warp a dark and light) 4 pairs of thread. Repeat
    B–C, 8 threads, 4 times. 32
C–D, second block (warp a dark and light) 4 pairs of thread. Repeat
    C–D, 8 threads, 4 times. 32
    Repeat from *B–D*, inclusive, 64 threads, to the desired width, (4
    times, 256 threads, for this rug) then add:

92

D–E, like first block, 4 pairs of thread. Repeat D–E, 4 times.   .   .   32
E–F, border (warp two dark threads in succession). Repeat E–F,
4 threads, 8 times.   32

WEAVING PLAN

The character of the weave is shown best in the two-harness threading in Figure 53. In weaving, when harness 1 (shed 1) is depressed, all sections like B–C have their light threads up and dark threads down; and all sections like C–D have their dark threads up and light threads down. When harness 2 (shed 2) is depressed, the opposite is true. This shows how the blocks occur. By weaving with an alternate light and dark weft, the light weft will make a light ridge if the light warps are raised, and the dark weft will make a dark ridge if the dark warps are raised. Weaving with the light weft on shed 1 for a space, and the dark on shed 2, results in a certain color contrast between adjacent blocks. By adding an extra light weft on shed 2, the dark will now occur on shed 1 and the light on shed 2, giving an entirely different effect and causing the formation of the blocks both warp-wise and weft-wise. Here are the sheds on either two- or four-harness looms. For these threadings, see Figure 53.

Two-Harness	*Four-Harness*
Shed 1 — depress harness 1	depress harnesses 1–3
Shed 2 — depress harness 2	depress harnesses 2–4

In designing Log-Cabin rugs you can easily achieve the four following effects:

Effect 1.   First block texture: Weave shed 1 (light), shed 2 (dark), shed 1 (light), shed 2 (dark). Repeat until the sections form squares.

Effect 2.   Second block: Weave shed 1 (dark), shed 2 (light), shed 1 (dark), shed 2 (light). Repeat to square the blocks.

Effect 3.   Solid dark color, any width: Weave alternate sheds, dark filler only.

Effect 4.   Solid light color, any width: Weave alternate sheds, light filler only.

The traditional Log Cabin is woven with alternate squares of (b) and (c) blocks, as shown in Figure 53. Between the blocks there will be two successive rows of the same color, such as a dark finishing the old block, and a dark starting the new. This change causes the interesting texture and color change of the Log-Cabin blocks.

In No. 1, Figure 53, the size of both blocks is the same. In No. 2, see how designs can be made to have regular side borders and centers by repeating one block oftener than the other. Carry out the same proportion in weaving for *plaid* effects. For *vertical columns*, Log Cabin usually is woven with a neutral weft color, which does not interfere with the dark and light vertical warp stripes.

93

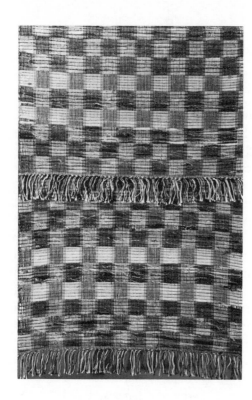

Fig. 54 — Log Cabin warp-face rug
in red, white, and blue with
red warp accents.

Courtesy — Mrs. Dan Koster

LARGE LOG-CABIN WARP-FACE RAG RUG
IN RED, WHITE, AND BLUE (Fig. 54)

This red, white, and blue rug is far lovelier in its actual form than the photograph shows. Between the blocks of black and white warps, bands of red warp threads act as both dividing lines and colorful accents, and these blend with wide red bands at the ends of the rug, hardly visible in the photograph. The filler is heavy blue denim and the rug is very sturdy and practical. The warp colors practically cover the filler which is the same throughout, the block changes being achieved by a second weft of black carpet warp, instead of an alternating weft of the same weight generally used.

WARP PLAN

Warp: Red, white, and black 8/4 carpet warp
Filler: Blue denim
Threads per Inch: 12
Width in Reed: 28 in., weaves down to 27 in.
Total Number of Threads: 340

THREADING PLAN

Use Figure 53 as a guide but make the *B–C* and *C–D* blocks 20 instead of 8 threads each.

94

A–B — Selvage. 4 bright red threads 4

B–C — Start with white warp (o), alternate with black warp (x) for 20 threads, 10 threads each.

A–B — Add four extra red threads again.

C–D — Start with dark warp (x), alternate with white warp (o) for 20 threads, 10 threads each.

Repeat this series of two full blocks with red accents, 24 threads each, all across rug, 6 times, 12 blocks. At end add *A–B,* 4 red threads.

WEAVING PLAN

Alternate heavy blue denim (d) with black carpet warp (cw) as follows:

Heading: Leave 4-in. fringe. Weave 10 rows red carpet warp as tabby, harnesses 1–3 then 2–4. (On two-harness loom, harness 1 then harness 2.)

Main Rug:

(a) Block: harnesses 1–3 (d); harnesses 2–4 (cw). Repeat to square the block.

(b) Block: harnesses 1–3 (cw); harnesses 2–4 (d). Repeat to square the block. Alternate (a) and (b) blocks to length desired. End with (a) block and red heading. For a red border, simply replace denim rags with red rags.

CHAPTER 14

Mattor-Weave Rugs

A POPULAR rug and mat texture known as the Mattor weave, originating in Scandinavia, has been brought to this country in recent years. It is built upon the same principle as the Log-Cabin weave, used so much in the southern mountains and New England as a durable, practical weave for rugs and runners. Since Mattor is strictly warp face, it can prove a very durable weave and wear-resistant rug surface.

The Mattor weave is most frequently woven on four or more harnesses, and this provides more design blocks for variety of both color and form. Log Cabin adheres to the shifting of two tabby combinations and two colors only, and may be woven either on a two-harness or four-harness loom.

TEXTURE AND DECORATIVE USE

The texture of Mattor rugs is exceedingly strong and closely woven. This rug lies flat and its surface is smooth and even. The feeling or texture of its surface depends on the quality of the warp. Since the design is in square or oblong blocks, this type of rug is useful for modern decorative effects as well as traditional settings of Scandinavian feeling. The figures are always simple and colorful, and several color tones may be blended in blocks within blocks, adding textural interest. The firm texture and simple designs of Mattor rugs make them most suitable for boys' rooms, game rooms, and halls.

DESIGN AND COLOR

The design in Mattor weave depends upon the use of two colors alternating with each other, with an occasional shift of each color to another shed. In Mattor there is also a greater freedom in the change of the lights and darks to other harness combinations than in Log Cabin. For instance, in the pattern of Figure 56, the dark color starts out on the block of harnesses 1–2, which puts the dark on both the 1–3 and the 2–4 shed. Then the light color takes over on harnesses 3–4. Later, reading the draft from right to left, the 1–2 block with the dark color is on harness 1, and the light color on harness 2, while the dark thread remains on either harness 3 or harness 1 for some time. Then the darks shift to harness 2 or harness 4, i.e., the other shed (notice vertical arrow at center of long 1–2 block). At points where this shifting occurs, a different color rises to the upper layer of warp threads when the shed is made. This causes a change in the pattern, as well as in the colors of the woven blocks. More than one pair of colors can be used.

MATERIALS

The warp is of heavy cotton or linen or closely spun wool. These threads are set close in the reed so as to form a warp-surface texture.

The weft should be fairly heavy to make the warp threads show well as the weft passes under them; the thicker the weft the more the warps are lifted over its round form.

By using a very heavy weft and alternating this with a fine weft, one set of warps and colors will appear. more predominant. To bring out the other set of warps, or the second series of color blocks, weave in an additional heavy row, which puts the fine weft on the shed last used by the heavy weft, and the heavy weft on the shed last used by the fine.

These two wefts, heavy and fine, may be of the same color as they do not show except at the selvages. A single weft would also give the division of the design blocks, but it is not quite so effective.

Fig. 55 — Corner of Mattor rug.

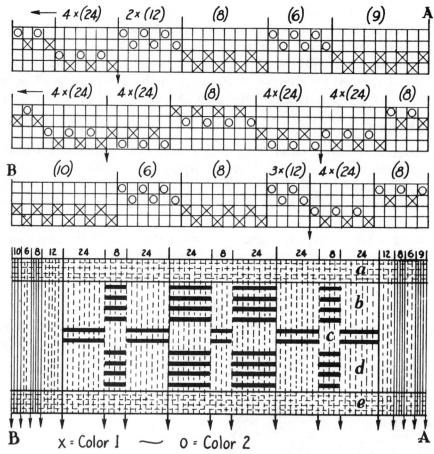

Fig. 56 — Mattor rug draft and design for rug in Figure 55.

EQUIPMENT

Mattor requires a sturdy four-harness loom, either jack or counterbalanced. The beater should be strong, and the reed such as to accommodate a close setting.

Two rug shuttles of equal size make weaving efficient as they alternate; but a rug shuttle also can be used for the heavy weft and a throw shuttle for the finer weft.

METHOD

Warp Plan

Warp: Cotton carpet warp 8/4 or 5/3 set at 15 to 20 per in.; or 10/5 linen or 4/4 cotton set at 12 to 16; or spun wool set according to its weight.

Weft: Two or four colors in groups of a heavy and a fine for each pair. For the heavier of the two wefts, use cotton rugro, woolen thrums, evenly cut rags, etc. For the finer weft, use rug-weave yarn, tufting cotton, finer rags, or coarse yarn such as 3/2 cotton or 4-strand, even carpet warp double. The wefts are practically covered by the warp, so they may be a cheap substance, but they must be durable.

Threading Plan. Choose two warp colors, x and o. If you wish to use more than two colors, choose another light and dark combination, and substitute this pair at sections desired in the threading. Or simply change one of the two colors of the first pair, such as a more striking dark color to be used in the border. Thread the draft of Figure 56 from *A* to *B*, following each section in order from right to left. Note that the groups of the upper draft which are marked off by vertical divisions correspond to the groups of the woven rug in the sketch below, marked off by vertical arrows. These divisions in both draft and drawing show how the colors shift from one shed to the other.

The warp of Figure 56 has 240 threads, 120 light and 120 dark. A selvage, 8 more threads, may be added:

Right Selvage: Harness 4 dark; harness 3 light; harness 2 dark; harness 1 light.

Left Selvage: Harness 1 light; harness 2 dark; harness 3 light; harness 4 dark.

Weaving Plan. For the filler, choose a heavy rag strip or rug yarn, and alternate with finer rug-weave yarn or tufting cotton, etc. Here are the possibilities for harness combinations:

Harnesses 4–1, alternating with harnesses 2–3
Harnesses 1–3, alternating with harnesses 2–4

Think out ways of combining harnesses with different color alternations:

To weave the rug in Figure 56, a, b, c, d, e (finished rug in Figure 55):

Section (a): Harnesses 1–3, coarse; 2–4, fine; alternate for space desired. Finish with 1–3, coarse.

Section (b): Harnesses 2–3, coarse; 4–1, fine; alternate for space desired. Finish with 2–3, coarse.

Section (c): Harnesses 4–1, coarse; 2–3, fine; alternate for space desired. Finish with 4–1, coarse.

Weave section (d) same as (b); section (e) same as (a).

For another variation, weave section (a) for a space, alternating harnesses 1–3, coarse, and 2–4, fine; end with harnesses 1–3 coarse. Now start the reverse coloring, following this last row with harnesses 2–4, coarse, harnesses 1–3, fine, and alternate, ending with harnesses 2–4, coarse. Repeat until ready for section (b).

For color changes within the same block, four colors are needed, such as: coarse brown with fine gold; fine brown with coarse gold. Weave any of the successions above, first with one set then with the other.

Weft-Face Rugs

Rugs in the weft-face technique are very soft, for the weft crowds down between the rougher warps; thus only the surface of the weft can be seen and felt. This is the type of rug made by the Indians in the famous Navajo tapestry rugs described elsewhere. In general, wool is the best filler to use. For a less expensive rug, use 4-strand cotton or rug-weave yarn or 3-ply rug yarn.

Following are the types of weft-surface rugs described in this book: Oriental tapestry rugs, Chapter 8; Navajo tapestry rugs, Chapter 9; Soumak rugs, Chapter 10; laid-in and imitation tapestry, Chapter 11; weft-face Monk's Belt, Chapter 15; three-harness weave, Chapter 16; and Indian Saddle-Blanket weave, Chapter 17. Below are the general rules for weaving all weft-face or weft-surface rugs.

TEXTURE AND DECORATIVE USE

Although pile rugs, with their deep-cut pile surface, are the softest of all rugs, weft-face rugs are a close second in giving foot comfort. A coarse, strong warp is buried beneath a weft which can be as soft and smooth as the weaver chooses. Since these rugs include those of tapestry design, they are not only desirable for their texture but for their design and color possibilities as well. Weft-face rugs generally are thick and firm as a result of the packing of the filler and, therefore, are suitable for living and dining rooms. In bedroom and bathroom, where soft surfaces are welcome, small weft-face rugs are gratifying.

COLOR AND DESIGN

The designs of weft-face rugs depend solely on the handling of the weft which alone is visible. Interesting effects are caused by the interplay of two or more weft colors, producing vertical columns, Figure 57, or by weaving successive sections of each weft color in horizontal stripes, No. 1,

Figure 48, or by using three or more colors in a rhythmic succession as in bound weaving, Figure 59. If tapestry-weave techniques are employed, the design potentials are limitless, with background and design wefts interlocking to form any figure chosen, worked out from a graph-paper guide. However, weavers who grow expert in weaving tapestry can create free designs inspired by the colors of the interlocking wefts.

The simplest way to weave in the weft-face manner is to use two well balanced colors and alternate them on a tabby combination or on opposites while weaving. This produces definite vertical columns. If an extra row of one of the colors is added, the columns shift, and the dark colors appear where the light were before, as shown in Figure 58.

For best effects in coloring use soft blends or contrasting hues. For laid-in designs, such as diamonds, triangles, etc., carefully planned accent colors against neutral backgrounds produce effective rugs (see E and F, Fig. 41). Plan the borders also in contrasting hues or in darker shades of the background color.

For guidance in designing rugs of weft-face texture, see Figures 37, 42, 43, 48, 57, and 58; also tapestry weaves, Figure 41, and weft-face Monk's Belt, Figure 52.

MATERIALS AND SETTINGS

Since only the weft shows, the warps must be set far enough apart to be covered. Carpet warp 8/4 or 5/3, set at 8 to 10 per inch, is used for medium-weight rugs woven with 3-ply rug yarns, wool rug yarn, or chenille filler. For heavier rugs, use pairs of carpet warp 8/4 or 5/3 set at 6 to 8 pairs per inch and woven with soft heavy filler. Heavy linen warp 10/5 and cotton 4/4 are good for very strong rugs; they should be set at 4 to 6 per inch and woven with 4-ply rug yarn, heavy wool filler, etc.

EQUIPMENT

Primitive weavers fastened their warps across poles and made a routine tie to hold warp threads apart at even distances. They packed down the weft with a sword, laying it in where desired with their hands. While it is possible and interesting to imitate this inexpensive method, especially in art or history classes, the person who weaves durable rugs today needs a sturdy floor loom, either two or four-harness. The essential requirement is a coarse reed for the wide setting of the warps, and a strong beater to pack the filler so closely against preceding rows that the warp is entirely covered.

METHOD

Since the weft-face type of rug covers the many techniques listed previously, the specific methods for each will be found in its chapter. The method of setting warps or pairs of warps far enough apart to enable the chosen filler

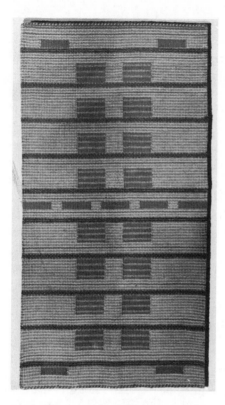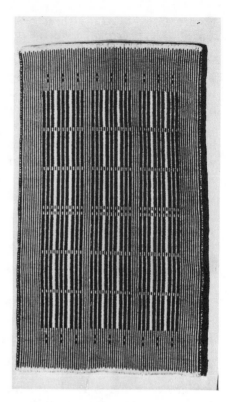

Fig. 57 — Weft-face Rugs. Left, "Apartment Building" design, red brick squares against tan; cross-bands, deep emerald; tapestry weave. Right, "Sharp Rhythm," woven on opposites in Summer and Winter; colors, natural, seal brown and emerald; dots woven on a pick-up stick.

Courtesy — Clem Smith

to cover them completely is common to all. The same is true of the need for heavy beating. In planning to weave rugs of weft-face texture, it is a wise plan to make a sample setting of the warp and weave a trial section across it with the weft, to be sure of getting the desired results.

A BEAUTIFUL WEFT-FACE ALLOVER ROOM CARPET (Fig. 2)

The effective beauty of the living-room rug in Figure 2 is due to its great simplicity and the sturdy quality of its cowhair filler, which resembles the jute rug yarn used in Figure 58. The threadling is "two-twills," and bands of dark twill weave alternate with the speckled bands of plain weave.

The technique is the same as that used for the run in Figure 58.

THREADING

The two-twills pattern: Harnesses 1, 2, 3, 4; 1, 2, 3, 4; 1, 4, 3, 2; 1, 4, 3, 2; 1, 4. Repeat all to width desired.

Dark Band: 4-in. plain weave or twill, dark brown cowhair (about the same thickness as rug jute). Dark lead gray is also effective.

Brown and Natural Speckled Band:

Edge of Band: Harnesses 4–1, brown; harnesses 2–3, natural. Alternate 3 times, 6 rows. End with natural, harnesses 2–3.

Speckled Center: Harnesses 1–3, natural; harnesses 2–4, brown. Repeat 8 times. End with harnesses 1–3, natural.

Edge: Harnesses 2–3, natural; harnesses 4–1, brown. Repeat 3 times. End with harnesses 2–3, natural.

Continue with next dark band.

WEFT-FACE RUG IN TWO-HARNESS MONK'S BELT (Fig. 52)

A practical type of weft-surface rug is the two-harness Monk's Belt. Its design appears in cheery columns or squares of color, making a bright rug for dark corners. Only one color is necessary for the warp since it is covered, but two alternating weft colors on separate shuttles are used in weaving. It is easy to weave; the two colors go right along in the treadling of the alternate harnesses. For the sketch of the finished rug border, see No. 1, right, in Figure 52.

Like Log Cabin, this pattern can either be woven in columns by continuing right along with the same weft color succession, dark, light, dark, light, etc., or it may be changed into blocks by throwing in an extra row of either color, i.e., a light after a light, or a dark after a dark, on the next shed of course, then continuing to alternate. The first column effect will be dark, light, dark, light; then change to light, dark, light, dark; then dark, light, dark, light; etc.

Fig. 58 — Close-up of rug stripes in weft-face technique. Design by Lili Blumeneau.

WARP PLAN

Warp: Carpet warp 8/4, 8/3, or 5/3
Weft: Two colors of rug filler
Threads per Inch: 12 or 15
Width: 24½ in. (weaves to 23 in), or 20 in. if set at 15
Total Threads: 304

THREADING PLAN

Plan No. 1. Uneven Blocks:

	Threads
Thread *A–B*, border (8 threads). Repeat 2 times	16
B–C, pattern (32 threads). Repeat 8 times	256
B to (*) only	16
B–A (read *A–B* backward) 8 threads. Repeat 2 times . . .	16
Total number of threads	304

Plan No. 2. Even Blocks: Checkerboard Effect:
All the blocks can be of the same size except the narrow border blocks. In this case start threading *A–B,* then follow with four units on harness 1, four on harness 2, etc. Keep repeating, then end with four on harness 1, and the border *B–A.*

WEAVING PLAN FOR BOTH DESIGNS

The effect of weft-face Monk's Belt when woven is that of two alternating blocks. Call the first block the (a) block; the second block, the (b) block. Use two shuttles, one with dark filler, the other with light.

(a) block: Weave harness 1, dark color; harness 2, light color. Repeat this succession as desired to form a row of squarelike motifs.

(b) block: Weave harness 1, light color; harness 2, dark color. Repeat as desired. The light shows up against the dark in previous row.

VARIATIONS IN EFFECT

For dark bands to outline the regular weave and to be inserted where desired, simply weave the above successions with only the dark shuttle. For light bands, weave with the light shuttle only. These dark and light bands are shown at upper right of drawing in Figure 52, No. 1.

One can add other colors for accents and contrasts. For instance, if weaving with one pair of colors, such as deep maroon and gold, one can change the gold to pale blue, and keep weaving with maroon and pale blue; or one can change both colors, the maroon to aqua, the gold to cream, or any desired combination.

CHAPTER 16

Three- and Four-Harness Krokbragd

THE three-harness weave offers splendid chances for striking color effects in step-like designs, Figure 59. This type of weave is known as *Krokbragd,* or "crooked path," and comes to us from Norway where it has been worked out in some unusual color effects. It is an ancient weave but one which will produce colorful surfaces of design suitable to modern decoration. In fact, the weaver who likes brilliant colors will glory in its daring color contrasts and ease of adding one color after another. The weaver should work like a painter, having at hand, ready for his "palette-shuttle," a bountiful supply of yarns of many colors. The weave is versatile, and it takes but the imagination of the weaver to achieve very beautiful effects.

TEXTURE AND DECORATIVE USE

The texture of three-harness rugs is heavy and matlike; in other words, it is a weft-face texture. The warp does not show, since the weft is packed down closely over it, with widely set warp threads to permit this. A lighter-weight weft is used than in the overshot technique of skipped spaces and binding tabby, for the wefts push against each other closely and add up to a soft heavy texture, especially pleasing to walk on. Use these rugs where soft foot comfort is desired. Their angular designs with brilliant color shadings make them suitable for interiors of modern decorative trend.

The weave may be adapted to other articles such as pillows, panels, purses, belts, chair-back sets, and table runners. For these a lighter-weight warp is used, such as 10/3 cotton or 16/2 linen set at 10 or 12 threads per inch, and a fine woolen filler. Germantown is excellent, used double for thicker effects. Cotton rug-weave yarn or cotton 4-strand filler may also be used.

DESIGN AND COLOR

This weave lends itself to designs of ascending and descending points of color, as well as triangular effects. One weft color replaces another; then a second is added, a third, etc., until there is an ascending series of tones. The charm of the pattern depends upon the blending or contrasting of these tones. The design at *H*, Figure 59, shows two colors, that at *I*, three, and at *J*, four. The succession of the treadles is often a simple repeat of harness 1, then harness 2, then harness 3; but the steps are obtained by the changes of the *color* succession, as well as the treadling. One of the most fascinating techniques known is to shade from color to color while the foot plays more or less the same tune. While the weave is called "three-harness," the same principle may be carried out in a four-harness plan. A threading for four-harness Krokbragd is given in *C*, Figure 59; and a finished rug in the four-harness type is shown in Figure 6, the rug in the background on the fireplace mantel.

MATERIALS

For rugs in three-harness weave use both warp and weft of good quality and durable texture, for this type of rug requires more time in weaving than many. It offers a splendid chance for colorful design in a weft-surface texture comparable to tapestry.

For warp, use the stronger grades of carpet warp, size 4/4 or 5/3; if you use 8/4, double it. Linen 10/5 is always good to use. While the warp is completely covered, this type of rug should last a long time; therefore, an expensive weft must not be used with a weak warp. Since the warp is set far apart, if the rug should have a fringe, add ends of wool yarn like the weft at the rug ends, and tie these in suitable groupings.

As for weft, rugs in three-harness weave are most effective when woven with soft heavy yarns, preferably wool rug yarn or a good grade of cotton filler, or carefully cut waste ends of wool fabrics from carpet mills. Wool filler is not only soft to the foot, but wears longer and is more soil resistant than cotton. In this weave especially, the lovely colors of wool rug yarn and its smooth texture produce effective rugs. In any one rug, use the same kind of weft throughout, such as all rayon, wool, or cotton, etc., and do not mix the wefts.

WARP SETTINGS

Heavy Texture: for heavy thick rugs
Warp: 4/4 or 5/3 cotton warp, or 8/4 double; or 10/5 linen warp, set at 4 to 6 per inch
Weft: Heavy wool rug yarn or cotton 4-ply rug filler
Medium Texture: for rugs of less weight or for wall hangings.
Warp: 8/3 or 8/4 cotton warp; or 10/2 linen warp, set at 8 to 10 per inch.
Weft: Medium-weight wool rug yarn, or Persian rug yarn, or Germantown yarn used double or triple, or cotton 3-ply rug-yarn, or rug-weave yarn.

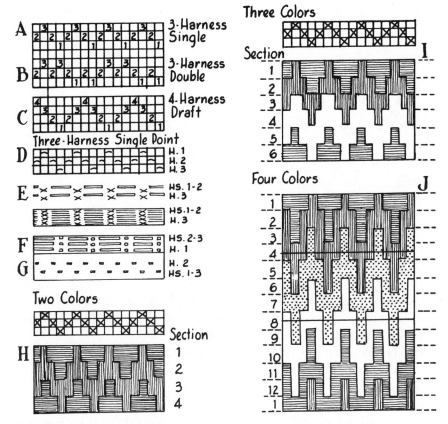

Fig. 59 — Design motifs of three-harness weave or Krokbragd;
draft for four-harness Krokbragd.

EQUIPMENT

To make a four-harness counterbalanced loom into a three-harness loom for threading the three-harness type, tie two harnesses together on the same beam so that they will move and act as one. Thread through one of them only. On a jack loom, any three harnesses can be used.

METHOD OF THREADING KROKBRAGD (Fig. 59)

Three-Harness Threading. There are two ways of threading — single or double points.

1. Single points, *A,* Figure 59. Thread harnesses 1, 2, 3, 2, and repeat.
2. Double points, *B,* Figure 59. Thread harnesses 1, 2, 1, 2, 3, 2, 3, 2, and repeat.

Four-Harness Threading

3. Thread as reverse twill, *C*, Figure 59. Thread harnesses 1, 2, 3, 4, 3, 2, and repeat.

TREADLE COMBINATIONS FOR THREE-HARNESS (Fig. 59)

There are six treadle conbinations: Harnesses 1 alone, 2 alone, 3 alone, 1 and 3 together, 1 and 2 together, 2 and 3 together. The tabby is harness 2 alone, then harnesses 1–3 together. Repeat. Use this tabby for headings at ends of rugs.

If a tie-up is preferred, prepare six treadles: Treadle 1, harness 1; treadle 2, harness 2; treadle 3, harness 3; treadle 4, harnesses 1–3; treadle 5, harnesses 1–2; treadle 6, harnesses 2–3.

For the various treadlings which make the columns and points shown, *D* to *J*, Figure 59, treadle as follows, finding the sections marked on the sketches. In all cases where two harnesses are used together, separate to single harnesses for closer-grained rug texture. For instance, at *E*, instead of harnesses 1–2, color (a); harness 3, color (b), treadle harness 1 alone, color (a); harness 2 alone, color (a); and harness 3 alone, color (b).

D. Three colors: (a), (b), (c): Weave harness 1 (a), harness 2 (b), harness 3 (c). Repeat.

E. Two colors: Weave harnesses 1–2 (a), harness 3 (b). Repeat.

F. Two colors: Weave harnesses 2–3 (a), harness 1 (b). Repeat.

G. Repeat. Two colors: (a), (b): Weave harness 2 (a), then harnesses 1–3 (b).

H. Two colors: (a), (b):
    Section 1. Harnesses 1–2 (a), harness 3 (b). Repeat as desired.
    Section 2. Harness 1 (a), harnesses 2–3 (b). Repeat as desired.
    Section 3. Harnesses 1–2 (b), harness 3 (a). Repeat as desired.
    Section 4. Harness 1 (b), harnesses 2–3 (a). Repeat as desired.

I. Three colors: (a), (b), (c):
    Section 1. Harnesses 1–2 (a), harness 3 (b). Repeat as desired.
    Section 2. Harness 1 (a), harnesses 2–3 (b). Repeat as desired.
    Section 3. Harnesses 1–2 (b), harness 3 (c). Repeat as desired.
    Section 4. Harness 1 (b), harnesses 2–3 (c). Repeat as desired.
    Section 5. Harnesses 1–2 (c), harness 3 (a). Repeat as desired.
    Section 6. Harness 1 (c), harnesses 2–3 (a). Repeat as desired.

J. Four colors: (a), (b), (c), (d):
This is the most effective of all the methods. Use contrasting colors.

For a background single color at the beginning, weave tabby with (a) only: Harness 2 alone; then harnesses 1–3. Repeat as desired. Then add the second color (b), and weave as follows:

Section 1. Harness 1 (b), harness 2 (a), harness 3 (a). Repeat about ¼ in. Omit the last harness 3 (a). Now reverse the colors, taking color (a) first.

Section 2. Harness 3 (a); harness 1 (b); harness 2 (b). Repeat about ¼ in. Add a third color (c).

Section 3. Harness 1 (c), harness 3 (a), harness 2 (b). Repeat ¼ in.

Section 4. Harness 1 (c), harness 3 (b), harness 2 (b). Repeat ¼ in.

Section 5. Harness 3 (b), harness 1 (c), harness 2 (c). Repeat ¼ in. Add a fourth color (d). Omit the first color (a). From now on the three steps listed below represent a continuous repeat which may be carried out in any four colors:

Section 6. Harness 1 (d), harness 3 (b), harness 2 (c). Repeat ¼ in.

Section 7. Harness 1 (d), harness 3 (c), harness 2 (c). Repeat about ¼ in.

Section 8. Harness 3 (c), harness 1 (d), harness 2 (d). Repeat about ¼ in. Add the next color. Repeat steps 6, 7, and 8, putting a new added color (e) where the former (d) was; and each color where the color of the previous letter was; i.e., put (e) in place of (d), (d) in place of (c), (c) in place of (b), (b) in place of (a), or take out. Keep adding colors thus, or reverse the colors.

The same directions shown for the single-point draft of *A,* Figure 59, also apply to the double-point draft, *B.*

METHOD OF WEAVING FOUR-HARNESS KROKBRAGD

Four-harness Krokbragd is quite similar to bound weaving and Indian saddle-blanket weave. The threading is reverse twill, and the weaving follows a consistent repeat of treadles, with change of color causing the desired effects. For materials, follow the same suggestions as for three-harness but set the warp at 6 to 8 per inch. No tabby is used, and the weft completely covers the warp, making a weft-surface fabric. Consult *C,* Figure 59, for threading.

Four-Harness Treadling:

Counterbalanced Loom: Treadle in succession harness 1 alone; harness 2; harness 3; harness 4.

Jack Loom: Treadle in succession: harneses 2, 3, 4 together, harnesses 3, 4, 1, harnesses 4, 1, 2, and harnesses 1, 2, 3.

SMALL ROSETTE WITHIN DIAMONDS

One of the most attractive figures is obtained by treadling as follows: There are 12 rows in one repeat; three colors are used. Read each row from left to right.

Row Harnesses	1	2	3	4
1.	Yellow	Yellow	Brown	Brown
2.	Brown	Yellow	Yellow	Brown
3.	Brown	Brown	Yellow	Yellow
4.	Green	Brown	Brown	Yellow
5.	Green	Green	Brown	Yellow
6.	Green	Brown	Brown	Yellow
7.	Brown	Brown	Yellow	Yellow
8.	Brown	Yellow	Yellow	Brown
9.	Yellow	Yellow	Brown	Brown
10.	Yellow	Brown	Brown	Green
11.	Yellow	Brown	Green	Green
12.	Yellow	Brown	Brown	Green

Fig. 60 — Indian weft-face ruglet, a photo of the rug described on page 66. Colors: red, gray, black and soft brown. Center design in tapestry weave.

CHAPTER 17

Indian Saddle-Blanket Rugs

TEXTURE AND DECORATIVE USE

An unusual and beautiful rug in two or more successive colors on a twill threading was created in this country by the American Indian. He wove it to secure a heavy mat surface for his saddle blankets. We now find this weave fascinating because of its mysterious color effects and useful because of its solid structure. Woven with cotton or wool rug yarn, it makes soft bedside rugs, floor runners for bungalows, seats for hard chairs or benches.

DESIGN AND COLOR

The four typical methods used for Indian saddle blankets, according to Gladys Reichard , author of *Navajo Shepherd and Weaver,** are known as "It is Woven," "Speckled," "Twill," and "Diamond." One of the advantages of this type of weaving is its attractive balance of soft color blends. Two or more colors are used in even balance, so that no one color stands out above the rest. The resulting color blend is not only pleasing but practical as it can be used with many color schemes. See Figure 61 for the character of these textures.

MATERIALS AND SETTING

The warp must be set far enough apart to be covered, for this is a weft-face texture. For thick, firm rugs, use 8/4 or 5/3 carpet warp doubled, or single strands of 4/4 cotton or 10/5 linen set at 6 to 8 per inch. The best filler is wool rug yarn or Germantown wool doubled or tripled, cotton substitutes, 3-ply rug yarn, or cotton rug-weave yarn.

For less heavy mats and cushions, set 8/4 or 5/3 carpet warp at 10 singles per inch and weave with blanket wool or 4-strand cotton.

* New York, N. Y.: J. J. Augustin, Publisher, 1936. Reprinted by Dover Publications, Inc., under the title *Weaving a Navajo Blanket.*

111

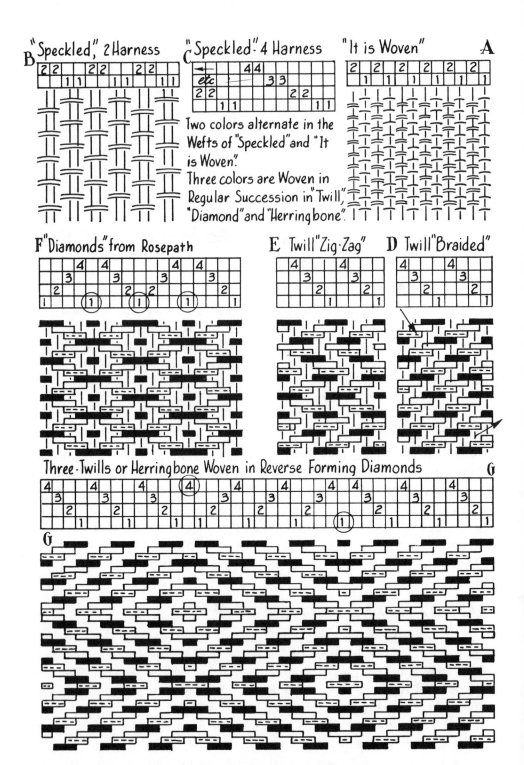

B "Speckled," 2 Harness   C "Speckled," 4 Harness   "It is Woven"   A

Two colors alternate in the Wefts of "Speckled" and "It is Woven".
Three colors are Woven in Regular Succession in "Twill", "Diamond" and "Herringbone".

F "Diamonds" from Rosepath   E Twill "Zig-Zag"   D Twill "Braided"

Three-Twills or Herringbone Woven in Reverse Forming Diamonds   G

G

Fig. 61 — Rugs in Indian Saddle-Blanket weave with variations.

EQUIPMENT

Indian saddle blankets were woven by the American Indian on warps stretched vertically between poles, and this arrangement served as his loom. To use this weave as a durable rug technique it is now necessary to have a sturdy four-harness floor loom with a large rug shuttle for each color of weft to be used.

METHODS

Blanket, "It is Woven." In this, the threading is tabby, *A*, Figure 61, and the weave is of two colors, alternating. The two-harness threading is alternate harnesses 1 and 2, and the four-harness threading is harnesses 1, 2, 3, and 4. The effect of weaving vertical columns of color by using two colors in this way is to give a color blend. It is fine for rugs, mats, and blankets or for a section of weaving between other weaves. Weave harness 1 then harness 2 alternately if threaded on a two-harness loom; and use a shuttle of the first color on harness 1, and a shuttle of the second color on harness 2. On a four-harness loom weave the first color on harnesses 1–3 and the second color on harnesses 2–4.

Speckled Weave (B and C, Fig. 61). This threading is planned so that two adjacent threads on one harness alternate with two on the other harness. On a two-harness loom, the threading is as shown at *B*, Figure 61; on a four-harness, as at *C*. When woven as tabby with two alternating wefts, the effect is as shown in the development below *B*. For four-harness threading, weave harnesses 1–3, then 2–4. For two-harness threading, weave harness 1, then harness 2. The speckled effect is more pronounced with alternating colors.

Twill "Zigzag" or "Braided" (D and E, Fig. 61). The threading is twill; the weaving is done with one or two, but preferably three successive colors. The final effect depends on interesting color combinations.

The Weave (*D*, Fig. 61). The succession of treadling follows the same plan as for regular twill weaving. Three successive colors are used, always in the same order. The texture of the pattern, visible along diagonal lines, seems to be quite independent of the trend of the colored stripes of the design, which appear to go in the opposite direction. For instance, in the sketch at *D*, the texture of the pattern goes from left to right as shown in the upward arrow, while the finished design appears in colored stripes going downward from right to left, as shown in the downward arrow.

Reversing (*E*, Fig. 61). Both the colors and the treadling can be reversed. By following all columns through, the order of colors will reverse at * on following page from A, B, C to C, B, A. To reverse both treadling and colors, follow columns through to **, harnesses 1–2 A. To reverse, go backward from here, starting at bottom of next left column and reading upward: 4–1, B; 3–4, C; 2–3, A; etc. See chart, top of page 114. Weave "twill-fashion."

Harnesses	Harnesses	Harnesses	Harnesses	Harnesses	Harnesses
1–2 A	1–2 B	1–2 C	*1–2 B	**1–2 A	1–2 C
2–3 B	2–3 C	2–3 A	2–3 A	2–3 C	2–3 B
3–4 C	3–4 A	3–4 B	3–4 C	3–4 B	3–4 A
4–1 A	4–1 B	4–1 C	4–1 B	4–1 A	4–1 C

It takes 12 rows for one complete round, up to *. Different effects are obtained by changing colors only at * and continuing to end; or by reversing sequence also at **.

Diamond (F and G, Fig. 61). In diamond, the weaving follows the same system as in "braided," just described, but the *threading,* instead of being a straight twill, must be a reverse twill or a herringbone. The resulting weave zigzags both horizontally and vertically. F shows diamonds from Rose Path; G shows diamonds from herringbone or three twills.

Although the diamond threading at F and G is different from the twill at D and E, the same weaving directions can be used for both. Applying the twill-fashion treadling given above for D and E to the drafts at F and G, the result is a texture of successive points. To produce the diamonds shown at F and G use the *"as-drawn-in"* method and reverse at points marked by circles in the drafts.

Weaving "as-drawn-in" means to use the succession of harnesses in the draft as a guide when weaving. For instance, if twill is threaded right to left, harnesses 1, 2, 3, 4, 1, 2, 3, 4, etc., use combinations of two harnesses in succession, as harnesses 1–2, 2–3, 3–4, 4–1, i.e., "twill-fashion." The same method is used for the reverse twill, harnesses 1, 2, 3, 4, 3, 2, 1, where one weaves harnesses 1–2, 2–3, 3–4, 2–3, 2–1, and repeats. At F in Figure 61 the draft reverses on the fifth note and becomes "Rose Path." There treadling "as-drawn-in" would be harnesses 1–2, 2–3, 3–4, 4–1, 3–4, 2–3, 1–2; and repeat.

Colors and Patterns. Three colors are used, as in "twill" or "braided," chosen from typical Indian colors, such as red, gray, black, and white. The effect of 3-tiered stripes or diamonds depends upon the fact that the number of harness combinations possible is not a multiple of three; but the number of colors used is. For instance, the standard twill weave has four treadling combinations, harnesses 1–2, 2–3, 3–4, and 4–1, so that, in the "Saddle-Blanket Weave," the use of an odd number of colors, such as three, with an even number of treadles, causes the colors to fall on different combinations after each round until all have been used. Then the succession starts all over again. The same colors must follow each other from start to finish, however, such as: red, gray, black; red, gray, black, etc. If one reverses the succession of the harnesses, i.e., to harnesses 4–1, 3–4, 2–3, 1–2, the order of the colors must also be reversed, such as black, gray, red. Any twill variation may be used for the threading, as herringbone, Rose Path, or diamond.

114

CHAPTER 18

Rag Rugs

THERE is something about rag rugs that captures the fancy. They indicate clean, crisp interiors, cheer and charm; they tell of the frugality of early days which unfolded in the creation of things both useful and beautiful. Whether we call them rag rugs, scatter rugs, or throw rugs, they fill the need for foot comfort in the American home at little expense. They are cheap, easy to keep clean, and replaceable with little effort.

Rag rugs can be woven at home on the simplest loom. There are many other kinds of weaving, but rag-rug weaving is the easiest to understand and the cheapest to do. The investment of a rug loom is soon paid for and later becomes a money earner. Many a weaver in a single month has woven enough rugs from long hoarded bags of rags and stockings to pay for a loom.

DECORATIVE USE

Today, rag rugs are used more than ever before — in period homes or modern cottages, in living rooms or children's nurseries, in bedrooms or bathrooms, on polished wood, tile, or linoleum floors; in fact, they appear in some form in most American homes. The secret of their perennial charm is that they offer such a chance for color harmony. They can be matched to any color scheme by using the tones of the room in the rag filler and adding border accents to match accessories.

Certain rag textures are used as the basis for an entire decorative scheme, such as the lightweight rag textures woven hit-or-miss of narrow rags, and used for upholstered porch or game-room furniture. Pillows, too, and chair-back sets, footstools, and couch throws, when dressed in a lightweight rag-rug texture, appear both pleasingly quaint and practical.

Many modern homemakers seek to decorate their homes in period furnishings and, whether they make or buy their own rugs, they cannot expect to find more suitable floor coverings than those woven of rags on a home loom, in the same way as were those of the period they duplicate.

Rag rugs fit well, too, into modern interiors, especially where light and color are desired — in dinette, kitchen, porch, or guest room. They serve to accent basic tones in cretonne or chintz drapes or chair covers. They can also act as a link between several disconnected colors, providing contrasts or blends of the tones in question.

BASIC DESIGN SUGGESTIONS

Rag-rug weaving is one of those things that began as necessity and ended as art. After mastering the rudiments of actual rugmaking, the weaver found adventure in creating designs. The different rags make exciting textures and the color changes can be intriguing, wrought either by placing weft color accents against backgrounds, weaving hit-and-miss sections, or again devising figures against a plain rug ground. And, while weft variations are numerous, there is almost as much chance for design variation in the warps. Some of the most attractive rugs show design in both warp and weft, appearing as gay plaids.

While some types of design are best for certain weaving setups, there are no hard and fast rules. Every weaver has his own individual taste and may elaborate on given principles to suit himself; if the results are pleasing, that is reason enough for doing it that way. However, we have at our disposal a wealth of ideas evolved by creative American handweavers, past and present, who have combined color, form, and texture in outstanding ways. Observing their designs for rag rugs, we can design ours as follows.

VERTICAL WARP STRIPES (Figs. 51, 52, 65, and 67)

Plan stripes for the warp. Weave either with a plain one-color weft which makes vertical stripes show clearly, or use a hit-and-miss weft which partly covers the stripes which show through as vertical halftones.

HORIZONTAL WEFT STRIPES (Figs. 41 and 68)

Use a plain one-color warp, such as natural, gray, tan, black, white, or a color, and add variety and contrast with colored weft borders at the ends of the rug, or at intervals throughout the rug.

STRIPES IN WARP AND WEFT; PLAIDS (Figs. 63, 65, and 70)

Place intermittent stripes in the warp. Add accents of color in the weft at about the same intervals or with interesting breaks of space. The background can be plain or of a soft mottled tone. Plaids provide nice designs with little effort; their color, especially in large rugs where there are joined strips, draws the eye away from the seams. This was the original idea of designing plaids in old Colonial carpets.

116

Fig. 63 — A rag rug lends charm to a fireplace.

ADDING DESIGN DETAILS (Figs. 41 and 48)

To give character and design appeal to a rag rug, regard the background as the foundation, and over this lay design motifs, such as laid-in figures, color tufts, or twisted wefts called arrows or bird wings or sea gulls flying. Both laid-in motifs and arrow borders are described in Chapter 9. Tapestry and laid-in methods, Chapters 8 and 11, also can be used to add such figures as diamonds, triangles, stepped or zigzag motifs, and blocks. Tapestry motifs should be simple to be effective. Since rug designs are before us so much of the time, too much detail becomes confusing. Work out all designs on graph paper first and simplify their outlines as much as possible.

VERTICAL STRIPES IN DECORATION

The easiest way to get design into a rug is to make a gaily striped warp, and weave with a plain weft. This appeals to beginners as the weft does not require frequent changing. Much can be said for the striped warp, especially valuable in rag rugs.

Warps with stripes are excellent to use for hallway rugs, wall panels, or portieres. The finished rug will add height to low rooms. Use them whenever the weft material is drab to add life and interest to the rug or to achieve a multicolored fringe.

WAYS TO DESIGN STRIPED WARPS (Fig. 65)

The regulation carpet warp, 8/4-ply, comes in a range of many beautiful colors dyed by the thread manufacturers. Plan to enjoy this extensive "palette" threading the warp roller with such colors as red and gold, blue, green and brown, with a dash of black or white here and there to set off these colors. To make a successful threading plan, use colored crayons on paper, or wind your changing warp colors around a cardboard so as to see the proportions. Before beginning, be sure that the warp colors are fast. Test a small amount of warp by washing in soapy water. In weaving across striped warps, plan to use either a plain neutral weft to allow the vertical stripes to show; or several colors of weft to make plaids.

RUG COLORS

Rug colors are much lower in value than at first imagined, forming backgrounds for other room colors. Therefore, in planning rag-rug colors, place them beside other rugs on the floor and note the difference. If one uses fresh rags, the bright new materials will produce rugs quite a bit gayer in effect than the usual rug, and very desirable to enliven the bedroom, dinette, or kitchen. However, to obtain more modulated colors, choose old rags softened by use but not too worn. To make low-toned colors try washing and sunning materials to fade them. This serves to make them permanently fast as well as to give them more mellow tones.

GOOD RUG SIZES

While one of the chief advantages in making woven rugs is that they can be planned any length or width to fit into any space, there are certain accepted rug sizes. They are helpful when weaving rugs for sale. The usual proportions followed are: 24 x 36 in., 24 x 48 in., 27 x 42 in., 27 x 54 in., 36 x 60 in., 36 x 72 in., and 50 x 72 in.

EQUIPMENT AND MATERIALS

Loom. A strong two- or four-harness loom is necessary for the rug directions given in this section. The essential quality of a loom on which to weave rag rugs is its strength. Heavy rugs must be woven on a floor loom; table looms usually are not strong enough to weave more than lightweight mats.

The cloth beam of a loom should be in such a position that it has plenty of space around it for winding the lengths of finished rag rugs, and there should be several rag shuttles for different colors of rags. The weaver should have a skein winder to wind skeins of dyed rags and a bobbin winder to wind weft for tabby portions at the ends of the rug or between the rag sections.

Warp and Settings. It is generally conceded that carpet warp 8/4, 8/3, or 5/3 set at 12 per inch makes a good texture. If set at 15 or 16, the warps are so close that the rug looks ridgey, hiding much of its color, and will not wear as long. At 12 per inch the warp and weft are fairly well balanced and the footwear is evenly distributed on both. When more color is desired, set at 10 per inch, but the rugs won't be quite so durable. For very heavy

118

rugs use pairs of carpet warp at 6 to 8 pairs per inch or 4/4 cotton warp or linen warp 10/5 at 6 singles per inch.

Shrinkage or "Take-Up." All warps shrink somewhat during weaving. The finished length of a rug is definitely lessened by the take-up caused by the insertion of bulky filler. As much as 15 per cent of the length is lost. In planning rug lengths, add one-sixth of the finished length for waste.

All rugs also shrink in width, becoming quite a bit narrower when taken off the loom than they were during weaving. The take-up depends on the weaver. A poor weaver often "pulls-in." Normal take-up is about 1 in. in 24.

Rag Wefts. Almost any kind of fabric can be used for filler. The final appearance of the rug depends upon how the rags are cut, handled, and combined. The width of the cut rag depends upon the weight of rug desired. Heavy wool suitings are cut as narrow as ½ to ¾ in.; lightweight cottons, stockings, rayon or silk, from 1 to 4 in. wide. Twist a piece of the cut rag to see how thick it becomes and cut it wider or narrower accordingly. Rags twisted firmly to pencil size are right for medium-weight rugs.

Cotton Rags. Cotton rags make attractive bedroom or nursery rugs, and are good for the kitchen or sun porch. Every housekeeper has plenty of discarded sheets, towels, cotton curtains, and aprons, and in a large family worn dress prints will be available and accumulate as fast as needed. If there are not enough used rags, buy cheap printed or plain material remnants at cotton sales or at a remnant counter. Slightly soiled goods can be obtained at bargain sales, and these materials can be washed.

Wool Rags. Suits, coats, skirts, and jackets, and especially woolen blankets, make wonderful material for the best and warmest rugs. Since these materials may have dark color tones, use such rugs in living rooms, hallways, or formal bedrooms. The rugs will be serviceable and soft to the feet. Great care must be used in cutting rags to get the same heft for all kinds of materials used. Even the weight by cutting different materials different widths. Cut straight-way of the goods, preferably along its length; if cut diagonally, it will fray badly, especially in woolen cloth.

Sweaters also can be used, but use them alone and do not combine them with regular smooth-woven wool cloth. Carefully cut sweater material will make a shaggy rug. The wool also can be unraveled and used for weaving in other ways.

Silk and Rayon Rags. Silk or rayon rags make rugs of more delicate character, as well as scatter rugs, couch throws, bedside rugs, seat mats, and dainty rugs for guest rooms. Use a ruler to get the proper width when cutting silk rags, for they must be cut wide to get the required bulk. Lightweight silk rag mats are made with strips ½ to 1 in. wide. For these, set the warp a bit closer and use a mercerized warp such as Perle 5 or 10/3, or even 16–3 Egyptian cotton at 20 per inch.

Silk Stockings. All knit goods, stockings, and jersey underwear should be used alone and not combined with regular cloth because knitted material stretches more. Stockings may be cut in continuous strips, beginning at the top and cutting round and round; or they may be cut across their width into loops and the loops put together like so many rubber bands attached in a row.

PREPARATION OF WARP MATERIAL

Warping a Plain Warp. For a smooth beam-type loom, warp by the regular chain method using a warping board or a revolving warp cylinder, shown at *A,* Figure 8. If the warp is very wide, warp in two sections.

For a sectional beam loom, use a warping creel. Place as many spools on the creel as desired for each 2 in. of warp. Warp 2 in. at a time.

Warping Striped Warps:

Method 1. On a Warping Frame. Wind colors consecutively. Plan a series of colors and proportions on graph paper. Let each square represent a certain number of warps. Carry the first color along until it changes. Tie on the next color at either the top or bottom peg, i.e., at the point of reversing; warp it the desired number of times; continue with the next color, etc.

Method 2. Warping in Groups. If the design consists of wide stripes of colors such as 4 in. of red followed by 2 in. of white, etc., warp each color its required number of threads, chain off, and be ready with a clean frame for the next color.

Method 3. On a Warping Creel. Use the sectional warping device and arrange the spools in the series desired, the most convenient being in repeats of 2, 4, or 6 in. Repeats of 2 in. make this method very fast and efficient. The spools will run along in the order desired on the creel such as 2 spools tan, 6 brown, 2 yellow, 2 flame, 2 yellow, 4 tan, 6 brown (24 threads for 2 in. at 12 per inch).

For stripes greater than 2 in. wide, plan a 4-in. stripe and warp in two 2-in. sections as follows: Arrange the colors for 2 in. Warp every other section on the loom, i.e., warp 2 in., skip 2 in., warp 2 in., etc., across the loom. Then change the colors, and warp the sections between. Do this with a 6-in. stripe as well, warping in three 2-in. sections. Also warp borders of 2 to 4 in. as described; then fill in the center of the rug with one color only from the creel. The creel provides an exact systematic way of making warp stripes, and the warp tensions resulting are all the same, thus assuring a perfect rug texture.

Rules for Cutting (A, Fig. 64). Cutting is preferable to tearing, for it avoids frayed edges which impede progress. Cut the cloth parallel to the warp and selvage whenever possible, for warp is stronger than weft and the rags are stronger cut this way. Cut circular goods, such as stockings or jersey, round and round in a spiral, or slice off in loops and lock them together. To save time, cut new material or large pieces of cloth as at *A.* First fold the material across the width several times like a loose bolt; then slice off sections with a sharp scissors or a paper cutter, *A,* arrow.

Rules for Tearing (B and C, Fig. 64). Some cloth can be torn without much fraying. It is faster than cutting, so test it. Furthermore, the usefulness of some rugs is not lessened by having a slightly rough texture. Always tear along the length of the cloth, parallel to the warp, as shown at *B.* It is better not to attempt to tear *across* materials, for warps are always fairly strong and wefts weaker. To tear rags quickly, fold the cloth lengthwise into two or three folds, and cut nicks in the cloth the desired distance apart as shown at *C.* Now tear through the gaps several strips at a time.

Starting Rags on Shuttle. Form a slipknot over the shuttle prong, and start winding. The rag also can be slit at its end and slipped over the point of the shuttle.

Joining Rags for Weaving (Fig. 64). Rag lengths measuring 4 yards and more do not need sewing. Wind them directly around the shuttle. For lengths

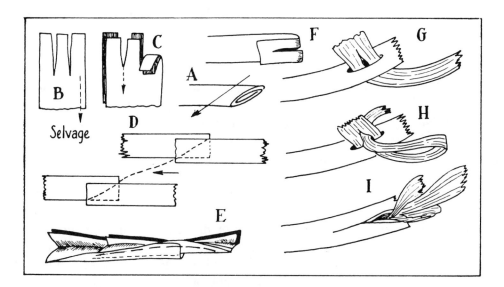

Fig. 64 — Cutting and joining rags.

shorter than this, however, select the preferred method among several shown in Figure 64.

Method 1. Piece rags together flat as shown in *D.* Lay the adjoining ends flat together, overlapping them 1½ to 2 in. Stitch diagonally across the overlapped part. If a sewing machine is used, do not cut the thread between stitchings, but run piece after piece right along. Tear the connecting thread later as indicated by the arrow, before winding strips into a ball.

Method 2. The strips also can be pieced with one fold. Lay two ends together, overlapping 1½ to 2 in. Fold them together lengthwise, and stitch diagonally across the overlapped part.

Method 3. Stitch with a double fold as shown in *E.* Lay the two ends together, overlapping 1½ to 2 in., fold over once, then once again. Stitch lengthwise. This method is good for weak materials or those that might form bunches if not folded and flattened down with the stitching.

Method 4. Piece together without sewing as shown in *F* to *I.* It is possible to put rag strips together without sewing; although this causes nubby joinings, these may be desirable. Moreover, lightweight rags joined in this way do not show much of a bulge.

First, cut slits about 1 in. long at the ends of the rag strips, by folding over as at *F,* and cutting with scissors. Leave at least ½ in. between the slit and the rag end. Slip one end of a second rag through the slit of first rag, as at *G.* Then bring the end of the first piece around to be inserted through its own slit, as at *H.* Draw tight, as at *I.*

Method 5. Silk-stocking loops: To join silk stockings, cut off sections from the stockings 3 to 4 in. wide on a paper cutter or with sharp scissors. Put several dozen loops on your right arm, and loop them off gradually with the left hand to form a chain of loops.

METHOD OF WEAVING

Two-harness rag rugs are woven in plain weave. Four-harness rugs may be either plain weave or twill. The weaver sorts the colors and makes either hit-or-miss joinings of any color or design, or separates the colors into piles and sews together the same colors or shades. Wound into balls, the rags are ready for the rug shuttle, and the weaver carries out his design plan on either a plain or striped warp.

The following rules should be observed.

Use Good Rags. Never use rags that are too badly soiled or too worn and old. There is no point in using inferior materials when time and effort are spent to make a rug of pleasing design. Firm rags that are washed clean and carefully cut go a long way toward producing a rug of quality.

Plan the Rag Width. If the same weight of cloth is used throughout a rug, cut all strips the same width. If different weights of material are used,

122

cut the heavy strips narrower so that, when they are twisted between the fingers, they will make filler of the same heft as the wider strips of less weight.

Rags for an average-weight rug should be cut into strips of such a width that when the rags are twisted tightly between the fingers they equal the diameter of a pencil. For heavier rugs, cut the strips wider; for lighter weight, narrower. This rule takes care of varying cloth weights.

Cut on the Square. Always cut the cloth on the square across either warp or weft, not diagonally; if possible, cut lengthwise with the warp.

Avoid Fabric Mixtures. It is best to use just one kind of fabric for any one rug. Cotton rags should be used with cotton only, silk with silk, wool with wool, jersey with jersey, synthetics with the same, because different kinds of fabrics stretch at different tensions, and rugs made of mixed fabrics pucker. This rule may be altered somewhat if a successive rhythm is used as, for instance, a row of wool followed by a row of cotton, and repeated throughout the rug. Successive rows of three kinds also can be used. The total texture in this case may remain fairly even, but to make sure, try out a sample length, washing and drying it.

Allow for Weft Slack. In laying-in weft rows, always place the rags on a slant so that a little extra length is allowed for take-up when the beater packs the row. This helps made a good selvage.

In weaving with silk stockings or jersey, allow even more slack for each row as the material is elastic and will shrink badly if this is not done. To allow for plenty of take-up, if the rug is very wide, slip the forefinger under the center of each row of filler, pushing it away from you in the shed, like the curve of a half circle.

Cutting Versus Tearing. Cut rags prove easier to work with than torn ones, for the edges are smoother for sewing and weaving. The frayed threads of torn rags often get in the way. However, some materials may be torn and not cause any difficulty, which may be determined by testing the material.

PURPOSE OF RUG DIRECTIONS

The following specific rug directions are given for two reasons: first, to guide weavers in making attractive warp plans and proportions of weft stripes with good color schemes; and second, to give those who are not weavers dimensions and designs for having their rugs woven by others. However, any weaver can get the general idea of the best designs from our directions and illustrations, and then create his own.

EIGHT DESIGNS FOR STRIPED AND PLAID RAG RUGS (Fig. 65)
1. ALTERNATE WARPS OR "PEPPER-AND-SALT"

The very simplest stripe design possible consists of alternate light and dark threads. Since the effect here is similar to that achieved by mixing

123

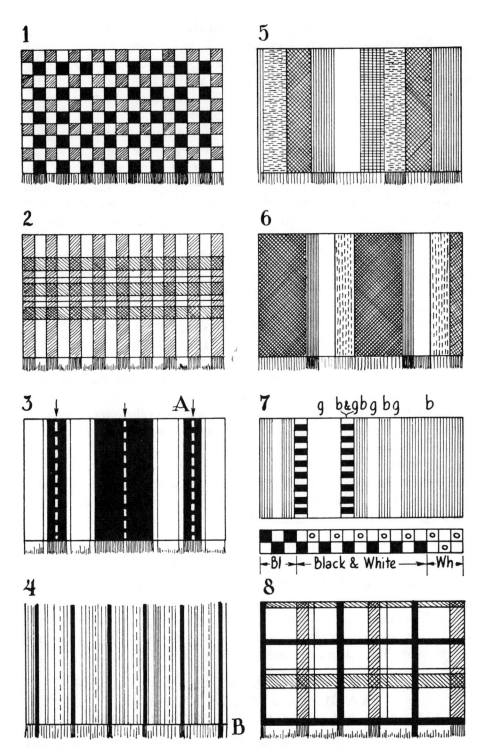

Fig. 65 — Eight designs for striped and plaid rag rugs.

124

pepper and salt, this design is called "pepper-and-salt." Not only black and white, but any two contrasting colors may be used. When a very heavy weft might tend to cover single warps, warp two darks and two lights in succession, but thread through separate heddle eyes: harness 1, dark, another harness 1, dark; harness 2, light, harness 2, light, etc. The alternate single colors or alternate pairs of color in the warp may be crossed with alternate colors in the weft, giving a pebbly appearance; or they may be crossed with wider bands of weft stripes. The two-color warp also ties up into an attractive fringe. Figure 65, No. 1, illustrates this design.

2. INTERMITTENT DARK AND LIGHT STRIPES

Stripes planned at regular intervals can be woven with the same series of stripes in the weft, making checks or rectangles. A good rug design develops from weaving checks at the rug ends, but keeping the long center of one color weft only. This gives columns of warp color connecting the checked designs at the ends. For warp, choose two contrasting colors, a light and a dark; thread one of these for 2 to 3 in.; then the other for the same space. Continue alternating the same width of each color. Weave as lengthwise stripes, or make the same size stripes in the weft with two similar colors, producing a plaid.

3. SYMMETRICALLY PLANNED WARP STRIPES

Repeats of dark and light colors, or any group of blending colors separated by accents, make beautiful rugs. Be sure to choose a restful design with spaces well balanced. Either continue repeating this, or plan a warp with a definite center and the same design on both sides. Break wide stripes by introducing an accent color, or place this accent at reverse points. Often a stripe elsewhere in the room decoration will be a guide in planning the rug stripes.

4. MOTTLED RUG WARPS

Use all your leftovers of warp of any color whatsoever and mix them up without rhyme or reason. It will form a most interesting and restful allover mottled effect with bright spots at points. Weave with one color of weft or varied weft stripes. This makes an especially nice fringe as shown at *B*, Figure 65.

5. WARPING A "RAINBOW" RUG—EQUAL BANDS OF MANY COLORS

Odd lots of colored carpet warp can be used for a warp of even bands of color, each 2 in. wide: brown, ivory, gold, flame, gray, etc. It makes a beautiful rug. The colors can also be arranged in the succession of rainbow hues. Either repeat or reverse the succession. A modernistic design results from warp bands of uneven widths. Weave as vertical stripes with one color of weft, or as plaids, changing the weft colors. If the same succession of colors in the weft as in the warp is used, a lovely harmony of many colored squares results.

6. ASYMMETRICAL STRIPE REPEATS

Some of our most interesting designs are asymmetrical. Choose a repeat of certain color proportions. Either continue repeating, or reverse. Very wide warp stripes in low colors can be accented by narrow ones in colors of stronger intensity. Even one single warp thread or a pair of warps in a very bright color adds life and sparkle to a rug. The asymmetrical stripes, too, are interesting in a tied fringe.

7. TRANSITIONS BETWEEN WARP STRIPES

A clever way to blend or join two contrasting stripes is to save a space between them in which to blend both. Take two colors, such as gold and brown, black and white, etc., and warp as adjacent bands but soften the break between them. Thread 2 in. of brown (b), then 1 in. of alternate gold and brown bands or single warps (b and g), then 2 in. of gold (g). The mottled stripe between them softens the break and forms a pleasant color tone. For a still closer transition, alternate single threads of each color for a space between the two strong colors. See the draft below, Figure 65, No. 7.

8. PLAID RUGS

In all of the above cases where there are definite stripes, the weft colors can be made to run in the same order and proportions and thus form plaids. Many carpets are woven as plaids, as shown in Figure 70.

Plan a warp with bands of color, wide and narrow. For a true plaid, weave the very same distances and colors along the weft. Continue repeating. In repeating a succession of weft colors, it is a good idea to make a paper pattern of one of the repeats and lay this along all the repeats, to be sure each band measures exactly the same.

TWO DESIRABLE TYPES OF COLONIAL RUGS (Figs. 66, 67)

EARLY PROVINCIAL PLAID RUG (Fig. 66)

The vivacious design of this rug in sharply contrasting colors would lend an air of cheer to any room. It is a traditional design and one which was very popular in Colonial days, the very earliest kind of rag rug or carpet made. It is an excellent design to combine with quaint antiques or to lighten up the rooms that are lived in most, the kitchen or breakfast nook.

It can also be used in rooms with four-poster beds and old furniture. It is the all-purpose rug, woven in repeating bands of several colors of your choice,

Courtesy — Charles Gilbert Beetem

Fig. 66 — Early provincial rug
with hit-and-miss borders.

Courtesy — Charles Gilbert Beetem

Fig. 67 — Color-blend rug in rag
carpet style combining two tones.

red, black, and white; or brown, tan, and blue against white with a touch of black for accent. Running down through the length of the rug on either side are two bright stripes of color about a foot apart — a traditional early American method of adding adornment. These stripes combine with the weft stripes to make plaids.

Directions (Fig. 66)

Size of Rug: 26 x 50 in. — finished size, 24 x 48 in.
Colors: Red, white, gray, and black
Threading Plan: Reading right to left across warp, top of rug photo, Figure 66
    5-in. white warp

2-in. striped bands (striped band consists of 8 green, 6 red, 5 tan, 6 red, 8 green)

12-in. white (center)

2-in. striped bands

5-in. white warp

Weaving Plan:

Heading; ½-in. plain weave with carpet warp

A. Light-colored band: 2 in. white

B. Dark-colored mottled stripe: a repeating stripe 5 in. wide, as follows:

5 rows bright red

5 rows black or blue

2 rows tan

2 rows gray

2 rows mottled

6 rows black

Alternate A and B as far as desired. End with either A or B.

COLOR-BLEND RUG — RAG-CARPET STYLE (Fig. 67)

This rug is quite modern American in adaptation and may be appropriately used with modern furniture. The same warp stripes may be used for this as were used in the Early Provincial plaid rug. The rug is divided into wide weft bands of a neutral shade, more often tan or gray, alternating with wide color bands of green or dubonnet, henna, hunter's green, old blue, rose, brown, and deep red. This same rug design, using sections of mottled rags in place of the wide dark bands, is shown in the fireplace rug, Figure 63.

With a striped warp, these wide bands cause plaids. Still brighter color bands may edge and accent these weft stripes. For instance, if the large bands are wine against neutral, weave two stripes of bright yellow and blue against them; if the blue and tan, use red and yellow stripes between.

Directions (See Fig. 67)

Size of Rug: 26 x 50 in. — finished size, 24 x 48 in.

Colors of Rug: Weft bands of dubonnet and ecru.

Accents of green and yellow.

Threading Plan: Same as Fig. 66 with side stripes.

Weaving Plan: Weave a heading with carpet warp, tabby, ½ in. wide.

First section, dark tone: 8-in. dubonnet

Following first section, two narrow bands of color: 4 rows bright green, 2 rows bright yellow.

Second section, light tone: 8-in. ecru

Following second section, two narrow bands of color: 4 rows bright green, 2 rows bright yellow

Repeat as desired; end with first section.

128

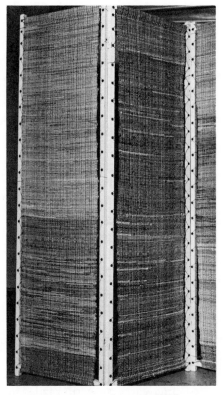

Courtesy — Florence Balliett

Courtesy — Detroit Handweavers Guild

Fig. 68 — Rug of silk rags woven on pattern threading.

Fig. 69 — A folding exhibit screen of panels woven with silk stockings.

A FOLDING SCREEN OF SIX PANELS WOVEN RAG-RUG FASHION OF SILK STOCKINGS (Fig. 69)

The materials of this screen, a project of the Detroit Handweavers' Guild, were donated by members who furnished rags of strong carpet warp in all colors and silk stockings cut in loops and linked together for the filler. The screen was used for exhibiting fabrics.

A multiple-colored warp was made carrying two natural colored threads in each five. The other three varied according to the supply. This warp was set 1 per dent in a 12-dent reed. The material was woven entirely in plain 2-harness weave. Metallic thread, some of it tarnished, was added at random. Texture was procured by loop joints, with added interest from the shaded nylons. The tightly stretched panels were laced with heavy brown thread over upholstery tacks on the side frames.

CHAPTER 19

Magic Color in Rag Carpets

ORIGIN OF THE HIT-AND-MISS CARPET

Just as the French are famous for their scrupulous saving of left-over food and its reappearance in the *soup de jour,* so our early American ancestors are to be remembered for their meticulous care in saving scraps of material for everyday floor coverings. The long process of spinning a thread, dyeing it, and finally weaving it into cloth had not been long forgotten at the time the first rag carpets were made in this country. The women of those provincial times knew the value of each tiny piece of material and very carefully saved it for the local weaver to work into a carpet for the best room of the house. Since all kinds and colors of cloth were balled together by the housewife, the weaver was obliged to weave them more or less as they were given him with the result that the final effect was an allover pattern still known today as the "hit-and-miss" carpet.

QUAINT RAG-CARPET TERMS

The names given to some of the color combinations are a reminder of historical events of that day. "Hit-and-Miss" seems to have been a collective term applied to all surface textures, but within this huge classification there was an attempt at certain designs, and we find a "Betsy Ross" carpet with stripes across the weft, a "Martha Washington" and "Mount Vernon" done in plaids, etc. In olden days, a large trade evolved from the making of the rag carpet, and this crept into the making and selling of standard types of hangings made from discarded silks from "milady's" wardrobe.

RAG MISCELLANY

The way in which the rags for the carpets were prepared is a story in itself. Rag sewing bees were one of the most popular diversions of the day, and in the summertime, hidden within vine-clad porches, a bevy of women, young and old, would be found sewing busily on all sorts of strips of textiles, afterward winding them into hard balls. Even little children helped gather rags, sort them, and hand them to the sewers. Anything and everything was put into the long trailing vine of rags, such as denim, gingham, corduroy, awning cloth, cretonne, flannel, silks, cottons, and wools. When several yards were completed, they were added to the roll; when several rolls were finished, they were sent to the weaver to be woven into rugs. Rag rugs and carpets captured the fancy of the folks of yore, and they were used everywhere in the home — for stairways, outdoor benches, or rush-seat chairs. The rag carpet was the large floor rug of the time, even in the finest homes.

DESIGN EXPANSION

As young America prospered, materials became more plentiful and the housewife became correspondingly selective. Then, instead of wrapping every color together, each color was balled separately so that the weaver had a better chance to express his own ideas by planning rugs that were more creative and individualistic. The chief design evolved during this Colonial period was the "crossbarred" carpet which replaced, to a great extent, the "hit-and-miss" technique. The warps still showed basic whites, tans, or ecru, but the weft colors crossed these neutral shades with bright stripes of varying dimensions which gave the rug its characteristic crossbars.

Both the "hit-and-miss" and the "crossbarred" carpets were in wide use from the Canadian provinces to as far south as Georgia and Louisiana. Almost every household of even modest means displayed at least one carpet, and this was usually in the living room. Other floor decoration had to be confined to small rugs that helped to dispel the chill of bare boards.

About 1750, a large emigration to the Great Smoky mountains of Kentucky and Tennessee had already begun. The Appalachians too were beginning to feel the ax of the pioneers who had left the coastal plains of Virginia, Georgia, and the Carolinas to settle the promising and beautiful "West." What was then the "West" is today considered the easternmost boundary of mountain ranges, but the hardships encountered in settling this country were just as great as if the wagons had been moving toward the Rockies. It is greatly to the credit of our forebears that not only did they bring practical tools to their new life but the means for maintaining beauty as well. As a result, with these settlers traveled the looms and spinning wheels which had served them so faithfully in the homes from which they came.

DOMESTIC CARPETS PROSPER

The rag carpet prospered and did not change greatly until approximately the year 1850. The use of wide colorful stripes in both warp and weft left little to be desired in the way of a decorative floor covering even though it was a style bounded by simplicity. Then the advent of power machinery cast the modest rag rug into almost total oblivion, at least for a time. Elaborate yarn and rag-filled carpets graced the homes of farm and city dwellers alike. More than ever before, the carpet began to take its place as a common and necessary fixture of the home.

If domestic carpets were now no longer a novelty, the imported variety certainly was. The wealthier families sought exclusiveness in foreign markets that offered a fancy assortment of expensive carpets as competition for our more modest yarn-filled coverings. These carpets were usually placed in the "most seen" rooms, either the living room, dining room, or master bedroom, while the familiar rag carpet still held sway in the rest of the house. But the foreign market was short-lived. About 1860, domestic manufacturers outpriced their competitors in Belgium, France, and Great Britain, and began to regain much of the trade they had previously lost. At this time also, what was known to many a Victorian parlor as the ingrain carpet came into style. Today it is considered "period," if not definitely bad taste, and remains little more than an historic item in the annals of this country's industrial progress. In sharp contrast to this is the lasting popularity of the original rag carpet which decorated the floors of the first settlers. It is loved today as it was then for its charm, its brilliance, and its practicality, and handweavers from Canada to Mexico still aim to create rag carpets for period rooms.

Two beautiful examples of early nineteenth-century carpets are shown in

Fig. 70 — Colorful rag carpet woven in a convent on Isle d'Orleans near Ste. Anne de Beaupré, Canada.

Figure 51. In these, the warp is wool and the weft is coarse linen and jute. The warp is set close enough to cover the filler and to show up the lovely vertical stripes.

ROOM-SIZE RAG RUG (Fig. 70)

This beautiful room-size rag rug or carpet was woven in a convent on the Isle d'Orleans near Ste. Anne de Beaupré. Its interesting warp design of green, lavender, and cerise, with an occasional bright yellow stripe, turns into a unique plaid when crossed with a silk-stocking weft in tan, yellow, and black. The warp used was somewhat finer than regular carpet warp, and may be duplicated very nearly with 10/3 mercerized cotton which comes in many colors. Choose any series of four good colors for a plaid in the proportions given below. Since the rug measures 60 in. wide and 80 in. long, divide it into two or three warp strips, of 20 or 30 in. wide each, always allowing 1 to 2 in. extra width for take-up.

DIRECTIONS FOR RUG IN FIGURE 70

Warp Plan

Warp: 10/3 cotton in colors
Weft: Rags, narrow strips of silk stockings
Threads per Inch: 20 (8/4 carpet warp may be used at 15 to 16 per inch.)
Size of Rug: 60 by 80 in.

Threading Plan

(Warp colors: cerise or red, yellow, lavender or tan, green)
Cerise, 10 in.
Yellow, ⅜ in.
Lavender, 3½ in.
Yellow, ⅜ in.
Green, 10 in.
Yellow, ⅜ in.
Lavender, 3½ in.
Yellow, ⅜ in.
Repeat all to width desired.

Weaving Plan

(Weft colors: tan rags or natural stockings; stockings or rags dyed black and yellow)
Tan, or stocking color, 10 in.
Yellow, ½ in.
Black, 2 in.
Yellow, ½ in.
Repeat all to length desired.

WARP-FACE CARPET OF JUTE OR LINEN FOR TWO- OR FOUR-HARNESS LOOMS

(Figs. 51 and 52)

A durable type of rag carpet is shown in Figure 51. Carpets like this are made of rag filler woven through a closely set warp of jute or linen. Bright border stripes show up well against the tan or linen-colored center and sides. The color count of these stripes is given in Figure 52.

This type of rug is one of the most durable. It was popular because of its practicality, for, with the closely set warp and the vertical design covering the filler, the weaver could use rags of any kind, dark or light, waste or otherwise. Warps can be of heavy 10/5 linen which comes in beautiful colors, or of heavy ply wools. Such carpets provide good uses for colorless rag fillers, and a wide range of colors in both linen and wool warps offers the rug designer a chance for the creation of effective vertical stripes.

LARGE RUGS FROM SMALL PIECES — FOR TWO- OR FOUR-HARNESS LOOMS

The dream of many a weaver is to make a coverlet. Still others are ambitious enough to plan a large floor rug. Many have succeeded in putting strips together in attractive ways, as shown in Figures 71, 72, and No. 1, Figure 94. Certain rug techniques are more suitable than others for this. Rug strips woven in Flossa, tapestry, Log Cabin, twill, or plain weave are all good. Two-block rugs lend themselves to joining together as the blocks alternate and the edges produce the same alternation. A very attractive exhibit rug was woven with stockings in blocks of blue, green, and natural on a sturdy table loom. This rug consisted entirely of strips of successive blocks. When the strips were joined, the blocks were made to alternate at the seams. The following rug is a good example.

LARGE RUGS FROM NARROW STRIPS (Fig. 71)

It is possible to make large rugs even if only a narrow floor loom is available. The rug shown in *A*, Figure 71, was woven with tabby background and small floral designs laid in with narrow colored rags, the floral figures alternating with plain ones. It is similar in appearance to a hooked rug but is made much more quickly. The rug is woven in narrow strips which are sewed together. Rugs of any size may be made this same way, but the loom must be strong so that the weft is packed down firmly. Steel or heavy wood looms should be used for this purpose.

DESIGN POSSIBILITIES

This rug of repeated design, *A, B, C,* Figure 71, has been chosen because of its simplicity. It is composed of design squares in a light color alternating

134

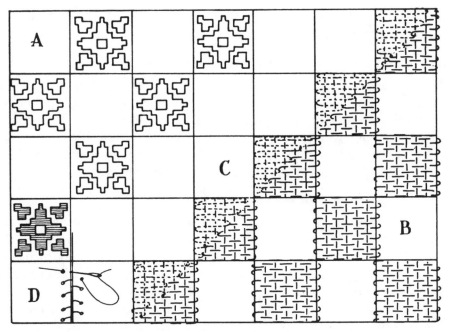

Fig. 71 — Plans for large rugs from narrow strips. Method of laying-in design blocks.

with plain ones in a dark color. The squares are either left plain or have a simple floral motif in the colors of the room. The background of the light squares is beige and the flowers are yellow, rose, lavender, or green, which are the predominating colors in the chintz of the room drapes. Squares of black or deep brown are stunning with laid-in figures of bright yellow, orange, pale green, etc.

Designs may be woven against the background by any of the following four methods. All of them may be employed on a two-harness loom, or a four-harness loom threaded to weave plain weave.

Method 1. The Flossa rug technique is used for the designs only, and the background spaces are woven of fine rags in plain weave. The design is woven in relief. Flossa bars are used for this part only, and the loops are clipped when finished. The Flossa loops may be cotton or wool yarn, with plain weave background of rags, and the Flossa rug technique is quite similar in effect to the hooked-rug technique, although it is done with much more speed (Figs. 26 and 27).

Method 2. The Indian Navajo tapestry method also may be used, Figures 40 and 41. Work in simple center motifs with change of color.

Method 3. The laid-in weave, Figures 43 and 46, is a simple way of adding design.

Method 4. The imitation-tapestry method, Figure 45, can be used to make a simple, diagonal design, *C,* Figure 71.

SUCCESSFUL DECORATIVE SCHEMES

Two or more contrasting colors usually are employed in draperies, walls, and accessories; and the effect is enhanced when some article is introduced into the room which contains a combination of these colors. In the informal type of room, where scatter rugs are preferable to an allover rug, designs can be planned in the room colors. Let the two predominating colors of the room be combined in this rug of alternate squares.

METHOD OF WEAVING STRIPS

Weave separate strips from 1 to 2 ft. wide, and join them together for the large rug. Set up a warp 13 or 25 in. wide with carpet warp at 12 threads per inch. Plan the length of the warp for each strip according to the length of the rug to be made, plus 15 per cent of this length for take-up, plus 2 ft. extra, as 1 ft. is wasted at beginning and end of warp.

As an example, for a finished strip 6 ft. long, make the warp 9 ft. long; for a 4-ft. strip, make the warp 7 ft. long, etc. However, if the cloth beam will hold more than one length, add only the strip length, such as 6 ft. plus shrinkage for each additional strip; the waste at the ends occurs only once for each series of strips. Again, if the cloth beam does not provide space for the winding up of one complete strip, plan to weave across the short width of rug, and sew strips crosswise together rather than lengthwise.

Divide each strip into even squares. If the strip is 6 ft. long divide it into six even squares alternating dark and light; if 4 ft., into four even 1-ft. squares, dark and light. Weave 1 ft. of plain rags dark; the next foot neutral light, and then alternate these. Start the second strip neutral light; the next square dark; etc. Then, when the strips are sewed together, the same alternation will occur the other way. See sketch *B,* Figure 71.

For a very simple rug, make alternate light and dark woven squares with no design, as at *B.* The squares at *C* show a simple but effective interlocking of two weft colors by the imitation-tapestry method, Chapter 11.

JOINING THE STRIPS (D, Fig. 71)

Rug strips are best joined with the figure-of-eight stitch, *D,* Figure 71. Match the sides accurately. Tack the strips together at intervals with sewing thread all along the lengths, so that, in the final sewing, you will not stretch one panel more than the other. Sew with 2-ply linen, either in a neutral color or a shade to match the strips. If no linen is available, use a strong cotton twine or carpet warp double, and run it through a waxer. It takes time to sew the strips together; therefore, a sewing cord should be used that will not wear out.

COMPLETE FLOOR COVERINGS FROM
SETS OF RUGS (Fig. 72)

A smart modern rug ensemble can be made to cover an entire room floor. Weave a set of rugs with or without borders. Plan them for a double purpose, either to use alone or to assemble in the shape of a large rectangle, as shown in Figure 72. Any one of the rugs can be used separately, and each rug can indeed be designed for a special purpose.

Rugs, long and short, may be woven to surround a table or bed, or to be used on three sides of a fireplace. The dotted lines suggest a bed or table bordered with rugs in twill texture.

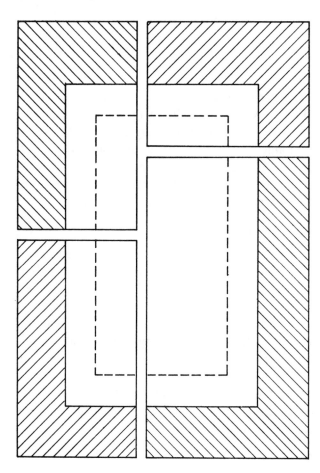

Fig. 72 — Complete floor coverings from sets of rugs.

PART VI *Rugs With Visible Warp and Weft Textures*

CHAPTER 20

Twill and Herringbone Rugs

FROM time immemorial, twill has been one of the most popular and practical weaves in the world. Folks like its texture of parallel diagonal lines, and the contrasting darks and lights of its warp and weft. It is durable, and the same setting woven as twill will last longer than when woven as tabby. Its ease of weaving delights the worker, for the design progresses rapidly with one swiftly flowing shuttle, and time is saved by not having to change from pattern to tabby as in regular 4-harness overshot pattern weaving.

TEXTURE AND DECORATIVE USE

The twill technique acts somewhat as a connecting link between plain weave and pattern weave. Like plain weave it is a one-shuttle weave, but like pattern weave it forms a definite figuration of design. It uses four harnesses, but a twill threading also is readily woven as plain weave.

Twill rugs have a texture with both warp and weft apparent. Usually more of the weft or filler shows, as this passes over two or more warps at a time instead of over single warps as in plain weave. The texture is smooth, the appearance of diagonal figure formations pleasing.

Decoratively speaking, the rugs are quite suitable to modern interiors. Sections of twill surfaces can be so threaded as to show opposite diagonal lines when woven, forming pleasing lights and shadows.

DESIGN AND COLOR

Twill sells itself to the rug weaver for many reasons, such as ease of workmanship, speed of weaving, and intriguing striped pattern surfaces with diagonals, diamonds, crosses, and radiating lines. Reversing the treadlings for

138

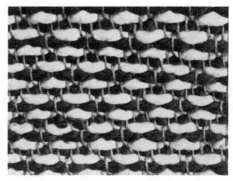

Fig. 75 — Close-up of rug textures in Rose Path and twill. Rose Path unit: dark warp, light filler. Twill unit: dark warp with weft in alternate rows of black and white.

straight twill will form vertical zigzags. Using a reverse twill in the draft results in horizontal zigzags and diamonds. The use of different colors in succession will form the most unusual and beautiful shadings. A few of the many possibilities are given in Figures 75, 76, and 77.

DESIGN VARIATIONS FOR TWILL AND HERRINGBONE RUGS (Fig. 76)

Try the suggestions below; then start creating designs of your own. Detailed directions for these rug designs follow the listing.

Straight Twill Rug, with no reverses. In rug No. 2, regard section *A,* one fourth of the sketch, as an entire rug. Simply thread as twill, harnesses 1, 2, 3, 4, and repeat.

One or Two Simple Reverses, rug No. 2, *B* and *C.* The twill lines can run across corners, *B,* or radiate from the center as in the small sketch, *C.*

Goose-Eye Motifs Repeated, rug No. 1. Section *D* represents one repeat.

Zigzag Design, rug No. 3. Twill threading, woven one way through *E,* reversed through *F.*

Herringbone End Borders and Vertical Stripes, rug No. 4. *G* represents one repeat.

Mottled Twill Textures, due to different treadlings possible instead of straight twill, Figure 75.

Following are the detailed directions for these various twill effects as shown in the rugs of Figure 76.

MATERIALS AND WARP SETTINGS

Suggested Fillers. One weft only is required. This brings out the design formations and makes a firm texture without the use of tabby, which is rarely used. For this filler, cotton rug yarn is satisfactory; wool rug yarn

139

produces rugs of more pleasing textural surface; wool thrums is a reasonable but good material to use. If you use rags, be sure to cut them evenly. Chenille or rug-weave yarn, or any filler of fairly light weight, produces excellent twill bath mats.

Warp Setting for Twill Threadings. For the most effective twill textures, set cotton carpet warp 8/4, 8/3, or 5/3 at 10 or 12 threads per inch; cotton 4/4 or linen 10/5 at 8 to 10 per inch. Cotton warps 8/4 and 8/3 may also be set at 15 or 16 per inch, since the filler usually passes over two warps at a time and sometimes over three leaving every fourth warp only showing. However, the more open setting, such as 10 to 12 per inch, shows the filler more attractively, as well as the trend of the diagonals.

WEAVING DIRECTIONS FOR TWILL AND HERRINGBONE RUGS (Fig. 76)

No. 1. Herringbone Threading, Woven as Goose-Eye

Warp Setting: For a rug 30 in. wide, set 8/4 or 5/3 warp at 12 threads per inch; total threads, 360. This same number of threads will make a rug 36 in. wide if set at 10 threads per inch.

Threading: *Harnesses 1, 2, 3, 4; repeat 15 times, 60 threads; change to harnesses 3, 2, 1, 4; repeat 15 times, 60 threads; total 120 threads. Repeat from the asterisk (*) 3 times, 360 threads. For a wider rug, repeat more times; for a narrower rug, repeat two times only.

Weaving: *Repeat harnesses 1–2, 2–3, 3–4, 4–1, once each, for 8 to 10 in. Change to harnesses 3–4, 2–3, 1–2, 4–1, for the same space. Continue repeating from the asterisk (*) for the desired length of the rug.

No. 2. Simple Reverses

Warp Setting: For a rug 30 in. wide and 42 in. long, set carpet warp double of 4/4 cotton or 3/2 mercerized cotton or its equivalent in size; or linen warp 10/5 at 10 threads per inch; or for a rug 25 in. wide, cotton 8/4 or 8/5 at 12 threads per inch. Total of threads in either case, 300.

Threading of large rug, *AB:* Repeat harnesses 4, 3, 2, 1 for 150 threads. Reverse to harnesses 2, 3, 4, 1 for 150 threads; total, 300 threads.

Weaving: Weave harnesses 3–4, 2–3, 1–2, 4–1 for 22 in.; then reverse to harnesses 1–2, 2–3, 3–4, 4–1 for the rest of the rug, 22 in.

Small sketch, *C,* with radiating lines from the center: Thread the same as for rug No. 2. Weave harnesses 1–2, 2–3, 3–4, 4–1, to the center of the length; then reverse to harnesses 3–4, 2–3, 1–2, 4–1, for the rest of the rug.

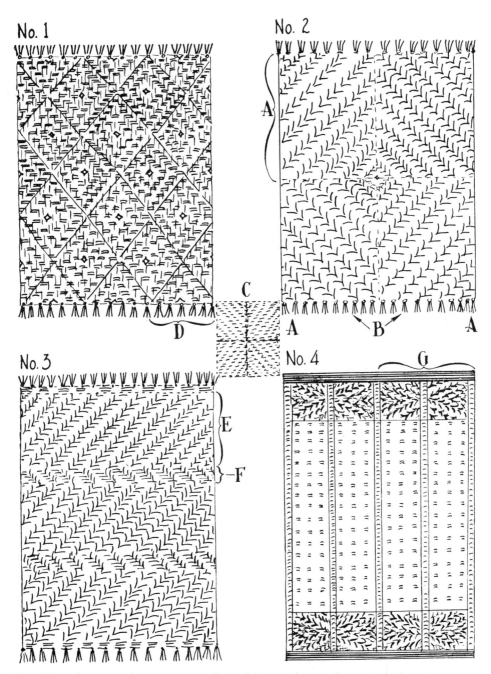

No. 1

No. 2

A

C

A

D

A

B

A

No. 3

E

~F

No. 4

G

Fig. 76 — Creative designs in twill and herringbone showing lights and shadows.

No. 3. Zigzag Design

Warp Setting: Set cotton warp 8/4, or 8/3 at 12 to 15 threads per inch; or cotton 4/4, or linen 10/5 at 10 threads per inch. Thread any number of times.

Threading: Repeat harnesses 1, 2, 3, 4 for the entire warp to the desired width.

Weaving: *Weave harnesses 1–2, 2–3, 3–4, 4–1 for 2 in.; reverse to harnesses 3–4, 2–3, 1–2, 4–1 for 10 to 12 in. Repeat from the asterisk (*) to the desired length. Add harnesses 1–2, 2–3, 3–4, 4–1 for 2 in.

No. 4. Herringbone End Borders and Vertical Stripes

Warp Setting: For a rug 36 in. wide, set carpet warp 8/4 or 8/3 at 12 threads per inch. Total threads, 433. For a rug 28½ in. wide, set carpet warp at 15 threads per inch. Total threads, 425.

Threading:

			Threads
Selvage:			
Harnesses 4, 3, 2, 1. Repeat 2 times.			8
Center:			
*Harnesses 4, 1, 4, 1, 4, 1, 4.		7	
Harnesses 1, 2, 3, 4. Repeat 15 times.		60	
Harnesses 1, 4, 1, 4, 1, 4, 1.		7	
Harnesses 4, 3, 2, 1. Repeat 15 times.		60	
	Total	134	

Repeat from the asterisk*, 134 threads, 3 times.		402
Add harnesses 4, 1, 4, 1, 4, 1, 4.		7
Selvage:		
Harnesses 1, 2, 3, 4. Repeat 2 times.		8
	Total	425

Weaving:

Hem and Heading:
  2-in. tabby, using carpet warp: Harnesses 1–3, 2–4. Use cotton rug filler for the pattern rows.

Border:
  Harnesses 4–1, 4 times. Tabby after each row.
  *Harnesses 1–2, 2–3, 3–4, 4–1, each once. Repeat these four rows from the asterisk (*) 5 to 10 times. No tabby necessary.
  Harnesses 4–1, 4 times. Tabby after each row.
  **Harnesses 3–4, 2–3, 1–2, 4–1, each once. Repeat these four rows from the double asterisk (**) 5 to 10 times.
  No tabby necessary.

142

Center:

Harnesses 4–1. Repeat for the center as far as desired, with tabby after each row. For another effect, weave the center of the rug "on opposites." Treadle any pattern combination, such as harnesses 1–2, and follow it with the opposite pair, 3–4, using rug yarn for each row, no tabby. Repeat throughout the center.

Border: Same as above.

TWILL AND HERRINGBONE AS CONNECTING LINKS (Fig. 77)

Both twill and herringbone can be used for one or more repeats to form a break between larger pattern motifs, as shown in the rug in Figure 77. Here the oval figures similar to honeysuckle are separated from the border and the center by herringbone stripes.

Threading Plan for a Twill and Diamond Rug. (Thread right to left.) Motifs are separated by brackets.

Border at Right Side: Harnesses (1, 2, 3, 4, 1, 2, 1, 2, 3, 2, 3, 4, 3, 4, 1, 4, 1, 2, 1, 2, 3, 2, 3, 4, 3, 4, 1, 4, 1) (4, 3, 2, 1, 4, 3, 2, 1, 2, 3, 4, 1, 2, 3, 4) (1, 2, 3, 2, 3, 2, 3, 4, 3, 4, 3, 2, 3, 4, 3, 4, 3, 2, 3, 2, 3, 2, 1) (4, 3, 2, 1, 2, 3, 4) (1, 2, 3, 2, 3, 2, 3, 4, 3, 4, 3, 2, 3, 4, 3, 4, 3, 2, 3, 2, 3, 2, 1) (4, 3, 2, 1, 4, 3, 2, 1, 2, 3, 4, 1, 2, 3, 4).

Center: (1, 2, 1, 2, 3, 2, 3, 4, 3, 4, 3, 2, 3, 2, 1, 2, 1)* (4, 3, 2, 1, 4, 3, 2, 1, 2, 3, 4, 1, 2, 3, 4). Repeat all of the center 4 times; the fifth time, repeat first motif only, to the asterisk *.

Border at Left Side: Read the wide border backwards, i.e., from the end to the beginning.

Weaving Plan. Note that most of the combinations occur for one row only, except for an occasional 3–4, 4 times.

Headings: Harnesses 1–2, 2–3, 3–4, 4–1, 3–4, 2–3. (Directions are still more simple with the 6-treadle tie-up. See Figure 81 and weave treadles 1, 2, 3, 4, 3, 2.)

Border: Harnesses 1–2, 2–3 (3–4, 4 times); 2–3, 1–2, 4–1, 3–4, 2–3, 1–2, 2–3, 3–4, 4–1, 1–2, 2–3 (3–4, 4 times); 2–3, 1–2. (Or, if using tie-up, treadles 1, 2, [3, 4 times]; 2, 1, 4, 3, 2, 1, 2, 3, 4, 1, 2, [3, 4 times]; 2, 1.)

Center: Same as the heading. Repeat to the length desired.

TWILL AND HERRINGBONE AS BORDERS

Both the straight twill and the reverse twill, Rose Path and herringbone, etc., make excellent borders for pattern rugs where a closely figured surface is desired to act as a background for a center of larger figures. A band of straight twill may form the outside edge. Then 4 or 5 inches from the edge this may be reversed to make a 2-in. strip of shadow running lengthwise, changing again to form the rest of the border or the ground for a

143

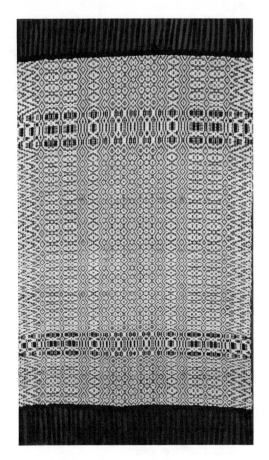

Fig. 77. — Rug in herringbone variations. The attractive side borders of white nylon filler show up effectively against the dark brown warp.

Courtesy — Florence Balliett

laid-in center. See Figure 76 for the interesting effects made possible by twill reverses. Here are some threadings which will prove useful for borders.

Twill Reverses

Threading Border: Harnesses 1, 2, 3, 4 (6 times); harnesses 3, 2, 1, 4, (4 times); harnesses 3, 2, 1, 2, 3, 4 (once); harnesses 1, 2, 3, 4 (2 times). Center of rug: Use the speckled weave, harnesses 2, 2, 4, 4, and repeat. Thread the border backward for the left side.

Weaving: Harnesses 1–2, 2–3, 3–4, 4–1, and repeat.

Herringbone Repeat

Threading: Harnesses 1, 2, 3, 4, 1, 2, 3, 4, 1, 2, 3, 4, 3, 2, 1, 4, 3, 2, 1, 4, 3, 2; repeat all. Start the chosen pattern for the center of the rug with harness 1. Use short Overshot patterns of diamond character.

Weaving Border: Harnesses 1–2, 2–3, 3–4, 4–1, and repeat. *Center:* Weave the center pattern such as diamond, "as-drawn-in."

144

Diamond or Enlarged Herringbone in Blocks

Threading: Harnesses 1, 2, 1, 2, 3, 2, 3, 4, 3, 4, 1, 4, 1, 4, 3, 4, 3, 2, 3, 2; repeat all. Start the pattern for the center on harnesses 1, 2, 1, 2. This border may also be repeated to make an entire rug in the diamond pattern (see Diamond Rug, Fig. 79).

Weaving: For the border at the base of the rug, weave harnesses 1–2, 2 times; 2–3, 2 times; 3–4, 2 times; 4–1, 2 times; 3–4, 2 times; 2–3, 2 times; repeat as desired. For the center of the rug, weave "as-drawn-in" according to the threading throughout the center. A row of tabby follows each pattern row throughout the border and rug. The alternating tabbies are harnesses 1–3, 2–4.

TWILL AND HERRINGBONE THREADINGS
FOR RAG RUGS (Fig. 76)

Rag rugs woven on a twill threading or any of its reverses are very attractive, for the texture of the weave lends character over all. Thread to any of the foregoing suggestions. The diamond threading in Figure 77 will result in a rug quite similar to the rag rug in Figure 51. Twill, planned with reverses, results in a stunning rug such as that shown in No. 4, Figure 76.

There are many ways to design twill rag rugs, and the threading is simple enough for anyone to handle. Make an outside vertical border any width, in plain weave or speckled basket weave, harnesses 1, 1, 2, 2, 3, 3, 4, 4; then add a straight twill center. Or, plan a twill border with a speckled center; or plan to use a repeated herringbone for the border, with a twill center, etc. Weave as twill: harnesses 1–2, 2–3, 3–4, 4–1; or reverse twill: harnesses 1–2, 2–3, 3–4, 4–1, 3–4, 2–3, and repeat.

WEAVING TWILL AND HERRINGBONE
ON OPPOSITES

Stunning modern textures grow out of the method, "on opposites." Twill and herringbone especially yield beautiful rugs. Set the warps far apart, such as eight pairs per inch, so that the opposite wefts will sink down against each other and form the typical twill angles, but with striking accents derived by the opposite treadlings in a contrasting color.

Weave: (Read left to right)
Harnesses 1–2, 1st color, followed by harnesses 3–4, 2nd color.
Harnesses 2–3, 1st color, followed by harnesses 4–1, 2nd color.
Harnesses 3–4, 1st color, followed by harnesses 1–2, 2nd color.
Harnesses 4–1, 1st color, followed by harnesses 2–3, 2nd color.
Continue repeating. After establishing the rhythm of these successions, try changing to other colors or reversing the two colors, producing shaded

145

effects. See the rug woven in two alternating colors in Figure 75, twill in black and white.

Bound Weaving. This weave produces a twill texture with successive color shadings. A twill or herringbone threading is set far apart in the reed, with carpet warp at 8 threads per inch. Two, three, or more colors are used, woven with the regular twill succession, harnesses 1–2, 2–3, 3–4, 4–1, or its reverse. Each row sinks down and binds the previous row, and the colors show up in diagonal formations. Effective series of colors are planned, such as brown, orange, and gold; or red, white, and blue; or shades of any color. For variation, the number of colors or their succession is changed. The method of weaving with several shuttles is shown in Figure 133.

In bound weaving, as in weaving on opposites, the warp threads should be completely covered, and the mat surface resulting is especially pleasing in twill rugs. Very adaptable are the threadings of Indian Saddle Blanket Weave, Chapter 17, some forms of which are really bound weave.

To be sure that the warp threads are covered, weave a small section as a try-out sample. If the warp shows, rethread to a wider setting. For instance, if your filler is fairly heavy, 4 pairs of carpet warp per inch or 4 heavy warps will give you a more satisfactory "Bound Weave" than 8 single warps. In this case you can rethread the 8 singles to 4 pairs per inch; or if your loom has 12 warps per inch, rethread to 6 pairs. Rethread 15 singles to 5 groups of 3 warps each. In all these cases, the groups of two or three warps are regarded as a single thread. The whole group is threaded through a heddle and from there through the reed dent. Any twisting of the threads in groups will not show since the warp is covered.

CHAPTER 21

Four-Harness Overshot Rugs

THIS group of handwoven rugs has many desirable Colonial Overshot patterns worked out by Colonial weavers. They are easy to weave, and when you have woven one you will understand the principle involved in all. Here are some of the beautiful figurations from which to choose rug motifs: diamonds, stars and roses, circles, wheels, crosses, tables, and bowknots. Countless patterns are shown in books on weaving and several successful rug patterns will be shown here.

One nice thing about four-harness Overshot rug patterns is that coverlets may be woven to match in the same figures and forms. In fact, from these patterns complete room ensembles can be designed, such as pillows, drapes, runners, coverlets, and rugs. Moreover, many large Colonial Overshot coverlet patterns may be reduced to motifs of the same proportions, but fewer threads, to make rugs to match.

While some modern weavers prefer methods with more closely bound filler than Overshot, experience has proven that the Overshot can be durable, useful, and beautiful. Rugs made by the following plans with limited Overshot spaces have lasted twenty years and are still strong, with unworn filler.

TEXTURE AND DECORATIVE USE

In weaving this type of rug, there are three distinct color values which contribute to their beauty of texture and usefulness in decoration:

1. The Overshot itself, or the heavy weft yarn, reaching across the warp opening to make one span of the design;

2. The "half tones" or small spots of color where the weft shows across short openings on each side of the Overshot;

3. The "tabby" background texture of in-and-out weave; this plain weave sets off the design blocks, and the half tones act as a blend between Overshot and tabby.

These textures contribute to an extensive and popular use of Overshot rugs in conventional and traditional settings, with the pattern forming an

147

allover repeat. The main figure in pattern color is made to stand out clearly with a contrasting background, giving two strong colors to play with as well as a third half tone combining both.

Overshot rugs look well in Colonial-period rooms but they also provide attractive design surfaces for modern rooms. An Overshot rug can combine the several colors of a decorative scheme and can serve as a basic background to the color scheme. Once an Overshot rug type is chosen, its color even more than its design places it in the home. Low-keyed colors make it functional yet inconspicuous for the living room, library, or hall. The rug brings out the darker colors of the room, holding the colors together by its own color blends.

A carefully planned color harmony can add a bright accent or two in rug borders, accessories, couch throws, and pillows. Pure colors of bright hue can make quite a different rug out of the same Overshot rug design. The Sunflower pattern, for instance, can be woven in low neutral tones for a large living-room rug, but may be reduced in size and woven in gay orange or flame for bedroom or nursery, and both are effective. Many of the patterns, such as the Cup-and-Saucer or Wheel of Fortune, Whig Rose, Chariot Wheel, Diamond, etc., are adaptable to almost any room in the home, with certain color limitations.

DESIGN AND COLOR

In Overshot rugs the colors are more dominant than in other types, for the pattern filler shows entirely across open spaces of the design, unmodified by the warp. This is very different from Summer and Winter or Crackle weave where the warp ties down the filler every fourth thread. We, therefore, get pure colors, and it is important to choose the color especially for the rug in question. More daring colors are used now than ever before, and the preferred can be selected, following the rule that whatever looks right *is* right. Gay colors also can be used, but they should be deeper than the colors of the room.

Hundreds of Overshot patterns are shown in books on weaving, from which designs may be chosen. Their contours can be round or square. Both the designs and colors in these patterns are beautifully distributed and blended.

In planning a design, a very important rule is not to have too long a skip in the Overshot itself, or the rug will not wear well. A skip should not be more than ¾ in. Skips of 1 in. or more are a hazard both for catching the loop and wearing out this portion of the rug rapidly.

FRINGE VERSUS HEM

Overshot rugs as well as rag rugs may have either a hem or a fringe with a heading. The color of these is important. If the warp is white and the filler dark, be careful to modulate these finishes accordingly.

148

For a hem, weave 2 in., using one of the colors of the rug for the weft. Plan a hemmed end in corresponding tone to the rest of the rug. A weft of very dark color modulates a white warp, and a dark warp can be lightened with a white weft. A white rug-end against a dark rug ruins the effect because of its sharp contrasting line. Hem finishes are shown in Figure 129.

For a fringe, leave 4 or more inches unwoven; then make a heading of plain weave for at least ½ in. Weave the same at the other end. When finished, tie several knots at intervals along the fringe temporarily so that they will not fray. A method of tying is shown in Figure 129. If a warp is white and the fringe itself stands out like a sore spot, dip it in dye to match some color in the rug.

MATERIALS

The most usual make-up of these rugs is a carpet warp of 8/4, 8/3, or 5/3 cotton, white or colored, or 10/2 linen; a pattern filler of 3- or 4-ply cotton or wool, generally colored; and a tabby or binder like the warp or about the same size.

Types of Filler. Several kinds of pattern weft can be used in Overshot pattern rugs.

Commercial Rug Cotton Filler (Called Rug Yarn or Rugro). This is a soft 3- or 4-ply cotton produced in skeins in all colors, by commercial thread companies, about the size of a pencil when tightly twisted. It makes excellent rugs that last many years, and if a good guaranteed grade is used the rugs will be fast to light and will wash well. The rugs should not be boiled or sent to the laundry; but they should be washed in a washing machine or by hand with soap and lukewarm water. A little lye put in the water will hold the color. A long soaking in suds, with very little machine washing, gives excellent results; moreover, it cuts washing time in half.

Wool Rug Yarn. This is a 3- or 4-ply wool yarn spun to just the right tension to make a soft beautiful texture. It comes in a wide range of graduated colors. Although more expensive than cotton, rugs of wool last more than twice as long and well repay the investment. Wool is the material to buy for a truly beautiful rug. Wool rugs, too, demand a much higher price than cotton, if the rugs are made to be sold.

Wool Filler. Some companies sell a knitted rug filler made of wool knitted into a chain either mottled or plain. Waste wool can be used in this way. It works up into a circular material that makes a beautiful springy fibrous rug. If you have much waste yarn, buy a tubular knitting gadget called "Hobby Knit" and make enough rug filler for a rug. Rugs made with this type filler are shown in Figures 46, 118, and 119.

Unspun Wool. It is also possible to use carded wool, unspun, that lies flat in smooth strips. This takes dye readily and makes a rug soft and pleasant to walk on. Use in rugs of short Overshot, or Summer and Winter or Crackle,

149

where a frequent tie-down prevents their fraying or fluffing up. This type of rug makes an excellent bath mat, soft to the foot and absorbent. It is possible to get carded wool, to dye the same, and to use it for colored unspun filler. The Crackle rug shown in Figure 98 was woven this way.

Wool or Cotton Rags. Wool rags from suitings, low in tone, can be successfully used for a pattern through brightly colored warps to lend them interest. The rags should all be about the same in color tone and type of cloth, otherwise the pattern figures will be broken by the color change. Cotton rags may be used, but for Overshot rugs with their rhythmic patterns the rags should be fairly plain and all of the same color. The design of the rug itself offers enough interest, without being interrupted by rags of mixed colors. Be sure too that the warp offers sufficient contrast to the rag color to make it stand out. Be sure to piece and cut carefully.

EQUIPMENT

A sturdy four-harness floor loom is necessary. The filler is carried by a heavy rug shuttle; the tabby by a throw shuttle.

TRADITIONAL TIE-UP FOR OVERSHOT PATTERN RUGS

Two types of tie-up are used on looms having more than two harnesses: direct tie-up and indirect tie-up.

Direct Tie-Up. In this tie-up, the harnesses are tied directly to the treadles, one to each treadle, and the weaver presses down the combinations he wishes, using both feet. He can make fourteen combinations: harnesses 1–2; 2–3; 3–4; 4–1; 1, 2, 3, together; 2, 3, 4; 3, 4, 1; 4, 1, 2; 1 alone; 2 alone; 3 alone; 4 alone; and the two tabby treadlings, harnesses 1–3; and 2–4. This method is advantageous in working out original textures, and gives free leeway. Most looms are so constructed that three treadles can be covered at a time when necessary, by using both feet, and placing one foot across two treadles.

Indirect Tie-Up. In this tie-up, the loom has intermediary bars called *lams* between the harnesses and the treadles. There are as many lams as there are harnesses, and each harness is tied to its respective lam which is placed under it and parallel to it. The number of harnesses desired is tied to a treadle, via its lam, so that each treadle contains a complete combination of two or three harnesses. The shed desired is obtained by pressing down one treadle only at a time. The method is advantageous in that one foot only is used for a treadling but it is limited because only as many combinations can be available as there are treadles; as a rule, there are six treadles. To obtain the other combinations the tie-up must be undone and another installed, again only six treadlings possible at a time.

On looms of more than four harnesses, the indirect tie-up method must be employed as the foot cannot cover the necessary treadles, and in this case more treadles are added accordingly. For four harnesses, however, the direct tie-up gives more liberty if the loom is adaptable.

Regulation Six-Treadle Tie-Up. Following are the harness combinations most often used for the indirect tie-up, and the treadles which correspond to them. Use this chart for the following rugs and all rugs in this book, if the tie-up is not otherwise specified. Note that the treadle number is the same as the first number of the corresponding counterbalanced harness combination, such as: harnesses 1–2, treadle 1, etc. This is simple to remember.

Treadles	Counterbalanced Harnesses		Jack Harnesses
1	1–2		3–4
2	2–3	Pattern	4–1
3	3–4		1–2
4	4–1		2–3
5	1–3	Tabby	2–4
6	2–4		1–3

NOTE: The directions given in this book, unless otherwise specified, are for counterbalanced looms. For jack looms, take the opposite two harnesses in each case — harnesses 3–4 instead of 1–2; harnesses 4–1 instead of 2–3; harnesses 1–2 instead of 3–4; and harnesses 2–3 instead of 4–1. The tabby can remain the same as in counterbalanced, or be its opposite — either succession is all right.

WEAVING AS-DRAWN-IN

While any of the harness combinations just given can be used and in any order and any number of times, there is an authentic way to weave a four-harness pattern which can be derived from the threading without any further directions or assistance. Divide the draft into its successive blocks with circles, and weave these circle combinations, passing from right to left on the draft (see draft for Wide Border Rug, Fig. 80).

To discover the outlines of the separate circles, regard each block as having two harnesses, such as harnesses 1–4, first circle. Close this in up to the point where a new harness comes in, such as harness 3 in the next combination. The first circle ends between harnesses 4 and 3. The next combination is clearly seen to be harnesses 4, 3. Therefore, begin the circle enclosing harness 4, and draw this circle around harnesses 4 and 3 until harness 2 comes in. Note that the two circles overlap. In patterns of this type, written with adjacent blocks in this way, there will always be an overlapping. Thus the first block is harnesses 4–1; the second block, harnesses 3–4; the third block, harnesses 2–3, etc.

When the entire pattern has been covered in this way, look at the first

151

block of four notes, harnesses 1, 4, 1, 4. Weave this with the pattern rows on the combination harnesses 4–1. In rugs, weave just about half as many times as there are notes in the block. For a 4-thread block of this kind, weave harnesses 4–1, twice; for a 5-thread block, see the third block, harnesses 2–3, weave two or three rows of the pattern; for a 6-thread block, three rows, etc. For a 2-thread block, weave once, or regard it as a transition between two larger blocks and do not weave at all. The 2-thread blocks can be omitted if desired in weaving rugs. Such a 2-thread block, harnesses 1–2, is shown several threads to the right of *B,* Figure 80. The tabby is disregarded in giving the count of the rows, but follows each pattern row if woven regularly.

To make it still easier to follow the draft, which is called "weaving-as-drawn-in" or weaving as threaded, jot down the successive blocks and the number of times to weave them in a column. This has been done in many of the rugs in the following weaving directions. Variations have been made in some from the true succession for certain design effects. However, all the following patterns in this chapter can be woven according to their draft.

WEAVING RUGS ON OPPOSITES

Heavy four-harness rugs result from weaving "on opposites." These are different from the regular Overshot pattern type. The tabby is omitted and each row of pattern filler is bound down with the next row of the same weight filler. In weaving "on opposites," use the harness combination for the binding row which is opposite that of the former row. Thus, if the weaving is done on harnesses 1–2 this row is followed with harnesses 3–4. In weaving on opposites the same kind of pattern filler is often used for both rows if a heavy rug is desired. The binding or "opposite" row may also be in a yarn of less weight, or even carpet warp used double. The resulting weight of the rug, however, will be much less. The "Blue-Ribbon Honeysuckle Rug," Figure 82, is woven in this manner.

Following are the combinations for weaving "on opposites." There are twelve regular harness combinations possible on a four-harness loom, in addition to the tabby on harnesses 1–3 and 2–4.

Combinations	*Opposites*
Harnesses 1–2	Harnesses 3–4
Harnesses 2–3	Harnesses 4–1
Harnesses 3–4	Harnesses 1–2
Harnesses 4–1	Harnesses 2–3
Harnesses 1–2–3 together	Harness 4 alone
Harnesses 2–3–4 together	Harness 1 alone
Harnesses 3–4–1 together	Harness 2 alone
Harnesses 4–1–2 together	Harness 3 alone

152

Harness 1 alone	Harnesses 2-3-4 together
Harness 2 alone	Harnesses 3-4-1 together
Harness 3 alone	Harnesses 4-1-2 together
Harness 4 alone	Harnesses 1-2-3 together

HOW TO WEAVE THE OPPOSITE BLOCKS

This method does not prevent the repetition of a pattern combination to make a block, because the harness combination followed by its opposite is repeated and all the warp threads will be securely tied since one shed locks the other. For instance, repeat harnesses 1-2, followed by harnesses 3-4 to make the 1-2 block. However, to show the outlines of the block effectively, choose a second color for the opposite or binding row. In planning a rug, choose two colors of good contrast or two quite different shades of the same color, and always use the second of the two colors for the binder or opposite row. Weave the rug with the usual succession of pattern blocks, but instead of tabby after each row substitute filler of the same or a little less weight than the pattern filler and weave this through on the opposite harness combination. Such a pattern would be woven as follows:

Harnesses 1-2, blue; 3-4, white. Repeat these two rows to square the block.
Harnesses 2-3, blue; 4-1, white. Repeat to square the block.
Harnesses 3-4, blue; 1-2, white. Repeat to square the block.
Harnesses 4-1, blue; 2-3, white. Repeat to square the block.
Continue in whatever order your blocks occur.

Three harnesses also can be used at a time followed by the opposite one harness; or one harness followed by the opposite three. However, precaution should be used to make sure that the particular pattern in question does not produce too long an Overshot when this is done. Using three against one is sometimes very effective for stronger color appearance on the side of longer pattern spans.

In rugs, weaving on opposites is best applied to Overshot pattern weaves of short Overshot; but it may also be applied to Summer and Winter, using harnesses 1-3 against harnesses 2-4 and harnesses 2-3 against harnesses 4-1. After only a few rows have been woven, a particular pattern can be recognized. Weaving on opposites can be used for new and interesting effects in Crackle Weave and Bronson, sometimes in combinations of two against two harnesses, again with one against three harnesses. In M's and O's rugs the weaving is also on opposites.

DIRECTIONS FOR OVERSHOT PATTERN RUGS

Figures 78 to 86 are good examples of Overshot pattern rugs. In each case, the draft and its effect when woven are given at the top of the pattern, and the directions for warping, threading, and weaving below the pattern. For other examples see Chapter 30 on rug borders.

153

Fig. 78 — A striking four-harness overshot pattern in two colors, one color predominant on each side. This is called the "Sunset" design.

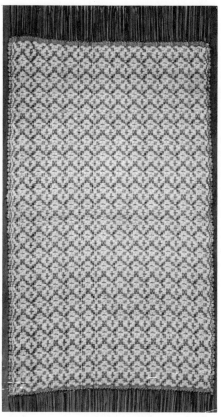

Fig. 79 — The diamond rug, a favorite overshot pattern.

THE DIAMOND PATTERN (Fig. 79)

Warp Plan

Warp: 8/4 carpet warp or equivalent
Weft: Pattern filler: rug yarn; tabby binder: like warp
Threads per Inch: 12
Width: 33 in., weaves down to 32 in.
Total Threads: 399

Threading Plan   *Threads*

Selvage: Harnesses 1, 2, 3, 4, (2 times)   8
Pattern: Harnesses 1, 2, 1, 2, 3, 2, 3, 4, 3, 4, 1, 4, 1, 4, 3, 4, 3, 2, 3, 2;
   20 threads (19 times) 380
Add harnesses 1, 2, 1   3
Selvage: Harnesses 4, 3, 2, 1, (2 times)   8
                                                  ————

                             Total Threads   399

Tie-Up

Regulation 6-treadle tie-up, given in Figure 80, and described in this chapter.

Weaving Plan

Leave 4 in. unwoven for fringe. Weave a ½-in. heading in tabby. Then start pattern rows, following each with a row of tabby.

Weave harnesses 1–2, 2 times; harnesses 2–3, 2 times; harnesses 3–4, 2 times; harnesses 4–1, 2 times; harnesses 3–4, 2 times; harnesses 2–3, 2 times.

Repeat these six combinations, twice each, 12 rows, throughout the rug. To finish the rug after the last repeat, add harnesses 1–2, 2 times. For a smaller diamond, weave each group once only.

WIDE-BORDER RUG (Fig. 80)

This rug has a border 4½ in. wide which completely surrounds a center of small diamond-shaped figures. It is equally effective as a single rug, bath mat, or long hall runner. It shows how the basic diamond figure can become an integral part of rugs with other design parts.

WARP PLAN

Same as for the preceding diamond pattern but with 22-in. width and 263 threads.

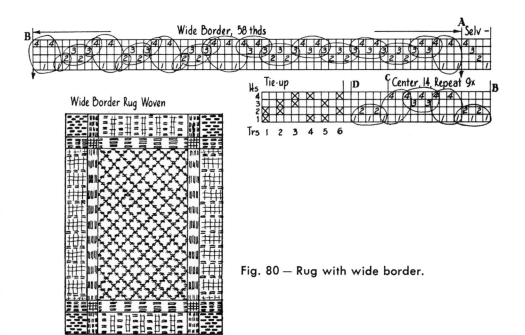

Fig. 80 — Rug with wide border.

155

THREADING PLAN

Follow draft, Figure 80.

	Threads
Selvage: 2 times	8
Border: A–B, once	58
Center: B–C, one repeat, 14 threads. Repeat 9 times	126
Add *C–D*	5
Thread border backward, *B–A*	58
Thread selvage backward, 2 times	8
Total	263

NOTE: For a wider or narrower rug, repeat the center *B* to *C* more or fewer times.

TIE-UP

Regulation 6-treadle tie-up, given in Figure 80.

WEAVING PLAN (Woven as drawn-in. Read down.)

Twill End: Harnesses 4–1 once
1–2 once
2–3 once
3–4 once
Beginning of Border: 4–1 twice
3–4 twice

Center of Rug: 4–1 twice
1–2 once
4–1 twice
3–4 once

Border Continued:

2–3 twice	4–1 twice
3–4 twice	2–3 twice
2–3 twice	4–1 twice
3–4 twice	2–3 twice
2–3 twice	4–1 twice
3–4 twice	*2–3 twice

Repeat these six rows of the center motif for 30 or more inches. Add harnesses 4–1, twice; 1–2, once; 4–1 twice; then weave the border backward, from the asterisk* to the beginning of the border.

THE ROSETTE PATTERN (Fig. 81)

This pattern makes a graceful rug design with its floral motif which may be woven either oval or all sides equidistant as shown here. Thread with carpet warp if heavy cotton rug yarn is used, or with toweling warp such as 10/4 or 10/3, or 16/4 for chenille or woolen ruglets of less weight.

WARP PLAN

Warp: Cotton 8/4, 8/3, or 10/3; or linen 20/2
Weft: Pattern filler: For 8/4 warp, cotton rug yarn or thrums. For 10/3 cotton or 20/2 linen, cotton rug-weave yarn or chenille.

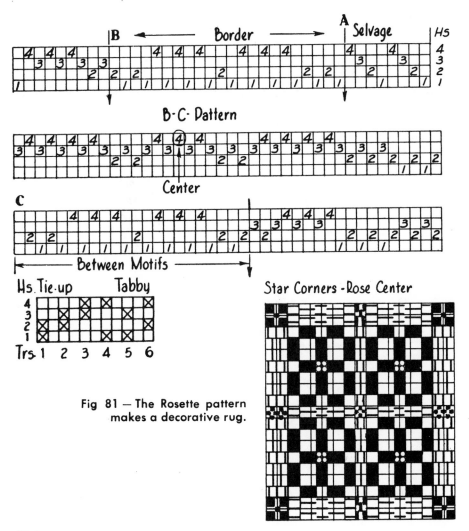

Fig 81 — The Rosette pattern
makes a decorative rug.

Tabby Binder: Same as warp
Threads per Inch: 12 for 8/4; 15 for 10/3
Width in Reed: 32½ in. (12 per inch); 26 in. (15 per inch)
Total Threads: 390

THREADING PLAN

	Threads
Selvage:	8
Border: A–B, 22 threads, once	22
Pattern: B–C, 88 threads, 4 times	352
Border at left side is incorporated in pattern	
Selvage at Left: Same as right selvage	8
Total Threads	390

157

TIE-UP

As given in diagram, Figure 81.

WEAVING PLAN

Follow each row of pattern with a row of tabby, alternating harnesses 1–3 and 2–4.

For star effect, weave "as-drawn-in"
Border:

Harnesses	Number of Repeats
1–2	2
4–1	4
1–2	2
4–1	4
1–2	2

Large Center Motif:

Harnesses	Number of Repeats
2–3	2
3–4	3
1–2	3
2–3	3
3–4	4
2–3	2

Center of Motif (3–4)	4
2–3	2
3–4	4
2–3	3
1–2	3
3–4	3
2–3	2

Between Motifs:

1–2	2
4–1	4
1–2	2
4–1	4
1–2	2

Repeat the center as desired. The last part of the center used between the larger motifs is like the border, so no extra border is required at the end.

For rose effect shown in Figure 81, weave:
   Border:

Harnesses	Number of Repeats
4–1	2
1–2	4
4–1	2
1–2	4
4–1	2

Large Center Motif:

2–3	2
3–4	2
1–2	2
3–4	2
2–3	4
3–4	2

Center of Motif (2–3)	2
3–4	2
2–3	4
3–4	2
1–2	2
3–4	2
2–3	2

Between Motifs:

4–1	2
1–2	4
4–1	2
1–2	4
4–1	2

WHIG-ROSE PATTERN FOR A BEDROOM RUG (Figs. 6 and 82)

No American Colonial pattern is more loved or frequently used by hand-weavers than the Whig Rose. It is called "Methodist Wheel" in New England, the "Philadelphia Flower Pot" in Pennsylvania, and the "Whig Rose" in the South. The contour of the pattern is circular, with a large center rose and four smaller roses at the corners, all combining to form a wheel or circle. It is a quaint pattern which goes well with antique furnishings when used for rugs, coverlets, couch throws, pillows, etc. In Figure 6, both the rug on the floor and that on the rug rack are in the Whig-Rose pattern.

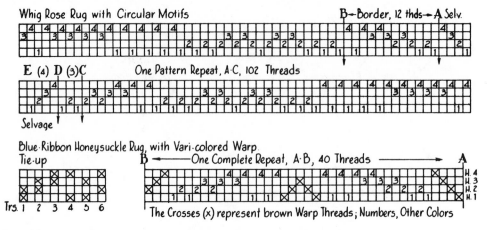

Fig. 82 — Two decorative rug patterns. The Whig Rose: a rug with circular motifs. The Blue Ribbon Honeysuckle rug with varicolored warp.

WARP PLAN

Warp: Carpet warp, 8/4 or 5/3; or 10/2 linen
Weft: Pattern filler: rug yarn. Tabby binder: same as warp
Threads per Inch: 12
Width: 28¼ in., weaves to 26½ in.
Total Number of Threads: 341

THREADING PLAN   *Threads*

Selvage:	4
Border: A–B, 12 threads once	12
Pattern: A–C, including the border, 102 threads	
Repeat A–C, 3 times	306
After the last time, add C–D	3
Border: Thread backward, i.e., B–A, once	12
Left Selvage: D–E	4
Total Threads	341

TIE-UP

Regulation 6-treadle tie-up given in Figure 82.

WEAVING PLAN

The pattern consists of the three units as follows: *A* border; *B* wheel consisting of small rose, large rose; small rose; *C* section between wheels. Start with the border, section *A;* continue with *B* and *C,* and repeat *B* followed by *C* throughout the rug. Finish with section *B,* followed directly by border *A* woven backward. Omit *C* the last time, as this leads on into

160

another wheel. For a rug 40 in. long, start with *A;* repeat *B;* then *C,* 3 times; finish with *B;* then border backward.

Star-Fashion. The Whig-Rose rug on the floor in Figure 6 is woven star-fashion.

(*A*) *Border Motif:*

Harnesses	Treadles	Number of Repeats
*1–2	1	2
2–3	2	2
3–4	3	2
4–1	4	2

Repeat from * once again.

(*B*) *Center Motif: Small Rose:*

1–2	1	2
2–3	2	2
1–2	1	1
2–3	2	2
1–2	1	2

Large Rose:

4–1	4	4
3–4	3	4
4–1	4	1
3–4	3	1
4–1	4	1
3–4	3	4
4–1	4	4

Small Rose:

1–2	1	2
2–3	2	2
1–2	1	1
2–3	2	2
1–2	1	2

(*C*) *Motif in Between Circles:*

4–1	4	2
3–4	3	2
2–3	2	2
1–2	1	2
2–3	2	2
3–4	3	2
4–1	4	2

Rose Fashion. The rug on the rack in Figure 6 is woven rose fashion. To weave thus, with roses of rounded contours, change the harness combinations in the foregoing directions for *B* and *C* as follows:

Change harnesses 1–2 to harnesses 2–3, but weave according to count for harnesses 1–2 at that place. For instance, at the beginning of the small rose, instead of harnesses 1–2, 2 times, weave harnesses 2–3, 2 times, etc.

Change harnesses 2–3 to harnesses 1–2, but weave according to count for harnesses 2–3 at that place.

Change harnesses 3–4 to harnesses 4–1, but weave according to count for harnesses 3–4 at that place.

Change harnesses 4–1 to harnesses 3–4, but weave according to count for harnesses 4–1 at that place.

BLUE-RIBBON HONEYSUCKLE RUG (Fig. 82)

This rug was planned to show the attractive design of the familiar Honeysuckle pattern in a slightly different way. The changing warp colors combined with the characteristic weft design form a unique effect in which the interest is in a warp of several colors with the weft all of one color. The pattern is also woven on opposites, as described in this chapter. The originality of this rug won for it first prize in the Wisconsin State Fair.

THE DRAFT

See Figure 82. The crosses represent brown threads. The numbers represent the other colors chosen — yellow, tan, and green.

WARP PLAN

Warp: Carpet warp 8/4 in colors (brown, yellow, tan, green)
Weft: Pattern filler: Cotton rug filler or a one-color rag weft evenly cut
Tabby Binder: Lighter-weight yarn, such as 4-strand or carpet warp double
Threads per Inch: 15
Width in Reed: 29 in., weaves to 28 in.

THREADING PLAN

Follow draft of Figure 82, *A–B,* from right to left

Heddles Needed:

Harness 1	122
Harness 2	110
Harness 3	99
Harness 4	110
Total Number of Heddles and Threads:	441

Begin at *A*. One repeat of pattern, *A–B,* has 40 threads. Repeat 11 times. Follow the warp colors from the table of repeats.

TABLE OF WARP COLORS AND REPEATS:

First Repeat: 4 brown, 14 yellow, 5 brown, 14 yellow. End on harness 1, the fourth thread from the end of the pattern.

Second Repeat: Start on harnesses 4, 3, 2, marked with crosses for brown, the last part of the first repeat. These 3 brown with 4 at beginning of pattern make 7 brown; then 14 green, 5 brown, 14 green. From now on, each repeat starts with 7 threads, 3 of these at the end of the last repeat, 4 of them at beginning of next repeat.

Third Repeat: 7 brown, 14 tan, 5 brown, 14 tan.

Fourth Repeat: 7 brown, 14 green, 5 brown, 14 green.

Fifth Repeat: 7 brown, 14 tan, 5 brown, 14 tan.

Sixth Repeat: 7 brown, 14 yellow, 5 brown, 14 yellow. This is the center of the warping plan; reverse from here.

Seventh Repeat: Same as fifth; eighth repeat, same as fourth; ninth repeat, same as third; tenth repeat, same as second; eleventh repeat, same as first. Add 4 brown warps to finish the design, harnesses 4, 3, 2, plus an added harness 1.

WEAVING PLAN

The rug is woven "on opposites," with heavy yarn such as rug yarn for a filler and a yarn like rug-weave yarn, lighter in weight for a binder on opposite harnesses, which takes the place of tabby. Since the color is in the warp, both filler and binder can be the same color, even neutral. For a very heavy rug, use a binder in the same material as the filler, i.e., regular rug yarn or the same size rags.

The treadlings given are for a sinking shed on counterbalanced looms. For a rising shed on jack looms, mark the column of filler, binder, and the column of binder, filler, and weave accordingly. Weave the filler first, and follow it with its opposite treadling in the binder row, using rug-weave yarn, 4-strand cotton, or carpet warp doubled.

Use two shuttles, one with heavier yarn, the filler, and the other with lighter-weight yarn, the binder. Leave 4 in. unwoven for the fringe.

Weave a ½-in. heading with carpet warp in the tabby, harnesses 1–3 and 2–4.

Border: Read left to right

Filler:		Binder:		Number of Repeats	
Harnesses	or Treadles	Harnesses	or Treadles		
3–4	3	1–2	1	1	2 rows
4–1	4	2–3	2	1	2 rows
1–2	1	3–4	3	1	2 rows
2–3	2	4–1	4	1	2 rows

Repeat this section once more.

Main Rug:

3–4	3	1–2	1	3	6 rows
4–1	4	2–3	2	3	6 rows
1–2	1	3–4	3	3	6 rows
2–3	2	4–1	4	5	10 rows
3–4	3	1–2	1	1	2 rows
4–1	4	2–3	2	1	2 rows
3–4	3	1–2	1	1	2 rows
2–3	2	4–1	4	5	10 rows
1–2	1	3–4	3	3	6 rows
4–1	4	2–3	2	3	6 rows
3–4	3	1–2	1	3	6 rows
2–3	2	4–1	4	1	2 rows
1–2	1	3–4	3	1	2 rows
4–1	4	2–3	2	1	2 rows
3–4	3	1–2	1	1	2 rows
4–1	4	2–3	2	1	2 rows
1–2	1	3–4	3	1	2 rows
2–3	2	4–1	4	1	2 rows

Repeat the main rug section two times for the length of the rug. Finish by weaving the border in reverse two times. End the rug with six to eight rows of carpet warp, tabby, and leave 4 in. for the fringe. Finish the rug by tying simple rug fringe.

LARGE CROSS AND TABLE RUG (Fig. 83)

This rug plan with large crosses alternating with tables is a most satisfying arrangement. It is quite suitable for living rooms, a man's room, or hallways. The large crosses move directly into the square table figures. The pattern may be woven in bright, cheery colors. The development of this design will be interesting as the motifs unfold while weaving. This is a variation of a basic rug pattern in *Foot-Power Loom Weaving* by Edward F. Worst,* one of America's weaving pioneers.

WARP PLAN

Warp: Carpet warp, 8/4 or equivalent
Weft: Pattern filler, 3- or 4-ply rug yarn
Tabby Binder: Same as warp
Width of Warp: 28 in.
Threads per Inch: 15
Total Threads: 420

*Milwaukee: The Bruce Publishing Company, 1924.

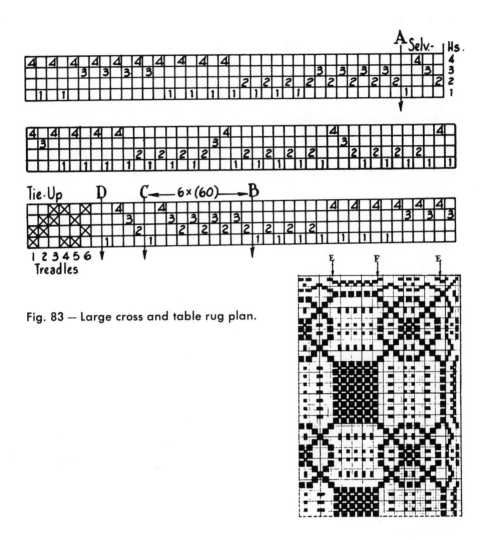

Fig. 83 — Large cross and table rug plan.

THREADING PLAN

	Threads
Right Selvage	4
Pattern: A–B, then *B–C* (154 threads). Repeat twice.	308
Pattern: A–B, once	94
B–C, once only	10
Left Selvage: C–D	4
Total Threads	420

TIE-UP

Regulation 6-treadle tie-up as in Figure 83.

165

Leave 4″ of warp for a fringe and weave a heading; or weave 2 in. for a hem. There are two ways of weaving the large cross and table rug.

1. Weave the border or cross, then the center or table. Now alternate the border and center throughout the rug and finish with the border. This is the method shown in Figure 83, *E, F,* etc.

2. Begin with the border. Then repeat the center only throughout the large portion of rug as desired. Finish the other end with the border.

Border: Large cross shown in *E,* Figure 83.

Harnesses	Treadles	Number of Repeats
2–3	2	4
1–2	1	4
4–1	4	4
3–4	3	4
4–1	4	4
1–2	1	4
3–4	3	2
1–2	1	4
3–4	3	2
1–2	1	4
4–1	4	4
3–4	3	4
4–1	4	4
1–2	1	4

Center of rug or table, shown in F, to be repeated as far as desired for method 2. Then add border woven backwards.

Center F:

Harnesses	Treadles	Number of Repeats
2–3	2	4
4–1	4	1

For method 1, repeat these units six times. Then alternate the border and this repeated center as far as desired. End with border woven backward.

ROSE AND STAR BEDROOM RUG WITH COLORED WARP (Fig. 84)

A Rose-and-Star rug with attractive twill border makes a pleasing pattern with dark warp setting off a light filler. The reverse also may be used. This particular rug was planned for the conservation of white rags, such as might be obtained from sheeting, towels, and underwear. If the warp is in one of the colors of the bedroom or the bathroom, such as old rose, blue, wine, green, or lavender, the effect is pleasing, as the toned warp outlines the white figures.

WARP PLAN

Warp: Cotton carpet warp 8/4, or linen 10/2 in a color
Weft: Pattern filler: White or light-colored rags
Tabby Binder: Same as warp
Threads per Inch: 12
Width: 28 in.; weaves to 26 in.
Total Threads: 333

THREADING PLAN

	Threads
Right Selvage: Harnesses 1, 2, 3, 4	4
Border: A–B, 12 threads. Repeat 4 times.	48
Pattern: B–C	115
Reverse Pattern: C–B, omitting repetition of C (harness 1) . . .	114
Border: B–A, backward. Repeat 4 times.	48
Left Selvage: Harnesses 4, 3, 2, 1	4
	Total Threads 333

TIE-UP

Regulation tie-up: same as Figure 83. Treadle 1, harnesses 1–2; treadle 2, harnesses 2–3; treadle 3, harnesses 3–4; treadle 4, harnesses 4–1
Tabby: Treadle 5, harnesses 1–3; treadle 6, harnesses 2–4

WEAVING PLAN

Use a row of tabby after each row of pattern
Border:

Harnesses	Treadles	Number of Repeats
1–2	1	2
2–3	2	2
3–4	3	2
4–1	4	2

Repeat these 4 rows 4 times — 16 rows

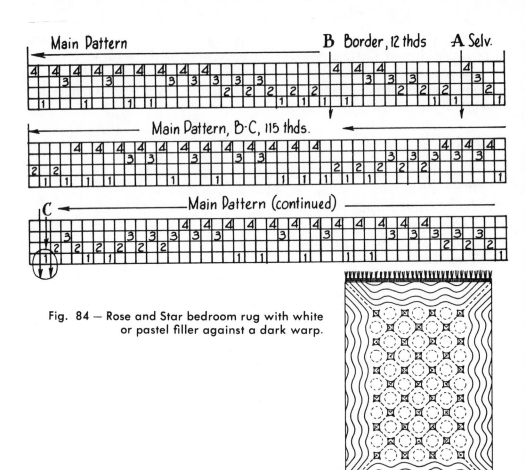

Fig. 84 — Rose and Star bedroom rug with white
or pastel filler against a dark warp.

Rug Center:
Motif A:

Harnesses	Treadles	Number of Repeats
1–2	1	3
2–3	2	3
3–4	3	3
4–1	4	2
3–4	3	1
4–1	4	1
3–4	3	1
4–1	4	2
3–4	3	3
2–3	2	3
1–2	1	3

Motif B:

4–1	4	3
3–4	3	2
4–1	4	1
3–4	3	1
4–1	4	1
3–4	3	2
4–1	4	3

Motif C or Center, 3 rows only on which to reverse pattern

2–3	2	1
1–2	1	1
2–3	2	1

For the complete rug, weave the border, then motifs *A, B, A, C, A, B, A,* and border backward.

For a longer rug, weave the border; then alternate *A* and *B* motifs as desired; add *A* as the last motif; then weave the border backward.

RUG WITH HANDSOME BORDER IN DOG-TRACKS PATTERN (Fig. 85)

In planning rugs for simple repeat patterns like the Dog Tracks, design a wide border to add interest and charm to the whole effect. The diagram shows that the border is about one fourth of the rug width. This border, when woven, forms large tables at the four corners, and makes a very satisfactory rug. In designing objects with borders, let the border be subdued with emphasis on the pattern, or give the chief interest to the border and let the pattern take second place. Chapter 30 describes rug borders.

WARP PLAN

For a rug 30 in. wide
Warp: Carpet warp 8/4, 8/3, or 5/3
Weft: Pattern filler: rug yarn, cotton or wool
Tabby Binder: Same as warp
Threads per Inch: 15
Width in Reed: 30½ in.
Total Number of Threads: 453
NOTE: For a wider rug, add 55 threads for each extra pattern repeat.

THREADING PLAN

Follow each section in order from right to left.

	Threads
Border: A–B	103
Center Pattern: B–D, 55 threads. Repeat 4 times.	220
Last or fifth time, *B–C* only	27

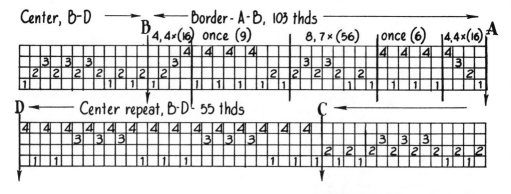

Center, B-D ——→ B ←—— Border- A-B, 103 thds ——————————→ A

4, 4×(16) once (9) | 8, 7×(56) once (6) 4,4×(16)

D ←—— Center repeat, B-D 55 thds C ←——————————

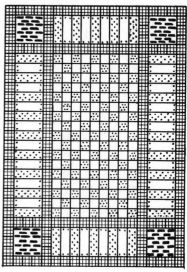

Fig. 85 — Rug with handsome border
in Dog Tracks pattern.

Border: A–B, left side 103

Total Threads $\overline{453}$

TIE-UP

Regulation 6-treadle tie-up same as Figure 83.

WEAVING PLAN

Border:

		Number
Harnesses	*Treadles*	*of Repeats*
4–1	4	1
1–2	1	1
2–3	2	1
3–4	3	1
Repeat these four rows four times.		
4–1	4	4

Border Table:

1–2	1	2
2–3	2	2

Repeat these four rows to square the corner.

Add	1–2	1	2
	4–1	4	4
	*3–4	3	1
	2–3	2	1
	1–2	1	1
	4–1	4	1

Repeat from * four times.

Motif A: Center of Rug:

2–3	2	3 or 4
1–2	1	3 or 4
2–3	2	3 or 4
1–2	1	3 or 4
2–3	2	3 or 4

Motif B:

3–4	3	3 or 4
4–1	4	3 or 4
3–4	3	3 or 4
4–1	4	3 or 4
3–4	3	3 or 4

Repeat *A*, then *B*, six times or more; finish the center of the rug with motif *A* once more. Weave the border backward. Each section, *A* and *B*, forms a dog track. If the tracks result in a form longer than a circle, reduce each combination to fewer repeats, either two or three times.

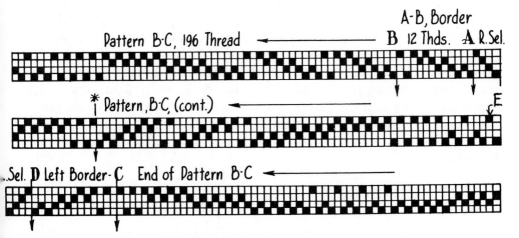

Pattern B-C, 196 Thread ⟵ — A-B, Border — B 12 Thds. A R.Sel.

* Pattern, B-C (cont.) ⟵ E

Sel. D left Border-C End of Pattern B-C ⟵

Fig. 86 — Draft for Wheel of Fortune rug in Figure 127. Use the regulation tie-up.

CHAPTER 22

The Summer and Winter Weave

SUMMER and Winter rugs are what their name implies. Planned for use throughout the year, they are woven with a light design on one side suggestive of the bright summertime and a corresponding dark on the other side, more suitable for winter weather. Figure 101 shows where the dark design areas of one side become light on the other. These rugs as reversible and therefore extremely useful. As shown in the Summer and Winter designs of Figures 87 and 94, each of these rugs is composed of two color tones. If they were turned over, the side that is not seen would show light for dark and dark for light. The rug in Figure 96 displays its "winter" or dark side, while that in No. 4, Figure 94, has "summer" and "winter" sides quite evenly distributed. See also the two-harness Summer and Winter method in Figure 95.

TEXTURE AND DECORATIVE USE

This two-in-one technique can be useful for decorative purposes, and it is economical as well, for it really gives us two quite different rugs for the work of making one. Many of the two-block rug designs in this book may be woven as Summer and Winter. See especially Figures 54, 89, 91, 93, 94, and 96.

Just as much can be said for the durability of Summer and Winter as for its beauty. The wise weaver uses it for articles subject to wear and tear such as seat mats, pillows, upholstery, coverlets, and, above all, rugs. It is one of our most durable rug forms. The texture can be heavy or light in weight, depending on the weft used, but it is always smooth and firm. In either case, the warp ties down the weft at every fourth thread and when correctly woven the texture of Summer and Winter appears as a diamond ground, *E*, Figure 88.

DESIGN AND COLOR

The modern home weaver makes good use of the two-color idea of Summer and Winter for charming design variations. An interior in dull subdued effects with the predominating blocks of the rug giving such tones

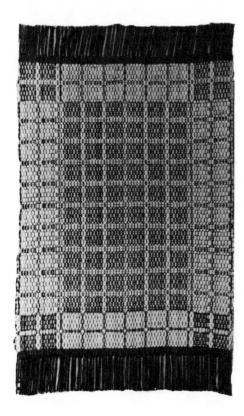

Fig. 87 — Summer and Winter bath mat with checkerboard center and two-block border.

as olive, rich brown, or rust may be featured, and just by turning the rug over a brand new color scheme appears at a moment's notice, showing the selfsame design spaces in gold or tangerine or flame. Contrasting textures can also be used to emphasize further the chameleonlike character of a Summer and Winter design. The warp and tabby always form one of the colors or textures, and the pattern threads the other.

The threading is so planned that there is a tie-down of the warp by the weft threads at every fourth thread, and this continues across the entire width, no matter whether the design blocks are light or dark. This makes it possible to produce long spaces of color and design without any fear of too long an overshot, and there are no dangerous gaps or loops, an undesirable and weakening feature in any textile. This frequent tie-down serves still another purpose; it enables the use of better threads for pattern weft with less danger of their wearing and rubbing, such as wool thrums, raytone, silk, bouclé, and chenille.

MATERIALS

The warp for Summer and Winter rugs is carpet warp 8/4, 8/3, or 5/3 set at 12 to 16 per inch; or cotton 4/4 or linen 10/5 at 6 to 8 per inch.

173

The pattern weft for Summer and Winter can be wool or cotton rug yarn, or evenly cut wool mill ends. The tabby is the same as the warp.

EQUIPMENT

A four-harness floor loom is required for two-block Summer and Winter rugs. An extra harness is required for each additional block. A three-block design requires five harnesses; a four-block, six harnesses; etc. See Figure ·101.

METHOD: PLANNING DESIGNS FOR SUMMER AND WINTER

Summer and Winter designs are planned in simple square or rectangular forms, quite adaptable to modern home decoration, while their traditional character suggests rugs and coverlets suitable for colonial interiors as well. In fact, this fascinating technique has a medium of design suitable to almost any type of home.

The designs for four-harness Summer and Winter are composed of two alternating blocks and only two. They are known as Blocks A and B. See their most simple alternation at the top of Figure 88, where dark blocks occur in row 1 in squares 1, 2, 3; 7, 8, 9, etc., and the light blocks alternate with these in row 2. All the blocks of this checkerboard rug design are equal,

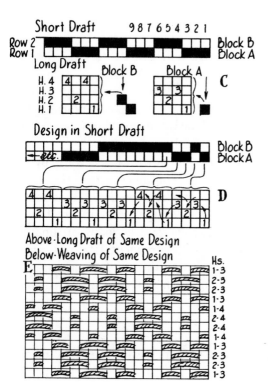

Fig. 88 — How to expand a short Summer and Winter draft to a long draft.

174

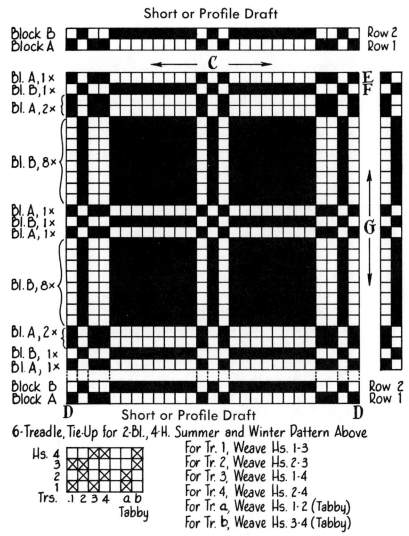

Fig. 89 — Summer and Winter four-harness two-block technique.
Short draft of a two-block pattern.

each composed of three squares in the draft. Compare this to Figure 89, where the blocks are of different sizes, but they also alternate in successive rows. The same is true of the rug in the lower left-hand corner of Figure 96, where space contrasts show most effectively, very large ones alternating with much smaller ones. The rule is: Wherever a line occurs between design spaces in Summer and Winter, and a new square or oblong appears over the line, either vertically or horizontally, the blocks will change so that the alternate tone or color shows.

How the A and B Blocks Are Woven. Making Your Own Design (Figs. 88, 89). Each of the two blocks consists of four warp threads only, *A, B,* and

C, Figure 88. The A block or unit is threaded harnesses 1, 3, 2, 3, and the B block or unit which alternates with this, harnesses 1, 4, 2, 4. The entire pattern on a four-harness loom is worked out by using these two blocks only, and the designer may do just what he wishes with them — repeat one for a long space, interrupt it with the other, alternate both equally, make the rug predominantly one or the other, etc. Moreover, since four-harness Summer and Winter designs are composed of two alternating blocks only, they may be worked out on graph paper, using dark and light blocks as shown. Best of all, they are so easy to plan that any weaver can enjoy creating his or her own Summer and Winter design.

There are two ways to go about it, either from a key diagram enlarged to a complete design, or from a complete design back to the key diagram. This diagram is necessary for threading.

Method 1. From Key Diagram to Design. Mark off two rows on graph paper, like those shown in the design strips at the top and bottom of the pattern, Figure 89. Next, fill in certain spaces on the lower row, 1, used for the A blocks, and then fill in the spaces between these on the upper row, 2, used for the B blocks. Make other little plans in this way, and see which seems to be the best proportioned. Use a simple repeat like No. 1, Figure 94; or plan a center repeat with a slight change for the border, like Nos. 3 and 6, Figure 126.

Such a design for a small bath mat or seat cushion is shown in Figure 89, short draft, top of sketch. To find out on paper how this will look when woven into cloth, mark off a similar two-row diagram vertically downward and at right angles to the other, as shown in the vertical draft at the right. Now connect the two diagrams by drawing lines vertically downward from the horizontal one, and straight across these from the vertical one. They cross each other at right angles, forming design spaces, square or rectangular, *C,* the final appearance of the design when woven.

Method 2. From Completed Design to Key Diagram. Mark off on graph paper the kind of square-block design which you would like to see woven into cloth. Use alternate spaces, shading them alternately light and dark as in *C,* Figure 89. To get the key diagram or design profile for threading, mark off two horizontal rows of squares about ½ in. below the complete design, as at *D,* Figure 89. Next project downward to these two rows, with dotted lines, all the vertical dividing lines of the design, as shown by the dotted lines. To get the A blocks for row 1, lay a ruler across the first filled-in row, at top, *E,* of the complete design, and duplicate the blocks of this row in row 1 of the key diagram. For the B row, look upward along the horizontal rows of the design to the first place where the blocks alternate. In this case it is the second row, *F.* Duplicate the blocks of this row along the squares of row 2 of the key diagram or design profile, *D.*

176

This small skeleton or draft, *D,* is known as the "profile" or "short draft" of the design. You will find a great deal of pleasure in working out block designs on graph paper, reducing them to design profiles and threading them to Summer and Winter in this way.

How to Thread the Design of A and B Blocks. See the design in short draft and its long draft enlargement *C, D,* and *E,* Figure 88. For each small square on row 1 of block A, enlarge the threading to harnesses 1, 3, 2, 3; and for each small square on row 2 of block B, enlarge the threading to harnesses 1, 4, 2, 4, *C,* Figure 88. The developed short draft is called the long draft, as shown in *D,* Figure 88. To thread a Summer and Winter pattern is simpler than an Overshot pattern, for all that is necessary is to follow the short draft or profile from right to left, replacing each A unit of the design profile with harnesses 1, 3, 2, 3; and each B unit with harnesses 1, 4, 2, 4, as shown in *C,* Figure 88. As an example, take the design profile at the top of Figure 89. It reads: right to left, block A, once, harnesses 1, 3, 2, 3; B once, harnesses 1, 4, 2, 4; A twice, harnesses 1, 3, 2, 3, 1, 3, 2, 3, etc. See *D,* Figure 88, for the draft enlarged thus far. Continue thus, B, 8 times, etc., following draft, Figure 89. The blocks, woven in detail, are shown at *E,* Figure 88.

How to Weave the Design of A and B Blocks. Summer and Winter also is easy to weave without directions, by reading each block of the profile from right to left, or developing the profile into its detailed threading, and weaving this as-drawn-in, *D* and *E,* Figure 88. This is written as the beginning of the long draft, as shown. Weave this long draft as-drawn-in. To do this, follow the curved arrows and weave each pair of threads connected by the arrows in succession: harnesses 1-3, 2-3, 2-3, 1-3; then harnesses 1-4, 2-4, 2-4, 1-4; then harnesses 1-3, 2-3, 2-3, 1-3; then again harnesses 1-3, 2-3, 2-3, 1-3; then harnesses * 1-4, 2-4, 2-4, 1-4. Repeat from the asterisk * 8 times for 8 units on the B row, shown in the short draft above *D.* Continue with harnesses 1-3, 2-3, 2-3, 1-3, etc. Use a tabby between each pattern row.

WEAVING FROM THE SHORT DRAFT

This can all be formulated in a rule by noting that all A blocks are woven 1-3, 2-3, 2-3, 1-3, and that all B blocks are woven 1-4, 2-4, 2-4, 1-4. Following this rule, weave directly from the profile, reading from right to left. Take this same draft, Figure 89, and weave the first dark block on row 1, harnesses 1-3, 2-3, 2-3, 1-3; then the next dark block on row 2, harnesses 1-4, 2-4, 2-4, 1-4, etc. It is very simple, each block showing which 4 rows to weave. These are the pattern rows. A row of tabby binder follows each.

TABBY OF SUMMER AND WINTER

To find the tabby, consult the long draft, Figure 88. Note that either harness 1 or 2 comes at every other note. This means that if harnesses 1-2

177

are woven together it will make one tabby, and obviously the other tabby will be on all the notes between or on the other harnesses, 3 and 4. The tabby of Summer and Winter becomes, therefore, harnesses 1–2, then 3–4.

Summer and Winter is usually woven with the tabby and begins with the 1–2 tabby after the first row of each block, i.e., after the 1–3 or the 1–4. Hence, the complete weaving of the Summer and Winter blocks, using the tie-up of Figure 89, would be:

A Block:

Harnesses 1–3 pattern treadle 1 followed by harnesses 1–2 tabby treadle 5
Harnesses 2–3 pattern treadle 2 followed by harnesses 3–4 tabby treadle 6
Harnesses 2–3 pattern treadle 2 followed by harnesses 1–2 tabby treadle 5
Harnesses 1–3 pattern treadle 1 followed by harnesses 3–4 tabby treadle 6

B Block:

Harnesses 1–4 pattern treadle 3 followed by harnesses 1–2 tabby treadle 5
Harnesses 2–4 pattern treadle 4 followed by harnesses 3–4 tabby treadle 6
Harnesses 2–4 pattern treadle 4 followed by harnesses 1–2 tabby treadle 5
Harnesses 1–4 pattern treadle 3 followed by harnesses 3–4 tabby treadle 6

These eight rows of either the A or B block represent their complete weaving. They are woven in the order in which they occur in the short draft, Figure 89, top, reading right to left, or in the development of the short draft into the long draft, *D,* Figure 88, which finally results in the finished fabric design at *C* and *G,* Figure 89.

SUMMER AND WINTER DIAMONDS

Why the Pattern Makes a Tie-Down. Consult *E,* Figure 88, and see the weaving of a few blocks on paper. See the first horizontal row woven, harnesses 1–3. This depresses all notes in the first block, harnesses 1, 3, 2, 3, except harness 2; it also depresses all notes in the second block except harnesses 2 and 4. This is true all the way across the draft, so that harness 2, recurring at every fourth warp thread, becomes a tie-down when weaving harnesses 1–3. Likewise, when harnesses 2–3 are woven, it leaves harnesses 1 and 4 outstanding so that harness 1, every fourth thread, becomes a tie-down. Harness 4 occurs at irregular intervals; hence it cannot be a tie-down. The same is true in the weaving of harnesses 1–4 and 2–4; the regular tie-downs are harnesses 1 and 2.

Note how the pattern at *E,* Figure 88, seems to form little bricks as it proceeds row by row. This peculiar texture is characteristic of Summer and Winter, forming minute diamonds which act as a background for the pattern blocks. However, to obtain these effective diamonds, known as the "true" Summer and Winter texture, always follow the first woven row of either block, i.e., harnesses 1–3 or 1–4 with the tabby on harnesses 1–2. If the wrong tabby is used, this effect is lost.

178

OTHER WAYS TO WEAVE SUMMER AND WINTER

There are other ways to weave a Summer and Winter pattern, if the granular diamond texture is not desired.

Weave in Pairs. The pattern rows will show up as closely formed pairs if the first row of each block, harnesses 1–3 or 1–4 are followed with the other tabby, harnesses 3–4, and kept on in regular alternation.

Also weave in straight pairs, harnesses 1–3, 2 times (each followed by tabby); harnesses 2–3, 2 times, with tabby, and repeat thus, changing over to harnesses 1–4, 2 times, and harnesses 2–4, 2 times when desired. For example, one complete pair is woven: harnesses 1–3, tabby 1–2, harnesses 1–3, tabby 3–4; then harnesses 2–3, tabby 1–2, harnesses 2–3, tabby 3–4; alternate thus.

Weave on Opposites Without Tabby. This gives a mottled texture. Weave harnesses 1–3, 2–4, each with pattern filler, and repeat. Tabby may be omitted as these combinations bind each other.

Weave Columns With Tabby. This makes a rather effective texture.

a) Weave harnesses 1–3, 2–3, 1–4, 2–4, pattern, each row followed by tabby, and repeat. This forms columns of the same color.

b) Weave harnesses 1–3, 2–3 (first color); harnesses 1–4, 2–4 (second color), each row followed by tabby. This forms alternate columns of different color.

Weave as Twill. Weave harnesses 1–2, 2–3, 3–4, 4–1. No tabby is required. Keep repeating. This forms a very interesting textural effect.

TIE-UP OF SUMMER AND WINTER

The tie-up for Summer and Winter is shown in Figure 89, below the design profile. The tie-up for a five-harness rug is shown at *D*, Figure 104. A direct tie-up also can be used with one harness to each treadle, as at *F*, Figure 104, with an additional harness 2 and harness 1 for the tabby. In weaving a block, in the latter tie-up, put down two treadles at a time, i.e., for the A block, treadles 1 and 3; treadles 2 and 3; treadles 2 and 3; and treadles 1 and 3, etc. This method is helpful when there are not enough treadles to tie the four combinations required for each block.

Summer and Winter can be woven with equal ease on counterbalanced or jack looms. See the 6-treadle tie-up of Figure 89 for counterbalanced looms.

On a jack loom, change treadle 1 to harnesses 2–4 instead of harnesses 1–3.
treadle 2 to harnesses 4–1 instead of harnesses 2–3.
treadle 3 to harnesses 2–3 instead of harnesses 1–4.
treadle 4 to harnesses 1–3 instead of harnesses 2–4.
Tabby (a) to harnesses 3–4 instead of harnesses 1–2.
Tabby (b) to harnesses 1–2 instead of harnesses 3–4.

179

CHAPTER 23

Checkerboard Rugs

CHARACTER AND TEXTURE

Checkerboard rugs are what the name implies, that is, rugs made in a block design of light and dark squares, all equal. Though one of the simplest types, these rugs are very effective with their gay contrasting colors and can be used almost anywhere. For the restful and simple check design shown in Figure 90, the weaver can choose between many pleasing loom techniques, all of which are constructed on the 2-block principle and can easily be arranged to weave into a rug surface of alternating light and dark squares. Moreover there are checkerboard rugs for both the amateur and advanced weaver, for the simple block-design principle can be adapted to two-, four-, and eight-harness looms. Among the two-harness types there are the familiar Log-Cabin or "Basket" weave, Figures 54 and 90; two-harness Monk's Belt, Figure 52; and a simple 2-block arrangement that resembles the four-harness Summer and Winter, and which we shall call two-harness Imitation Summer and Winter, Figure 95. Among the four-harness types, there are Mattor, Figures 55 and 56; Summer and Winter, Figures 87 and 96; Monk's Belt, Figure 91; M's and O's, Figures 93 and 96; African Vogue, Figures 91 and 97; Bronson, Figures 92 and 96; and Honeycomb, Figure 91; and for those who have multiharness looms, the six- and eight-harness twills can both be arranged in two alternating blocks; and two-color eight-harness double weave makes an exciting 2-block rug, Figures 91 and 102.

DESIGN AND COLOR

The checkerboard design meets a need for the simple and practical rug. The many linoleum and tile patterns used in modern homes show what good use has been made of the block system by designers of floor coverings. This chapter shows how dark and light blocks of the same size may alternate checkerboard fashion and Chapter 24 shows the great variety of forms possible

180

when the blocks are broken up into larger and smaller units providing interesting border and center proportions.

Design a hall rug or a rug for a game room in any of the techniques described in this chapter. The colors you choose for warp and filler determine the contrast between the blocks. Good color combinations are brown and gold, green and gray, black and white, blue and ivory, rust and yellow, aqua· and henna, cream and dubonnet.

DECORATIVE USE

Since checkerboard rugs combine two colors and textures, one can readily see how desirable they can be for kitchens and dinettes. For the same reason, as well as because of their simple structure, they fit into boys' rooms and recreation rooms. In fact they are very useful and practical in many places, with sizes of blocks and colors varied to suit the decorative mood. For living rooms and hallways, dark colors or shades of a color are appropriate with the blocks fairly large; for hallways, choose colors that will bring life and light into a shadowed spot. Wherever 2-block rugs are used, they can be planned to pick up the color notes in the rest of the room.

MATERIALS AND EQUIPMENT

The equipment for these rugs varies from two- to eight-harness looms, depending on the method chosen. Since the checkerboard category of rugs covers so many different techniques, and since we shall only briefly describe how to adapt them to the checkerboard 2-block system in this chapter, it would be well for the weaver to look up more detailed directions for the materials and method used for each type in the chapter which explains it more fully.

VARIATIONS OF CHECKERBOARD RUGS

Checkerboard rugs in the design of Figures 90, 91, and 92 may be woven in two- or four-harness Log Cabin, Mattor, M's and O's, Summer and Winter,

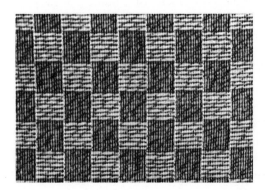

Fig. 90 — Log Cabin checkerboard rug, woven with jute on a rust and cream warp.

Bronson, African Vogue, Honeycomb, and 2-block eight-harness. For each draft, make the (a) and (b) blocks of that technique the desired size, and of equal size; then alternate them and end with the (a) block. A few suggestions for the size of the blocks are given in the following directions. Some are woven with rug yarn without tabby; others require a tabby binder. These blocks, when written in print, read from left to right, but in threading, thread the succession given from right to left on your loom as usual.

The chief thing to remember in designing rugs in any of the techniques given here is to know the texture with which you are working. If there are frequent tie-downs of the filler by the warp, the pattern blocks can be any size, such as in Summer and Winter and Crackle. Log Cabin can have blocks of any size, because its structure is entirely plain weave; eight-harness twill blocks can be any size because the structure of the weave is twill. In African Vogue, since all harnesses occur in each block and since there are no long skips, the weaver has a free hand to use any proportions. However, M's and O's and Bronson are most practical in blocks of 1½ to 2½ in., otherwise the texture will sag somewhat where the opposite treadlings occur; Overshot is best limited to blocks of 1 to 1¼ in. unless a block is interrupted with a tie-down of the two other harnesses at its center, for the skip of filler which occurs on the right side of the rug will be the length of the block; in Honeycomb the same is true except that this skip occurs on the wrong side of the fabric and there are no skips on the right side, so that one can use somewhat larger blocks. However, the reverse texture will not be smooth. Since rugs have more wear than any other handwoven item these differences should be known and respected.

DRAFT WRITING OF CHECKERBOARD PATTERNS

A knowledge of the structure of 2-block designs greatly simplifies many techniques so that drafts for them can be easily written. All the techniques in the chart on page 184 are merely composed of two alternating blocks. To make a 2-block rug, therefore, in fact a 2-block design for any fabric — upholstery, drapes, or table cloths — alternate the two blocks that make up the particular weave chosen. In checkerboard rugs these two blocks are the same size and very easy to plan; in the next chapter rugs are planned with the two blocks in varying proportions.

In planning a checkerboard rug for a game room, the best procedure is the following. First choose colors that would look well in the room. For example: plan a red filler on a black warp. Next decide what size block is suitable. If a large block is required for effect, choose a technique in which large blocks may be used. Glance down the right-hand column of the chart which follows to see the size block each technique can make. We will choose Summer and Winter, blocks of any size, and make the blocks for the game room 8 in. square. To find out how many threads per inch are required; see the next column. At 12 threads per inch, an 8-in. square would take 96 warp threads. Note in the next column that Summer and Winter has 4 threads in each (a) and (b) unit. Repeat each unit 24 times to make a large square check for the rug.

The size of our blocks is determined and the number of repeats for the (a) and (b) units are figured. This constitutes a rug plan. Simply alternate the (a) unit with the (b) unit 24 times, for the entire rug to the width desired. On paper this plan appears as in the short draft at the top of Figure 88, except that here there are only three units in each block. All of the techniques in the chart below can be simplified to a short draft in this way, following, of course, the suggested sizes for the blocks. This chart should help the weaver understand how very simple it is to write drafts when the underlying principles are known.

CHART OF TWO-BLOCK RUG UNITS FOR DIFFERENT TECHNIQUES

On page 184 are given the threadings of the (a) and (b) units for the separate techniques possible to use for 2-block rugs. These can either be for checkerboard rugs, Chapter 23, or rugs with blocks of planned proportions, Chapter 24.

LOG-CABIN CHECKERBOARD RUG IN TWO COLORS
(Two- and Four-Harness Looms [Fig. 53])

The Log Cabin is a valuable rug technique producing a firm durable texture in plain weave and blocks of any size. Two alternating colors are used. The two-harness method comes out exactly the same as the four-harness. When threading the loom, simply alternate the (a) and (b) units to make the blocks. Call the two colors: light (o) and dark (x).

Two-Harness Log Cabin Units:
   (a) unit: Harness 1 (x); harness 2 (o); harness 1 (x); harness 2 (o)
   (b) unit: Harness 1 (o); harness 2 (x); harness 1 (o); harness 2 (x)
Four-Harness Log Cabin Units:
   (a) unit: Harness 1 (x); harness 2 (o); harness 3 (x); harness 4 (o)
   (b) unit: Harness 1 (o); harness 2 (x); harness 3 (o); harness 4 (x)

WARP PLAN

A rug 30 in. wide weaves down to 29 in.
Warp: 8/4 Cotton
Filler: Cotton rug yarn or smoothly cut rags, two colors
Threads per Inch: 12
Total Threads: 360

183

CHART OF TWO-BLOCK RUG UNITS FOR DIFFERENT TECHNIQUES

Name	(a) Unit	(b) Unit	Threads per Inch	Maximum Block Size
Log Cabin, two-harness two colors: (x) and (o)	Harness 1(x); harness 2(o); Repeat once	Harness 1(o); harness 2(x) Repeat once	12, 15, 16	Any size
Log Cabin, four-harness two colors: (x) and (o)	Harness 1(x); harness 2(o); Harness 3(x); harness 4(o)	Harness 1(o); harness 2(x) Harness 3(o); harness 4(x)	12, 15, 16	Any size
Overshot on Opposites	Harnesses 1, 2, 1, 2	Harnesses 3, 4, 3, 4	12, 15, 16	1½ in. or 4 in. if with tie-downs
Honeycomb	Harnesses 1, 2, 1, 2, 1, 2	Harnesses 3, 4, 3, 4, 3, 4	12, 15, 16	2 in.
Summer and Winter	Harnesses 1, 3, 2, 3	Harnesses 1, 4, 2, 4	12, 15, 16	Any size
Bronson	Harnesses 1, 3, 1, 3, 1, 2	Harnesses 1, 4, 1, 4, 1, 2	15, 16	3 in.
M's and O's	Harnesses 1, 2, 1, 2, 3, 4, 3, 4	Harnesses 1, 3, 1, 3, 2, 4, 2, 4	12, 15, 16	2 in.
African Vogue	Harnesses 1, 2, 1, 4, 3, 4	Harnesses 2, 1, 2, 3, 4, 3	10, 12	Any size
Six-Harness Twill	Harnesses 1, 2, 3	Harnesses 4, 5, 6	10, 12	Any size
Eight-Harness Twill	Harnesses 1, 2, 3, 4	Harnesses 5, 6, 7, 8	10, 12	Any size
Eight-Harness Double Face Weave: two colors: (x) and (o)	Harnesses 1(x); 3(o); 2(x); 4(o)	Harnesses 5(x); 7(o); 6(x); 8(o)	8, 10	Any size

Note: Consult this chart for threading plans and block units of all rugs in this and the following chapters.

184

THREADING PLAN

For 2-in. blocks:
(a) Block: Repeat 6 times, 24 threads
(b) Block: Repeat 6 times, 24 threads
Total of both blocks: 48 threads

	Threads
Repeat these 48 threads, 7 times	336
Add (a) unit only	24
Total	360

WEAVING PLANS

Two-Harness Loom. Choose filler in two colors, dark (x) and light (o).
Heading: Carpet warp for heading — same color as warp. Weave plain weave, harness 1 then harness 2. The two colors of filler only are used for main rug.
Main Rug: Use filler only. (a) Block: Harness 1 (x); harness 2 (o). Repeat to square the block.
　　　　　　(b) Block: Harness 1 (o); harness 2 (x). Repeat to square the block.
　　　　　　Alternate the (a) and (b) blocks to length desired.
　　　　　　End with (a) block and heading.
Four-Harness Loom. Choose filler in two colors, dark (x) and light (o).
Heading: Weave plain weave, harnesses 1–3 then 2–4 with carpet warp.
Main Rug: Use filler only. (a) Block: Harnesses 1–3 (x); harnesses 2–4 (o). Repeat to square the block.
　　　　　　(b) Block: Harnesses 1–3 (o); harnesses 2–4 (x). Repeat to square the block.
　　　　　　Alternate the (a) and (b) blocks to length desired.
　　　　　　End with (a) block and heading.

A CHECKERBOARD RUG IN MONK'S BELT BLOCKS (Fig. 91)

The Monk's Belt can be so arranged as to make gay rugs with square blocks in Overshot. The effect is shown in Figure 91. It is attractive because light lines run through the dark blocks, and dark lines through the light blocks. This is caused by inserting a portion of the other block into the weaving of each block. See the draft, where the first block (a) on harnesses 1–2 is interrupted by two threads on harnesses 3–4; and where the second block (b) on harnesses 3–4 is interrupted by two threads on harnesses 1–2. The interruption or occurrence of a small portion of an opposite block is called a "tie-down."

The blocks as shown are equal in size and simply alternate. *ABC* forms the first or (a) block, 4 in.; *DEF* forms the second or (b) block. To make a rug predominantly dark on one side and light on the other, make the *ABC* block twice as large as it is by repeating *A* to *B*, 12 threads, 7 times, making *AB*, 84 threads, plus *BC*, 10 threads, total 94 threads; and make the *DEF* block half as large by repeating *DE* once only, making *DE*, 12 threads, plus *EF*, 10 threads, total 22 threads. Alternate this long *ABC* block, 8 in., with the short *DEF* block, 2 in.

WARP PLAN

Warp: Carpet warp 8/4, 8/3, or 5/3; or linen 10/2
Weft: Chenille, rags, or cotton or wool rug yarn
Threads per Inch: 12
Width: 27½ in.; weaves to 26½ in.
Total Threads: 330

THREADING PLAN

		Threads
Selvage: 4	. . . .	4
ABC (46); *then DEF,* (46): Total of these two blocks		
92 threads. Repeat 3 times	. . . .	276
Add *ABC* only (46)	. . . .	46
Selvage: 4	. . . .	4
	Total Threads	330

For a wider or narrower rug, repeat *A–F* more or fewer times. Always end with *ABC* plus the selvage.

TIE-UP

Treadle 1: harnesses 1 and 2; treadle 2: harnesses 3 and 4. Tabby: treadle 3: harnesses 1 and 3; treadle 4: harnesses 2 and 4.

WEAVING PLAN

Alternate blocks (a) and (b) in the following. End with block (a). Weave a row of tabby after each pattern row. Tabby is harnesses 1–3, 2–4.

(a)

Block ABC:

Harnesses	Repeats	Treadles
1–2	3 times*	1
3–4	3	2

Repeat 3 times
Then harnesses

| 1–2 | 3 times* | 1 |

(b)

Block DEF:

Harnesses	Repeats	Treadles
3–4	3 times**	2
1–2	1	1

Repeat 3 times
Then harnesses

| 3–4 | 3 times** | 2 |

*If *A–B* has been repeated 7 times in draft to make a rug predominately dark on one side, repeat harnesses 1–2, 6 or 7 times at this point.

**If *D–E* has been threaded once only in draft, repeat harnesses 3–4 once or twice only at this point.

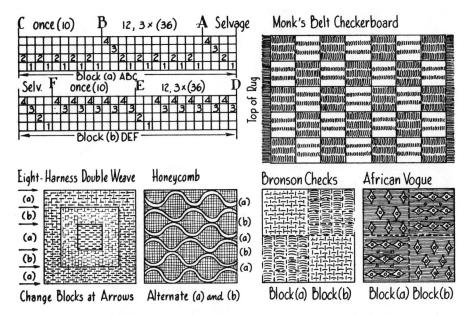

Fig. 91 — Checkerboard rug in Monk's Belt blocks. Two-block designs in Bronson, African Vogue, Honeycomb, and eight-harness double weave.

HONEYCOMB CHECKERBOARD (Fig. 91)

This technique produces a beautiful checkerboard, very effective for a modernistic texture. It is woven with sections of pattern weft divided by rows of tabby. In Honeycomb, the pattern weft is finer than the tabby. The pattern filler and tabby weft change places, so to speak, the tabby being much heavier than the pattern and separating the finer pattern sections with heavy rows which follow the contour of the pattern blocks. This makes a very interesting rug texture. The threading is always Overshot but with limited block sizes.

WARP PLAN

Warp: 8/4, 8/3, or 5/3 carpet warp set at 12 per inch; or 10/5 linen or 4/4 cotton at 8 to 10 per inch
Weft: Pattern, 4-strand mat cotton, rug-weave yarn; tufting cotton or lightweight chenille
Tabby: Heavy rug yarn

THREADING PLAN

Same as Monk's Belt, Figure 91.
Selvage: Harnesses 1, 2, 3, 4

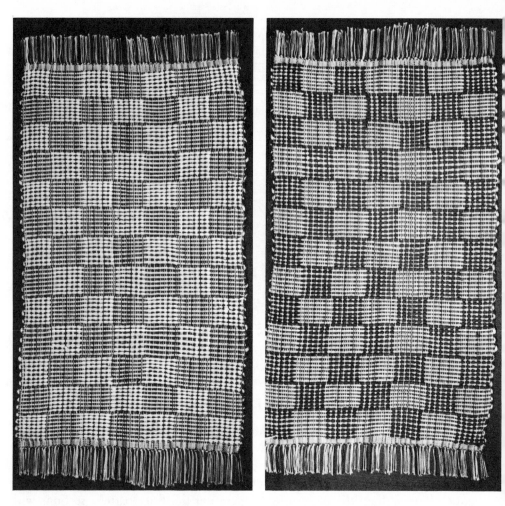

Fig. 92 — Rug with Bronson blocks woven on opposites. Light blocks on one side become dark blocks on the other.

Main Rug: For 3-in. blocks:
    Repeat the (a) block, *ABC*, once (22 threads).
    (This consists of *A–B*, once [12] plus *B–C*, once [10].)
    Repeat the (b) block, *DEF*, once (22 threads).
    (This consists of *D–E*, once [12] plus *E–F*, once [10].)
    Alternate the (a) and (b) blocks. End with the (a) block.
    For wider (a) blocks, repeat *A–B* several times; add *B–C*.
    For wider (b) blocks, repeat *D–E* several times; add *E–F*.
Selvage: Harnesses 1, 2, 3, 4

188

(a) block: Harness 1 alone; harness 2 alone. Weave with pattern weft, the lighter-weight weft; repeat these two rows 3 times, six rows in all, or more to square the block. With tabby weft, the heavier weft, weave harnesses 1–3; follow directly with harnesses 2–4, making two rows of tabby after the pattern block. Repeat all (8 rows) for 2 to 3 in.

(b) block: Harness 3 alone: harness 4 alone. Weave with pattern weft; repeat these two rows 3 times or more to same size as (a) block. With tabby weft, weave harnesses 1–3 and 2–4. Repeat all (8 rows) for 2 to 3 in.

Alternate (a) and (b) blocks, 3 in. square each, as desired. End rug with (a) block.

SUMMER AND WINTER RUG WITH ALLOVER CHECKERBOARD PATTERN
(Like the Center Portion of Figure 87)

This is a good rug texture because of its durability of structure and beauty of texture. A row of tabby binder follows each pattern row. The blocks can be any size; in Summer and Winter the filler is tied down every fourth warp thread, reinforcing the fabric.

WARP PLAN

Warp: Carpet warp 8/4 or 5/3 set at 10 to 12 per inch
Weft: Pattern filler: wool or cotton rug yarn; thrums or chenille
Tabby binder: Same as warp
Tie-Up: Same as given in Figure 89. Pattern treadles: treadle 1, harnesses 1–3; treadle 2, harnesses 2–3; treadle 3, harnesses 1–4; treadle 4, harnesses 2–4
Tabby treadles: treadle 5, harnesses 1–2; treadle 6, harnesses 3–4

THREADING PLAN

Selvage: Harnesses 1, 3, 2, 4 — repeat as desired.
Main Pattern: For 8-in. blocks:
Repeat (a) block, harnesses 1, 3, 2, 3, 20 times (80 threads).
Repeat (b) block, harnesses 1, 4, 2, 4, 20 times (80 threads).
Alternate (a) and (b) blocks to desired width; end with (a) block, 20 times.
Selvage: Harnesses 1, 3, 2, 4 — repeat as desired.

WEAVING PLAN

Tabby for heading at end of rug: Treadle 5 (harnesses 1–2); treadle 6 (harnesses 3–4).

Main Rug:

(*a*) *Block:*

The tabby following each pattern row is here written at its right.

PATTERN:	*Harnesses*	*Treadles*	TABBY:	*Harnesses*	*Treadles*
	1–3	1		1–2	5
	2–3	2		3–4	6*
	2–3	2		1–2	5
	1–2	1		3–4	6

Repeat these 8 rows to square the block.

(*b*) *Block:*

	1–4	3		1–2	5
	2–4	4		3–4	6*
	2–4	4		1–2	5
	1–4	3		3–4	6

Repeat (a), then (b) as desired. End with (a).

*For more compact rug blocks, keep repeating each block up to asterisk (*) only. (Two pattern rows and two tabby rows.)

BRONSON CHECKERBOARD RUG (Figs. 91 and 92)

This technique is suitable for soft-textured bath mats. Attractive texture blocks are woven "on opposites" or as pattern and tabby. See Figure 91.

WARP PLAN

Warp: Carpet warp 8/4 or 5/3 set at 15 per inch; or
   linen 10/5 or cotton 4/4 or 3/2 at 12 per inch
Weft: Wool or cotton rug yarn
Tabby binder: Like warp

THREADING PLAN

Selvage: Harnesses 1, 2, 1, 2.
Main Texture: For 2-in. blocks at 15 per inch:
   Repeat (a) block, harnesses 1, 3, 1, 3, 1, 2 five times — 30 threads
   Repeat (b) block, harnesses 1, 4, 1, 4, 1, 2 five times — 30 threads
   Alternate (a) and (b) blocks as desired. End with (a) block.
Selvage: Harnesses 1, 2, 1, 2.

TIE-UP

Pattern: Treadle 1, harnesses 1–3; treadle 2, harnesses 2–4; treadle 3, harnesses 1–4; treadle 4, harnesses 2–3
Tabby: Treadle 5, harness 1 alone; treadle 6, harnesses 2, 3, 4 together.

Read across horizontal rows below.

"On Opposites." One shuttle only. For tabby heading at ends, alternate treadles 5 and 6 (harness 1 alone and harnesses 2, 3, 4 together).

(*a*) *Block:*

Harnesses	Treadles	then:	Harnesses	Treadles
1–3	1		2–4	2

Alternate these two rows to square the block.

(*b*) *Block:*

1–4	3	then	2–3	4

Alternate these two rows to square the block.

For complete rug, alternate (a) and (b) blocks. End with (a) block.

As Pattern and Tabby. Two shuttles: heavier pattern filler and lighter tabby binder. For tabby heading at ends, weave with tabby thread only: treadles 5 and 6 (harnesses 1 alone and 2, 3, 4 together). In weaving the blocks, follow each pattern row with a row of tabby. Read across:

(*a*) *Block:*

Pattern		Tabby	
Harnesses	Treadles	Harnesses	Treadles
1–3	1	1 alone	5
1–3	1	2, 3, 4	6

Repeat these four rows to square the block.

(*b*) *Block:*

Pattern		Tabby	
Harnesses	Treadles	Harnesses	Treadles
1–4	3	1 alone	5
1–4	3	2, 3, 4	6

Repeat these four rows to square the block.

Alternate (a) and (b) as desired. End with (a).

M'S AND O'S CHECKERBOARD RUG (Fig. 93)

The left rug shown in Figure 93 is the rug that made the blind weavers of Gettysburg famous. This rug can be woven in one and one half to two hours. With a black and white warp, or one of dark color, light blocks show up most effectively. It is a one-shuttle weave.

The M's and O's rug method is a find to any rug weaver, for the design itself comes up in alternating pattern and plain-weave blocks, and no binder is needed. In Figure 93 the M's and O's blocks measure 2 in. square.

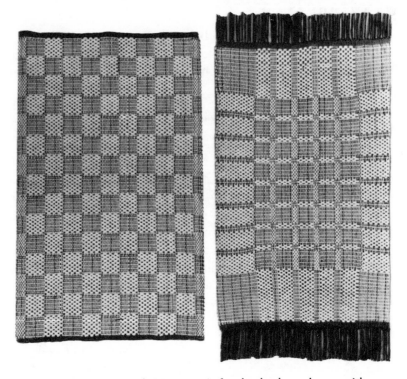

Fig. 93 — Two M's and O's rugs. Left: checkerboard rug with white rayon on a dark green warp. Right: same warp threaded to a border pattern around a checkerboard center.

WARPING PLAN

Warp: Carpet warp 8/4, 8/3 or 5/3 set at 15 or 16 per inch

Weft: Rug yarn, cotton or wool. The pattern weft produces tabby as well as pattern.

Tie-Up: Treadle 1, harnesses 1–2; treadle 2, harnesses 3–4; treadle 3, harnesses 1–3; treadle 4, harnesses 2–4. For tabby-like textures at ends of rugs woven as a heading: treadle 5, harnesses 4–1; treadle 6, harnesses 2–3

THREADING PLAN

Selvage: Harnesses 1, 2, 3, 4; 1, 3, 2, 4 — 8 threads

Main Pattern: For 2-in. blocks:

Repeat (a) block, harnesses 1, 2, 1, 2, 3, 4, 3, 4, (3 times) — 24 threads

Repeat (b) block, harnesses 1, 3, 1, 3, 2, 4, 2, 4, (3 times) — 24 threads

Alternate (a) and (b) blocks. End with (a) block.

Selvage: Harnesses 1, 3, 2, 4; 1, 2, 3, 4 — 8 threads

192

Leave fringe and make a ½-in. heading: harnesses 4–1, treadle 5, alternating with harnesses 2–3, treadle 6, using carpet warp.

(*a*) *Block:* harnesses 1–2 (treadle 1); then harnesses 3–4 (treadle 2); repeat to square the block.

(*b*) *Block:* harnesses 1–3 (treadle 3); then harnesses 2–4 (treadle 4); repeat to square the block.

Alternate the (a) and (b) blocks as far as desired for length of rug. End with (a) block, then ½-in. heading and fringe.

To thread the second rug of Figure 93 with wide borders around a center simply repeat the (a) block given above six to eight times for the border, then alternate three repeats of the (b) block with one repeat of the (a) block throughout the center, finishing with (a) block repeated as on first side. Weave the (a) block to square the corner, then alternate (b) and (a) blocks in the dimensions shown for the center.

AFRICAN VOGUE CHECKERBOARD RUG

This technique provides unique and charming diamond-figured blocks, as shown in Figure 91. It has no tabby, and the pattern weft should be full and soft. It lends itself to effective rugs and will make a thick, firm, and practical rug texture planned as a checkerboard design in equal blocks. For a full analysis of this technique, see Chapter 24, "Block-Design Rugs," and also Figure 97, and its directions for weaving. Simply thread the (a) and (b) units to equal sizes, and use the same weaving directions as for Figure 97, "Rug Arrangement in African Vogue Blocks."

Block-Design Rugs

CHARACTER AND TEXTURE

Some of the most popular modern rugs depend for their effect on texture contrast, which takes priority over color change. In 2-block rugs the color tones of the alternating blocks are partly caused by the change of texture resulting from the character of the weave and the break between the blocks. The surface designs are also controlled by the warp and weft relationships which change with the block threadings.

In the last chapter the various textures possible for planning rugs with equal blocks were described; rugs with blocks of unequal sizes can also be grouped in many beautiful rug effects (see Figure 94, 3 and 4, and Figures 95 and 96). Both checkerboard and 2-block rugs in varying proportions present two subtly contrasting textures due to the rhythm of two alternating design blocks, whereas in other rugs the surface effect is caused in quite different ways, such as with pattern and tabby, the changing of colors in tapestry and pile, etc. This makes the 2-block rug most welcome for the weaver seeking unusual rug fabric effects.

The changes of color apparent between the alternating blocks, providing relating color tones or shades of color, are often due to the dominant and subdued hues of this texture in the weave. Sometimes the warp shows predominantly in one block, and the weft in the other, making it possible to plan blocks of two different colors. Again some techniques, such as Log Cabin and Bronson on opposites, allow for the use of alternating wefts of two contrasting colors, and these will predominate in their respective blocks. Finally, in Summer and Winter, a block that appears light on one side will appear dark on the other and vice versa. Hence the weaver has available a countless variety of both texture and color variations.

This same 2-block principle may be applied to the weaving of any fabric whatever. Upholstery and heavy drapes may be woven in the same 2-block

194

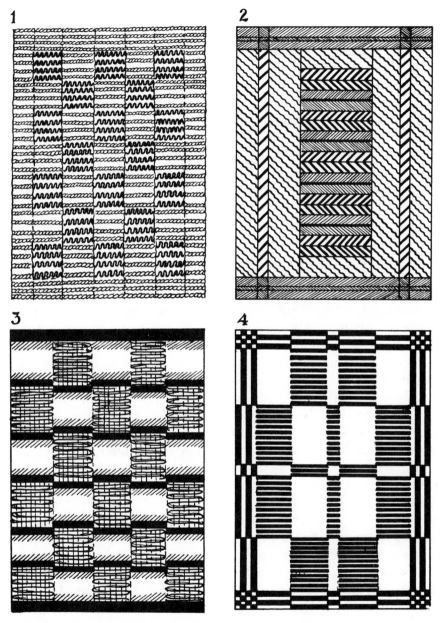

Fig. 94 — Four attractive rugs designed on the two-block principle. No. 1: Large 6' x 9' two-color rug in blocks of twill or Summer and Winter sewed together. No. 2: Rug on a twill threading with reversed twill side borders. No. 3: Rug design suitable for tapestry. No. 4: Summer and Winter design with borders in narrow units.

design texture as a rug. A firm, close-grained texture is produced by Summer and Winter and Log Cabin; soft, thick surfaces derive from weaves with no tabby such as African Vogue, M's and O's and Bronson on opposites, while Honeycomb offers a pitted texture outlined by curving lines. The weaver can plan the size of blocks and their arrangement, then choose the technique and texture desired for their development.

DECORATIVE USE

When weaving rugs either to decorate a home or for a commercial outlet, the weaver should consider the many attractive effects obtainable from the wide range of textural design in 2-block rugs. They are equally useful with the traditional colonial or modern forms of decoration, since the weaver can plan the blocks in any proportion and choose a particular texture. Tailored designs and blocks of firm texture make ideal rugs for living rooms and hallways; closely packed weaves with no tabby produce soft surfaces for bedroom rugs and bath mats; blocks in gay colors look well in dinettes and patios.

DESIGNING TWO-BLOCK RUGS

Handweavers, when designing rugs, can make good use of the block principle and work to advantage with graph paper, alternating two blocks of any size. The colors of the warp and filler chosen may be such as to form a pleasing contrast. With these colors in mind, develop a plan giving predominance to one or the other in the weaving, by making large blocks where the filler will show, small ones where the warp will show, or vice versa. The method of design is easy to understand. Make a plan on graph paper, Figure 89. Make the first horizontal row of blocks in any size, leaving spaces between. Call this Row 1, and the blocks, (a) blocks. For the second row, fill in spaces between those of the first row. Call this Row 2, and the blocks (b) blocks. Keep alternating the blocks on these two rows in the proportions desired.

Borders can be planned by varying the sizes of the center blocks with those near the selvage, as shown in Figure 126, Chapter 30. One type, No. 6, shows large blocks of the main part of the border contrasting in size to small blocks at the outside edge; another type, No. 3, shows a border entirely composed of repeated (a) and (b) blocks, while the center is simply a repeated expanse of one of these blocks, either dark or light. In Figure 96, the border of each rug design is one large repeated block.

STRUCTURE AND DESIGN OF TWO-HARNESS TWO-BLOCK PATTERNS (Figs. 53 and 95)

Two-Harness Two-Block Rug in Log Cabin (Fig. 53). Log Cabin is one of the most popular and durable of the rug textures. It is a plain weave on

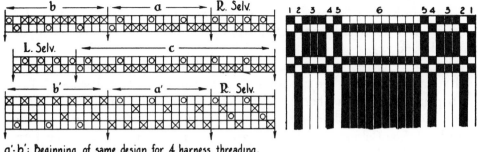

a'·b': Beginning of same design for 4 harness threading.
For section c', repeat first 12 thds. of section a', then add H.1, light.

Design 1. Two-block rug with dark center. In the figure at right, the dark portions correspond to the (a) block, the light to the (b) block. The center (c) is same as (a). The 4-harness draft a'b' produces the same effect.

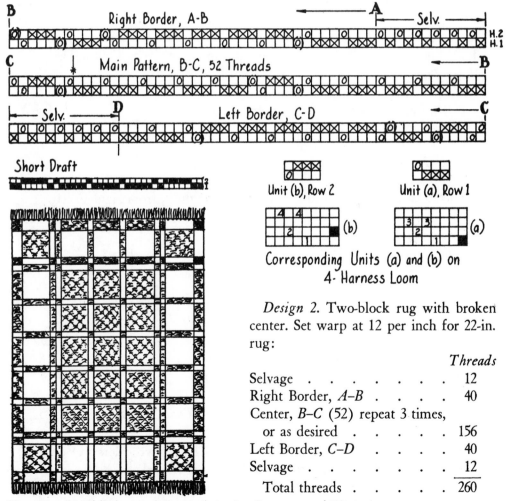

Unit (b), Row 2   Unit (a), Row 1

Corresponding Units (a) and (b) on
4-Harness Loom

Design 2. Two-block rug with broken center. Set warp at 12 per inch for 22-in. rug:

	Threads
Selvage	12
Right Border, *A–B*	40
Center, *B–C* (52) repeat 3 times, or as desired	156
Left Border, *C–D*	40
Selvage	12
Total threads	260

Fig. 95 — Two-block, two-harness imitation Summer and Winter rugs.

197

two- or four-harness looms. For the two-harness plan, use the (a) and (b) units as given for checkerboard, with 8/4 carpet warp in two colors: light (o) and dark (x).

(a) Unit: Harness 1 (x); harness 2 (o); harness 1 (x); harness 2 (o)
(b) Unit: Harness 1 (o); harness 2 (x); harness 1 (o); harness 2 (x)

To plan a rug in two-harness Log Cabin with blocks of different sizes, follow the profile or short draft given in Figure 95, substituting the four threads of Log-Cabin (a) unit for each note on harness 1, and the four threads of the (b) unit for each note on harness 2. Or plan blocks in any proportions, and repeat either block to the width desired. The Log-Cabin rug in No. 2, Figure 53, shows a plan with narrow unit repeats at the sides, and larger ones to make the body of the rug.

Two-Harness Two-Block Rug in Imitation Summer and Winter (Fig. 95). A rug or mat pattern for a two-harness loom can result in a design effect quite similar to the four-harness Summer and Winter. The warp may be in one or two colors; but with two colors, indicated by the x's and o's of the draft, Figure 95, the technique shows up more effectively. Follow Design 1.

Warp Plan
   Warp: 8/4 carpet warp or equivalent
   Weft: Rug yarn or rags, two colors
   Threads per Inch: 10 to 12
   Width in Reed: 29 in., weaves to 27 in.
   Total Threads: 352

Threading Plan
   Thread each section in order as given on the draft, from right to left.

			Threads
Selvage			8
Border: Section a		13	
Section b		13	
Section c		25	
Section b, read right to left		13	
Section a, read right to left		13	
Total border			77
Center: Repeat Section b 14 times			182
Second Border: Same as first end: a, b, c, b, a			77
Selvage			8
		Total Threads	352

Weaving Plan
   See the diagram at the right of the draft. Choose two colors (x) and (o) in the same weight of rug yarn; no tabby binder is used.

   Heading: Weave 1 in. in plain weave, harness 1; then harness 2 with carpet warp.

198

Border:

Section 1, Block (a): Weave harness 1, color x; harness 2, color o. Repeat these two rows six to ten times to form a dark corner square, labeled 1, Figure 95.

Section 2, Block (b): Weave harness 1, color o; harness 2, color x. Repeat six to ten times to form the next dark square, 2, progressing diagonally downward to the left.

Section 3: Repeat Section 1 enough times to square Section 3.

Section 4: Same as Section 2.

Section 5: Same as Section 1.

Center: Section 6: Repeat Section 2 as many times as desired to make a square or oblong center. Follow with the same border as at the first end.

STRUCTURE AND DESIGN OF FOUR-HARNESS TWO-BLOCK PATTERNS (Fig. 96)

Designs in two contrasting blocks are easy to thread and weave because of their simple repeating structure. The very same block units used for checkerboard rugs in Chapter 23 are used for the creation of rugs in planned proportions, such as those of Figure 96. The same 2-block design may be written in many techniques, which means that the order of the blocks and their same proportions are preserved, but that they appear dressed in different textures. The general appearance of these various textures is described below so that the weaver will be better equipped to plan the sizes of the blocks and the resulting appearance of color and texture relationships. For the varying repeats, use the same units as for checkerboard rugs in chart of 2-block rug units, page 184.

Four-Harness Log Cabin. This produces two contrasting blocks with two colors in each combined in such a way that in block (a) one of the colors predominates, and in block (b) the other color predominates. Both blocks appear in a mixture of two colors, with one color giving the key in each case. The general effect is granular, like a pepper-and-salt surface. The texture is firm as in plain weave, hence the blocks may be any size whatever. A well-planned rug in Log Cabin is shown in 2, Figure 53.

Overshot on Opposites. This technique produces blocks of contrasting colors with the color of the filler showing boldly. The Monk's Belt design is of this type. The size of the blocks is limited to 1 in. unless there is a tie-down to interrupt the overshot in which the filler appears as a loop on the right side of the fabric. This method is very desirable because of the pureness of the weft colors which are not covered by warp for a space. It can be nicely handled with blocks longer than 1 in. by interrupting the block with two notes of the two harnesses not in the block, running these twill-wise, *B,* in Figure 91. In applying this rug technique to the planned proportions of Figure 96, simply use the same blocks as in Figure 91: (a) block, *ABC;*

199

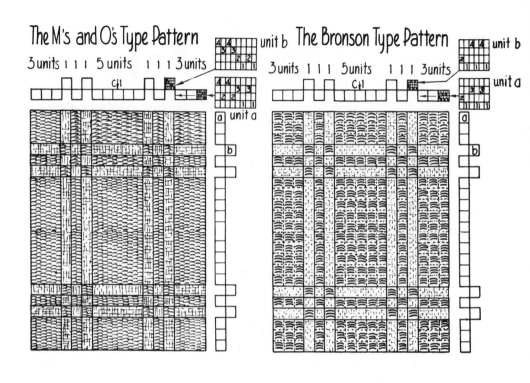

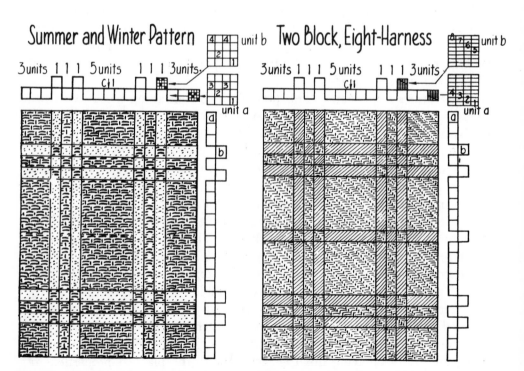

Fig. 96 — Sketches showing the same two-block pattern in four techniques.

(b) block, *DEF*. Alternate these according to the number of repeats planned for each.

Honeycomb. The threading is the same as for Overshot, "on opposites," but the blocks appear as depressions within the texture rather than as weft passes lifted above the rug surface. Like Overshot, the blocks should be limited as there is an "undershot" of weft on the wrong side of the cloth, but the right side is well bound. Limit the blocks to 1 in. between tie-downs. The draft in Figure 91 is suitable. However the (a) block can be repeated many times as long as it is tied down after 10 warps by a few threads of the other block, as at *B*.

Summer and Winter. Summer and Winter produces firm blocks with the pattern filler securely fastened into the texture by a tie-down of the warp that covers the weft every fourth thread. The blocks, therefore, may be of any size. Their color, however, is not so pure as in Overshot, because they are modified by the recurrence of the warp color crossing them. See (a) and (b) units, Figure 96.

Bronson. Blocks are characterized by columns of short weft overpasses which are tied down at every sixth warp thread. These blocks alternate with blocks in plain weave. The blocks should not be larger than 3 in. See (a) and (b) units, Figure 96.

African Vogue. In this intriguing technique, developed by Helen Allen, each of the (a) and (b) blocks appears in two colors with dark diamond units in one, set off by a light background, and light diamond units in the other, set off by a dark background. The blocks may be of any size whatever since the filler is tied down at close intervals throughout. In applying this technique to Figure 96, for (a) unit, use harnesses 1, 2, 1, 4, 3, 4; (b) unit, harnesses 2, 1, 2, 3, 4, 3. See also African Vogue Rug, Figure 97.

M's and O's. In this technique all the blocks appear of the same color, but blocks in plain weave alternate with blocks in the M's and O's texture weave, and the total effect, therefore, is of two alternating blocks. Single blocks should not extend over 2 in. See (a) and (b) units in Figure 96.

Eight-Harness. The damask effect of two alternating blocks is produced by the twill lines of block 1 running in an opposite direction from the twill lines of block 2. Only one weft is used. The blocks appear as light and dark because of their shadowed lines. Blocks of any size may be designed as the texture is twill and held firmly by its own successive rows. See (a) and (b) units in Figure 96.

WRITING THE DRAFTS

The same design is arranged so that it can be woven in these several ways by making a profile picture or condensed form of the draft. The profile is arranged on graph paper with the succession of blocks as appearing

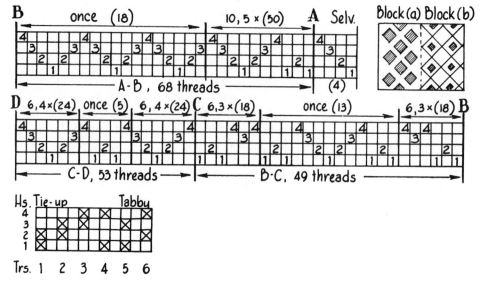

Fig. 97 — Rug arrangement in African Vogue blocks.

in the original design. Then each filled-in square of the profile is enlarged or replaced with its detailed block.

As an example, plan a small bath mat 20 in. wide on a loom; the warp is set at 10 per inch, total threads 200, with 4 threads of selvage on each side. Arrange the blocks of the design as shown in Figure 96. The 2-row layout of blocks above each rug is a picture of the design developed below it. Call the lower row the (a) row and the upper row the (b) row. Each design is exactly the same but worked out in a different texture. The succession of blocks is the same, but the inside of each shows that they are threaded differently. Read off this succession of blocks as follows: right to left: (a) row, 3 units; (b) row, 1 unit; (a) row, 1 unit; (b) row, 1 unit; center (a) unit as far as desired; then (b) row, 1 unit; (a) row, 1 unit; (b) row, 1 unit; (a) row, 3 units. At the right of each draft of Figure 96, note the enlargement of the (a) and (b) blocks to its particular detailed threading.

For example, in Summer and Winter as a rug texture, each unit will have 4 threads. This means that the first three (a) units will take 12 threads, the next (b, a, and b) another 12 threads, making 24 threads for the border on each side, or 48 in all. This, deducted from 200, leaves 152 threads for the center or 38 repeats of the (a) unit of 4 threads each. For a wider border double the number of (a) and (b) units as they occur on each row, leaving fewer repeats for the center.

To thread the design of Figure 96 as M's and O's, enlarge the (a) block to harnesses 1, 3, 1, 3, 2, 4, 2, 4; and the (b) block to harnesses 1, 2, 1, 2, 3, 4, 3, 4. To thread the same design as Bronson, enlarge the (a) block to harnesses

202

1, 3, 1, 3, 1, 2, and the (b) block to harnesses 1, 4, 1, 4, 1, 2. The same design may be written in any technique where two alternating blocks make up the texture, i.e., in all the techniques listed in this chapter and shown in the chart of 2-block rug techniques, Chapter 23. However, if the loom has been warped with a constant figure such as 200 warps to try out these various techniques, the larger the block (such as 8 threads in M's and O's), the fewer the number of repeats of the pattern to take up the warp threads.

RUG ARRANGEMENT IN AFRICAN VOGUE BLOCKS (Fig. 97)
(A Four-Harness Two-Block Pattern)

WARP PLAN

Warp: Cotton 8/4; 8/3 or 5/3; or linen 10/2
Weft: Rug yarn, 2 colors
Threads per Inch: 10 to 12
Width in Reed: 25 in., weaves to 24 in.
Total Threads: 295

THREADING PLAN

	Threads
Selvage	4
A–B	68
B–C	49
C–D	53
C–B	49
B–A	68
Selvage	4
Total:	295

Note that the last 2 items, *C–B* and *B–A,* are same as first two threaded backward.

TIE-UP

Harnesses	*Treadles*
1–2	1
2–3	2
3–4	3
4–1	4

WEAVING PLAN

Weave with two contrasting colors, no tabby. The first color is shown in parentheses. The second color is shown without parentheses.

Before weaving the main rug of successive blocks given below, weave a heading of 1 in. tabby, harnesses 1 and 3, then 2 and 4 (treadles 5 then 6).

MAIN RUG

There are four sections in the weaving marked *A, B, A',* and *B'.* Any weaving plan shifts from one to the other of these. Read each block down.

Harnesses	Treadles	Harnesses	Treadles	Harnesses	Treadles	Harnesses	Treadles
A:		*B:*		*A':*		*B':*	
(1–2)	(1)	(3–4)	(2)	(3–4)	(2)	(1–2)	(1)
3–4	2	1–2	1	1–2	1	3–4	2
(4–1)	(4)	(2–3)	(3)	(4–1)	(4)	(2–3)	(3)
2–3	3	4–1	4	2–3	3	4–1	4

Effect 1, block (a) shown in sketch, Figure 91.

Weave *A, B, A', (B')** Repeat all.

Effect 2, block *B* shown in sketch, Figure 91.

Weave *B', A', B, (A)** Repeat all. Finish with 1 in. tabby weave.

Important: Omit last (*B'*), if progressing from block (a) to block (b); and omit last (*A*), if progressing from block (b) to block (a).

CHAPTER 25

Crackle-Weave Rugs

THE Crackle weave delights the rug maker for it not only offers a durable texture over the entire surface of the rug but the blocks also form large simple connecting units of design. It is a four-harness weave and, like Summer and Winter, the weft is tied down at every fourth warp thread with no long floats; this makes it possible to plan for colorful wefts to extend over long block spaces as far as desired. The weave has certain unique characteristics. It is known as *Jämtlandsvaev* in Sweden, and was discovered and introduced to American weavers by Mary Meigs Atwater, author of the *Shuttlecraft Book of American Handweaving*.

Study the directions closely and when you have memorized the four blocks, you will understand how to weave the rugs in Figures 98, 99, and 100.

TEXTURE AND DECORATIVE USE

Both sides of rugs woven in Crackle weave are equally intriguing and effective. The solid color over certain blocks on one side appears over other blocks on the opposite side. Both warp and weft are apparent in the fabric which is smooth and closely bound.

The Crackle weave provides a tool for the development of lovely new texture effects, with block designs formed by horizontal and vertical intersections of pattern changes. It is adaptable to modern interiors, and especially good for rugs; it is used also for upholstery and heavy drapery.

DESIGN AND COLOR

There is great freedom of design, as the blocks are not limited in length. A Crackle design is governed by the space covered by any one repeated block and the movement of the blocks before and after it. Crackle-weave blocks seem to proceed in large steps, their progress anticipated and modulated by the combining of the last block with the new, the latter appear-

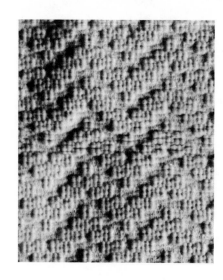

Fig. 98 — Texture of
Herringbone Crackle rug
with pattern weft of
unspun wool.

Courtesy — Clara McNulty

ing more dominant. This is caused by the overlapping of woven blocks in the weave's structure. From the standpoint of design, it makes possible soft blends of color in suggestive lights and shadows. Colors never appear pure; they are subtly modified by the warp with single warps at intervals allowing more weft color to show, and groups of warps at other points covering the weft so that very little of its color shows. It is a technique that offers the adventurous weaver unlimited scope in the creation of space shadings and beautiful color effects. Wefts of two or three colors also can be used for still more interesting combinations.

WARP SETTING AND MATERIALS

Warp: Carpet warp 8/4 or equivalent, set at 12 per inch, makes the best setting for Crackle rugs. For very heavy rugs, use 10/5 linen warp or 4/4 cotton, or 8/4 double, set at 8 to 10 per inch. The warp may also be set with vertical bands of color which when woven correspond to the width of the blocks and form stunning effects. In Figure 99, red warp is used across Block 1, and this is repeated 16 times. Block 2 in black, Block 3 in white, and Block 4 in gray are each repeated 16 times. Shades of a color can also be used in this way for successive Crackle-weave blocks.

Weft: With warp at 12 per inch, use wool rug yarn or rug chenille for pattern filler to make a rug of good quality. Cotton rug yarn is also satisfactory. Covered by the recurrent tie-down warps it will wear well. For very heavy rugs, use wool yarn or chenille double across the 10/5 or 4/4 warp at 8 or 10 per inch. Evenly cut strips of woolen suiting may also be used.

EQUIPMENT

A sturdy four-harness floor loom is required, either jack or counter-balanced. In weaving, harnesses are balanced two against two.

METHOD: NATURE OF THE WEAVE AND OVERLAPPING OF BLOCKS

In Crackle weave, each pattern shed weaves across two blocks at the same time, resulting in an overlapping of woven blocks. The reason for this is that instead of there being only two harnesses together (such as harnesses 1, 2, 1, 2) in each design block, like Overshot, there are three harnesses in each Crackle-weave block (such as harnesses 1, 2, 1, 4). The appearance of these three-harness blocks, however, is due to the threading; the treadling is the same as in Overshot. Here is the threading for the four Crackle-weave blocks:

Blocks	Overshot	Crackle
No. 1 — Instead of harnesses 1, 2, 1, 2 — thread		1, 2, 1, 4
No. 2 — Instead of harnesses 2, 3, 2, 3 — thread		2, 3, 2, 1
No. 3 — Instead of harnesses 3, 4, 3, 4 — thread		3, 4, 3, 2
No. 4 — Instead of harnesses 4, 1, 4, 1 — thread		4, 1, 4, 3

Each Crackle block combines two Overshot blocks thus:

Block No. 1 (Harnesses 1, 2, 1, 4) combines Overshot blocks, harnesses 1–2, and harnesses 4–1, and will show whenever harnesses 1–2 or 4–1 are woven.

Block No. 2 (Harnesses 2, 3, 2, 1) combines Overshot blocks, harnesses 2–3 and 1–2, and will show whenever harnesses 2–3 or 1–2 are woven. Warp threads on harnesses 1–2 appear in both of these blocks and will spread through both, overlapping the other, when either one is woven, thus acting as a blend between them. This is what makes Crackle such a subtle, charming, and different weave.

Block No. 3 (Harnesses 3, 4, 3, 2) combines harnesses 3–4 and 2–3.

Block No. 4 (Harnesses 4, 1, 4, 3) combines harnesses 4–1 and 3–4.

Another way to think of the Crackle design structure is this. Each harness combination, such as harnesses 1–2, occurs in two entirely separate blocks, such as:

Block 1 — Harnesses 1, 2, 1, 4
Block 2 — Harnesses 2, 3, 2, 1

It, therefore, fulfills a double purpose as a block of its own and as a connecting link between itself and the next block. When weaving harnesses 1–2, wherever Block 1 is threaded (harnesses 1, 2, 1, 4), a pure block of color will be interrupted only by the tie-downs on harness 4. However, the same color also will appear wherever Block 2 (harnesses 2, 3, 2, 1) is threaded, interrupted only by the note on harness 3, since three of the threads on Block 2 are either on harness 1 or 2. At the same time, wherever Block 3

207

is threaded (harnesses 3, 4, 3, 2), a shadow of color will show over harness 2; and wherever Block 4 is threaded (harnesses 4, 1, 4, 3), a shadow of color will show over harness 1, since only one thread of each will show whenever the weaving of Block 1 reaches them across the warp.

To make each woven block result in interesting distributions of overlapping blocks, have two blocks with strong color and two blocks with a suggestion only of color.

If Block 2 (harnesses 2, 3, 2, 1) is woven after Block 1, there will be strong color next to the color previously filled by harnesses 1 and 2, but other areas will occur in new spots. This recurrence of color makes the steps in Crackle most effective, as shown in Figure 99. This overlapping of color cannot be avoided, but it may be regarded as adding to the beauty and charm of the texture.

HOW TO WEAVE THE BLOCKS

Follow each row of pattern filler with a row of tabby.

Block 1 — Harnesses 1, 2, 1, 4 — is woven as in Overshot: harnesses 1–2. However, all the way across this block, while harnesses 1 and 2 are depressed, harness 4 will stay in the upper shed above the weft. Thus it is tied down, prevents a skip, and makes it possible to repeat the block in the threading as far as desired.

Block 2 — Harnesses 2, 3, 2, 1 — is woven harnesses 2–3, and harness 1 acts as the tie-down across this block.

Block 3 — Harnesses 3, 4, 3, 2 — is woven harnesses 3–4, and harness 2 acts as the tie-down.

Block 4 — Harnesses 4, 1, 4, 3 — is woven harnesses 4–1, and harness 3 acts as the tie-down.

In any Crackle block, if two harnesses are woven, the other acts as a tie-down.

DESIGN IN CRACKLE WEAVE

In designing with Crackle technique, the four blocks may be used in any succession and for any distance, observing the following rules:

1. Repeat each block as far as desired; then change to the next block. There is no limit to the length of a block.

2. Add one or two notes "twill fashion" between the end of one block and the beginning of the next if necessary to prevent a "flat," i.e., two odd or two even harnesses in succession. In adding the connecting harness, look at the harnesses used in the following block at left. You will find that the last note or harness in this block will answer the connecting purpose. The added connecting notes are marked by circles in Figure 99; by arrows in Figure 100. Thus harness 1, Figure 99, is last note of Block 2, harnesses 2, 3, 2, 1.

3. Check the draft thoroughly to be sure that there are no skips or overshots

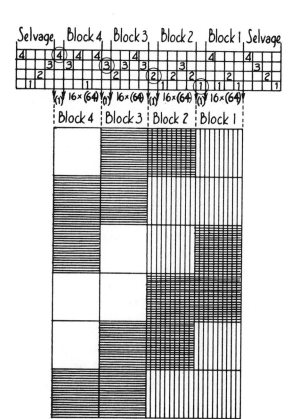

Fig. 99 — "Modern Step"
Crackle pattern.

of more than three warp threads on the same two harnesses without a tie-down on a third harness.

4. If, at any point on the draft, there is such an overshot of more than three threads, such as harnesses 1, 2, 1, (2), there is a mistake. To correct it, omit the last harness, such as harness 2 in the circle, and replace it with the harness that is its opposite, in this case harness 4.

5. To produce a texture with no overlapping of the blocks, omit one entire block when planning the draft. For instance, in the blocks numbered above, use Blocks Nos. 1, 2, 3, but not No. 4; or Nos. 2, 3, 4, but not No. 1, etc. The texture will still be Crackle, but the blocks will be more clearly outlined.

CRACKLE RUG DESIGN NO. 1.
MODERN STEP PATTERN (Fig. 99)

For the simplest rug design, arrange blocks in sequence and repeat each one to make a large block, all four blocks of the same size. This "step" pattern has become very popular. Its compactness of texture and simple effective spacing of design produces a rug of modern feeling so welcome to the handweaver of today and useful in many homes. Extensive possibilities for

209

rich color effects are given by the division of the warp into successive bands of different colors. Each repeated block is threaded throughout in a color of its own, which appears blended into adjacent colors by the manner of weaving Crackle.

WARP PLAN

For a rug or bath mat 22 in. x 36 in., plan warp in four colors; see threading plan.

Warp: 8/4 Carpet warp, four separate colors

Weft: Pattern filler: Rug yarn, color less brilliant than warp colors
Tabby binder: One of warp colors

Threads per Inch: 12

Width in Reed: 22½ in.

Total Threads: 268

THREADING PLAN

Right Selvage . . . . 4 ⎫
Block 1 (harnesses 1, 2, 1, 4): Repeat 16 times . 64 ⎬ 69 threads, color 1
  Add* harness 1 to connect with next block . 1 ⎭

Block 2 (harnesses 2, 3, 2, 1): Repeat 16 times . 64 ⎫ 65 threads, color 2
  Add harness 2 . . . . 1 ⎭

Block 3 (harnesses 3, 4, 3, 2): Repeat 16 times . 64 ⎫ 65 threads, color 3
  Add harness 3 . . . . 1 ⎭

Block 4 (harnesses 4, 1, 4, 3): Repeat 16 times . 64 ⎫
  Add harness 4 . . . . 1 ⎬ 69 threads, color 4
Left Selvage . . . . 4 ⎭

(Figure 99, added notes encircled)

TIE-UP

Treadle 1, harnesses 1–2; treadle 2, harnesses 2–3; treadle 3, harnesses 3–4; treadle 4, harnesses 4–1. Tabby: treadle 5, harnesses 1–3; treadle 6, harnesses 2–4. Note that this is the regulation 6-treadle tie-up, same as in Figure 100.

WEAVING PLAN

Tabby: Harnesses 1–3 (treadle 5); then harnesses 2–4 (treadle 6). Repeat.

Four different block effects are given here. In weaving it is best to develop each one to square. Read each row from left to right. The pattern weft is always followed by tabby.

---

*The added notes between blocks prevent a "flat." The rule is that an odd harness must be followed by an even one, and an even by an odd. See Rule 2 under "Designing."

Block 1. Harnesses 1–2; pattern (treadle 1); harnesses 1–3; tabby (treadle 5)
Harnesses 1–2; pattern (treadle 1); harnesses 2–4; tabby (treadle 6)
Repeat these four rows as desired.

Block 2. Harnesses 2–3; pattern (treadle 2); harnesses 1–3; tabby (treadle 5)
Harnesses 2–3; pattern (treadle 2); harnesses 2–4; tabby (treadle 6)
Repeat these four rows.

Block 3. Harnesses 3–4; pattern (treadle 3); harnesses 1–3; tabby (treadle 5)
Harnesses 3–4; pattern (treadle 3); harnesses 2–4; tabby (treadle 6)
Repeat these four rows.

Block 4. Harnesses 4–1; pattern (treadle 4); harnesses 1–3; tabby (treadle 5)
Harnesses 4–1; pattern (treadle 4); harnesses 2–4; tabby (treadle 6)
Repeat these four rows.

Work out further variations after seeing the effects of these four blocks.

CRACKLE RUG DESIGN NO. 2. RUG IN HERRINGBONE CRACKLE WEAVE (Fig. 100)

The soft bedside rug shown in Figure 98 was woven with unspun wool, laid through the warp in carded lengths. The Crackle weave with its frequent tie-downs of the warp makes this possible.

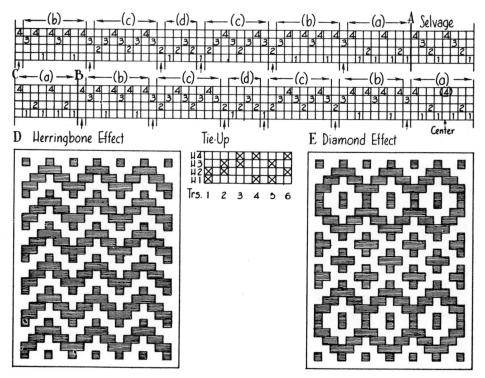

Fig. 100 — Herringbone Crackle rug pattern.

211

This Crackle-weave rug is the same as that of Figure 98. It is so designed as to form a herringbone pattern of large connecting blocks when woven as a repeat, as shown in the diagram at the left in Figure 100, or as a closed diamond when woven with a reverse as shown in the diagram at the right. The blocks are used in the following succession in the draft, the circle designating a reverse point at center, and arrows connecting links.

Block 1.   See (a) in draft — harnesses 1, 2, 1, 4. Weave as harnesses 1–2.
Block 4.   See (b) in draft — harnesses 4, 1, 4, 3. Weave as harnesses 4–1.
Block 3.   See (c) in draft — harnesses 3, 4, 3, 2. Weave as harnesses 3–4.
Block 2.   See (d) in draft — harnesses 2, 3, 2, 1. Weave as harnesses 2–3.

WARP PLAN

Warp: 8/4, 8/3, or 5/3 cotton, or 10/2 linen
Weft: Tabby: Same as warp
   Pattern: Rug yarn, rugro, rug wool, evenly cut wool rags
Threads per Inch: 12 or 15
Width and Total Threads: See "Threading Plans."

THREADING PLANS

	Rug 18 in. wide	*Rug* 25 in. wide	*Rug* 34 in. wide
Right Selvage	8	8	8
Main Pattern, A–B: 100 threads			
(2 times)	200	(3 times) 300	(4 times) 400
Add B–C after Last Repeat . .	7	7	7
Left Selvage	8	8	8
Total	223	323	423

TIE-UP

Regulation 6-treadle tie-up as given in Figure 100.

WEAVING PLANS

Follow each pattern row with tabby: harnesses 1–3 (treadle 5); and harnesses 2–4 (treadle 6).

Design D. Herringbone Effect.   Figure 100, left.
   Harnesses 1–2 (treadle 1). Repeat as desired.
   Harnesses 4–1 (treadle 4). Repeat as desired.
   Harnesses 3–4 (treadle 3). Repeat as desired.
   Harnesses 2–3 (treadle 2). Repeat as desired.
   Keep repeating these four blocks.

Design E. Diamond Effect. Figure 100, right.

Harnesses* 1–2 (treadle 1). Repeat 4 to 8 times.

Harnesses 4–1 (treadle 4). Repeat 4 to 8 times.

Harnesses 3–4 (treadle 3). Repeat 4 to 8 times.

Harnesses 2–3 (treadle 2). Repeat 4 to 8 times.

Harnesses 3–4 (treadle 3). Repeat 4 to 8 times.

Harnesses 4–1 (treadle 4). Repeat 4 to 8 times.

Harnesses 1–2* (treadle 1). Repeat 4 to 8 times. This 1–2 block forms center; reverse from here. Continue reversing from end to start and back again, between asterisks, but do not double the reverse blocks, harnesses 1–2.

CHAPTER 26

Rugs on Looms of More Than Four Harnesses

ON MULTIHARNESS looms, such as from five- to eight-harness, rugs can be designed with many more pattern changes than on a four-harness loom. Whether it be twill, Overshot, or Summer and Winter, for each added harness there appears another block to give greater range for the development of the design motifs. In Overshot multiharness patterns, the addition of more blocks means more design detail, a greater number of units, and a more gradual connection between units. These permit more gradual curves and closer blending of forms. In twill, the additional harnesses result in twill textures in opposing blocks of lights and shadows, the twill lines running one way in one block and the opposite way in all adjacent blocks. This technique, known as "damask texture," is impossible on a four-harness loom.

Possibly Summer and Winter benefits more than any other technique by the greater range of blocks in multiharness looms. Four-harness Summer and Winter provides only two alternating blocks, but for each added harness there is another block for design purposes. A five-harness loom makes 3 blocks; a six-harness, 4 blocks; a seven-harness, 5 blocks; and an eight-harness, 6 blocks. Thus, a four-harness Overshot pattern that the weaver finds pleasing can be translated into the firmer rug texture of four-block Summer and Winter on 6 harnesses with the very same design effect. This is of great advantage in rug weaving, for Overshot, because of its loops of pattern weft, is a far less desirable technique than Summer and Winter which provides a more durable texture by tying down every fourth thread.

Bronson, on more than four harnesses, is very much like Summer and Winter, making another block for each added harness. The Bronson weave has worked into some attractive rugs. Pattern units with very short overshot can be planned and woven with a heavy yarn for the pattern and carpet warp or twine for the tabby binder — all of which makes a stunning rug texture.

All in all, multiharness patterns for rugs provide for great variety and beauty of design and texture. Those who have looms of more than four harnesses

Fig. 101 — Reversible Summer and Winter rug in a
three block design, five harnesses required.

can put them to use weaving rugs with unusual borders and interesting center patterns. Following are suggestions for rugs woven in each of the afore-mentioned techniques on looms of more than four harnesses.

MULTIHARNESS TWILL (Fig. 102)

The principles of twill, on either six- or eight-harness looms, offer the weaver a number of delightful patterns and textures. Twill sells itself to the rug weaver for many reasons: its use of one shuttle only; consequent speed of weaving with no need for tabby binder; simplicity of threading and weaving structure; durability of texture; and its production of many varied and beautiful pattern figurations, such as diagonals, diamonds, crosses, and radiating lines. Twill rugs are adaptable to interiors of yesterday and today. Some Colonial rugs were made in twill and the most modern of interiors call for their subtle simplicity.

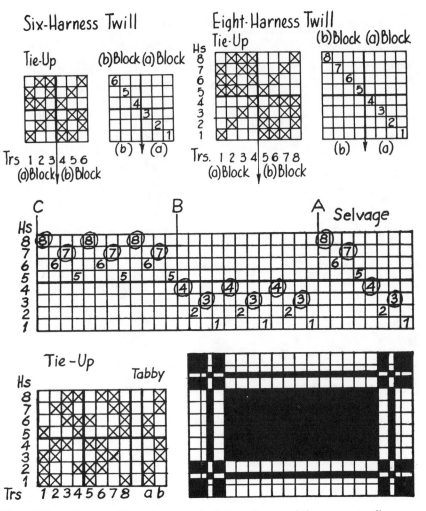

Fig. 102 — Above: Threading and tie-up for multiharness twill patterns. Below: An eight-harness reversible double weave rug draft in two colors.

Eight-harness, 2-block twill patterns carry out the alternating block system described for Summer and Winter, Bronson, M's and O's, Log Cabin, and Honeycomb, either with blocks of the same size, Chapter 23, or blocks of planned proportions, Chapter 24. On a four-harness loom, two alternating blocks of twill texture cannot be woven, because it takes four harnesses to make one twill succession. Consequently, the six- or eight-harness loom provides a tool for weaving two blocks against each other, with twill lines running in opposite directions, which in itself results in beautiful textural effects, Figures 96, 102. Or again, pleasing design surfaces can be made with blocks of plain weave alternating with blocks of twill, Figure 103.

216

SIX- AND EIGHT-HARNESS CHECKERBOARD.
TWO BLOCKS OF SAME SIZE (Fig. 102)
EIGHT-HARNESS, TWO-BLOCK PATTERN (Fig. 102, Right)

Warp Plan

Warp: Cotton 8/4, 8/3, or 5/3; or linen 10/2 set at 10 or 12 per inch

Weft: Rug wool, rug-weave yarn; cotton rugro, or evenly cut thrums. No tabby.

Threading Plan

For large 7-in. blocks in pleasing twill texture, thread

Selvage: Harnesses 1, 2, 3, 4, 5, 6, 7, 8.

Block (a): Harnesses 1, 2, 3, 4. Repeat 18 times, 72 threads.

Block (b): Harnesses 5, 6, 7, 8. Repeat 18 times, 72 threads.

Alternate these two blocks. End with (a) block and selvage.

Tie-Up. See Figure 102. If plain weave at ends of rugs is desired, add two extra treadles, treadle 9, first tabby: harnesses 1, 3, 5, 7; and treadle 10, second tabby: harnesses 2, 4, 6, 8.

Weaving Plan. Leave fringe or weave hem. For plain weave at ends, weave alternately treadles 9 and 10, using carpet warp. The main part of the rug is woven as twill with no tabby binder. To secure a good edge, use two shuttles and alternate them, locking or crossing the two fillers at the selvage.

Alternate (a) and (b) blocks to length desired. End rug with (a) block.

(a) *Block:* Weave in succession treadles 1, 2, 3, 4. Repeat to square or size desired.

(b) *Block:* Weave in succession treadles 5, 6, 7, 8. Repeat to square or size desired.

Add (a) block at end, then plain weave hem or fringe.

SIX-HARNESS, TWO-BLOCK PATTERN (Fig. 102, Left)

Warp Plan. Same as for eight-harness.

Threading Plan

Selvage: Harnesses 1, 2, 3, 4, 5, 6.

(a) *Block:* Thread harnesses 1, 2, 3. Repeat as desired.

(b) *Block:* Thread harnesses 4, 5, 6. Repeat as desired.

Alternate these two blocks as desired. End with (a) block, then selvage.

Tie-Up (Fig. 102). If plain weave at ends of rug is desired, add two treadles, treadle 7, first tabby, harnesses 1, 3, 5; and treadle 8, second tabby, harnesses 2, 4, 6.

Weaving Plan. Leave fringe or weave hem. For plain weave alternate treadles 7 and 8.

For a good selvage use two alternating shuttles of the same filler.

(a) *Block:* Weave in succession treadles 1, 2, 3. Repeat to square.

217

(*b*) *Block:* Weave in succession treadles 4, 5, 6. Repeat to square. Alternate (a) and (b) blocks as desired. End with (a) block.

TWO-BLOCK EIGHT-HARNESS RUG PATTERN
(Fig 96)

BLOCKS OF DIFFERENT SIZES FORM BORDERS AND CENTERS

Rug patterns of two blocks, such as those in Figure 96, may be designed in various pleasing proportions for an eight-harness loom, using the profile method. The twill texture shows an attractive allover weft surface on one side with the other side of the same section in warp color; or both sides can be evenly distributed as to color. The texture is a coarse twill, quite suitable for rugs and runners.

For threading, use the same directions as given for the threading of the (a) and (b) blocks described above for Figure 102, and weave accordingly; but square the sections as you progress through them, so that the design developed vertically will correspond to the profile written horizontally, with center as long as desired.

TWO-BLOCK SIX- AND EIGHT-HARNESS

Both six- and eight-harness twill are actually composed of two blocks which may be woven so as to form checkerboard squares. The threading and tie-up for these are given in Figure 102, and the weaving is fully described in Chapter 24, "Block Designs." Charts showing the relationship of two-block twill to other techniques are shown in Figure 96. In these diagrams and directions, one can use the two blocks of the six-harness twill in the same manner as the two blocks of the 8-harness.

While these close twill effects on multiharness looms are effective, weavers with six- or eight-harness looms will discover a still sturdier type of rug in the double-face eight-harness technique, described below.

PRACTICAL TWO-COLOR DOUBLE-FACE EIGHT-HARNESS RUG

An attractive and serviceable rug with blocks of two contrasting colors results from the arrangement shown in Figure 102, lower draft. There are two thicknesses, each tied down at intervals by warp threads that come through from the other surface, and these show up as interesting accents of opposing color, which gives the background texture lively little specks of design to break the allover ground. The result is a delightful two-color pattern but with a thicker more satisfying rug texture than many of our techniques provide. Good colors are bright red and dark brown or black, rust and natural, black and gray, brown and cream, blue and light gray, green and black.

WARP PLAN

Two colors of Perle 3, or carpet warp used double.
The second color is circled in the draft, Figure 102.
Filler: Same two colors of rug yarn
Threads per Inch: 10
Width in Reed: 29 in.
Total Threads: 292

THREADING PLAN

This rug is 29 in. wide, with a border of several alternating blocks and a center of one of the blocks repeated to make one large block.

	Threads
Right Selvage	8
Thread First Motif; A–B (12), 4 times	48
Thread Second Motif; B–C (12), once	12
Thread: A–B, 2 times	24
Thread: B–C, 9 times (center)	108
Thread: A–B, 2 times	24
Thread: B–C, once	12
Thread: A–B, 4 times	48
Left Selvage (same as right selvage)	8
Total Threads	292

WEAVING PLAN

For heading at ends of rug, weave treadles (a); then (b); harnesses 1, 2, 5, 6; then harnesses 3, 4, 7, 8. Use carpet warp for this plain weave.

For weaving the blocks prepare two shuttles of two different colors of rug yarn, x, y.

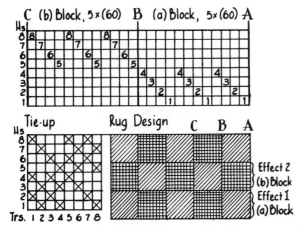

Fig. 103 — An eight-harness rug pattern with alternate blocks of twill and plain weave.

219

Block No. 1	Treadles	Harnesses	Colors
	1	1, 2, 3, 5	Red (x)
	2	1, 3, 4, 7	Red (x)
	3	4, 6, 7, 8	Brown (y)
	4	2, 5, 6, 8	Brown (y)

Repeat these four rows to square the first block at lower right corner of woven rug.

Block No. 2	Treadles	Harnesses	Colors
	5	1, 2, 4, 6	Red (x)
	6	2, 3, 4, 8	Red (x)
	7	3, 5, 7, 8	Brown (y)
	8	1, 5, 6, 7	Brown (y)

Repeat these four rows to square the next block, running diagonally upward to the left from first corner block.

Alternate blocks No. 1 and No. 2, squaring each block in order, running diagonally upward to the left, all across rug. You may make an exception to this squaring process at the center of the rug where the woven block may be as long as desired.

EIGHT-HARNESS DOUBLE-FACED CARPETING (Fig. 102), Upper Draft

This carpeting forms a firm, durable double-thick texture, as strong and practical as that acquired by the two-warp, double-beam rug in Figure 109, and especially desirable for those using eight-harness looms, for no extra warp beam is necessary. A two-color checkerboard results, the warp all of one color, and the checks or blocks formed by the use of two alternating colors in the filler. This texture is one of the best possible to use for rugs.

WARP PLAN

Warp: 4/4 cotton carpet warp, or 12/2 linen, or 8/4 double
Weft: Tabby for headings: same as warp
   Filler: two colors of rug yarn, Lily's or Maysville 3-ply
Threads per Inch: 12, set single in a 12-dent reed

THREADING PLAN

Use eight-harness twill, Figure 102, above; harnesses 1, 2, 3, 4, 5, 6, 7, 8. Repeat.

WEAVING PLAN

Block No. 1	Treadles	Harnesses	Colors
	1	1, 5, 6, 7	Dark
	2	1, 3, 4, 5	Light

3	3, 5, 7, 8	Dark
4	1, 2, 3, 7	Light
5	2, 5, 6, 7	Dark
6	2, 3, 4, 6	Light
7	4, 6, 7, 8	Dark
8	1, 2, 4, 8	Light

Repeat all 8 rows to square the block.

Block No. 2

Weave treadles in same order as block No. 1, but reverse colors.

EIGHT-HARNESS RUG PATTERN WITH BLOCKS OF TWILL ALTERNATING WITH BLOCKS OF PLAIN WEAVE (Fig. 103)

For an interesting rug on an eight-harness loom, try this 12-thread block. The finished fabric will be a surface of alternating blocks, twill alternating with plain-weave.

WARP PLAN

Warp: 8/4 or 8/3 carpet warp; or 10/2 linen
Weft: Use rug yarn 3-strand or rug-weave yarn
Threads per Inch: 12, 15, or 16.
Width: 25 in. if at 12 per inch; 21 in. if at 15 per inch

WEAVING PLAN

Selvage: Harnesses 1, 2, 3, 4, 5, 6, 7, 8 8
Thread A–B: 12 threads. Repeat 5 times 60
Thread B–C: 12 threads. Repeat 5 times 60

Total	120 . . . 120

Repeat all once again 120
Add A–B: Repeat 5 times 60
Selvage: Harnesses 5, 6, 7, 8, 1, 2, 3, 4 8

Total Threads   316

For a rug wider than 25 in., repeat A to C more times. Always end with A to B.

WEAVING PLAN

See effects of rows in Figure 103.

Effect 1. Treadles 1, 2, 3, 4 each once; repeat to square to form first row of blocks.

Effect 2. Treadles 5, 6, 7, 8 each once; repeat to square to form second row of blocks.

Repeat as far as desired.

End with Effect 1.

221

MULTIHARNESS SUMMER AND WINTER

For multiharness Summer and Winter make the tie-up as desired to bring down the succession of blocks or the combinations planned, D, Figure 104, with the first tabby on harnesses 1–2. The second tabby should be on all the other harnesses together. Harnesses 3, 4, 5, if a five-harness pattern; 3, 4, 5, 6, if six-harness; and 3, 4, 5, 6, 7, 8, if eight-harness.

Some of the most beautiful handwoven coverlets and rugs are the result of multiharness patterns. These produce pattern blocks with extensive space variations, as shown in the six-harness Pine-Tree design, Figure 105. Here too the system is clear and easily understood. See the long draft in E, Figure 104. Here there are 6 blocks altogether: the (a) block on harness 3 — harnesses 1, 3, 2, 3; (b) block on harness 4 — harnesses 1, 4, 2, 4; (c) block on harness 5 — harnesses 1, 5, 2, 5; (d) block on harness 6 — harnesses 1, 6, 2, 6; (e) block on harness 7 — harnesses 1, 7, 2, 7; and (f) block on harness 8 — harnesses 1, 8, 2, 8.

The tabby is written by the same principle as four-harness, since either harness 1 or harness 2 occurs every other note. Hence the first tabby is harnesses 1–2, and the second tabby consists of all the notes between, or all the other harnesses, 3, 4, 5, 6, 7, 8. If the pattern is only five-harness, the second tabby would be harnesses 3, 4, 5 together, etc.

Note that the short draft, F, Figure 104, has only 6 horizontal rows of checks, yet it is an eight-harness pattern. The first row shown is the (a) block, on harnesses 1, 3, 2, 3. In Summer and Winter, either four-harness or multiharness, the tabby is never written in the short draft. This saves space and time. Hence, there are always two more harnesses than shown in any short draft of Summer and Winter. They are, of course, clearly developed in the long draft, and that is one reason why this is written out for clarity. Moreover, for each added block of any Summer and Winter design created, one more harness will be required.

The weaving of multiharness Summer and Winter may also be as-drawn-in, or according to any plan the weaver wishes to make, for many blocks can be combined any way desired. Authentically the (a) block would be woven as in four-harness, harnesses 1–3, 2–3, 2–3, 1–3, (each row followed by tabby, harnesses 1–2 alternating with harnesses 3, 4, 5, 6, 7, 8); (b) block, harnesses 1–4, 2–4, 2–4, 1–4, etc. The other blocks would follow the same plan; (c) block, harnesses 1–5, 2–5, 2–5, 1–5, etc.

FIVE-HARNESS RUG DRAFT (Figs. 101 and 104)

A typical Summer and Winter rug in a multiharness pattern is shown in Figure 101. In five or more harnesses, the block areas progress in steps, and the dark steps on one side of the rug correspond to the lighter steps or spaces on the other.

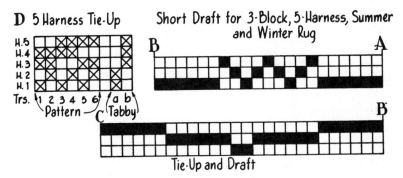

D 5 Harness Tie-Up   Short Draft for 3-Block, 5-Harness, Summer and Winter Rug

Tie-Up and Draft

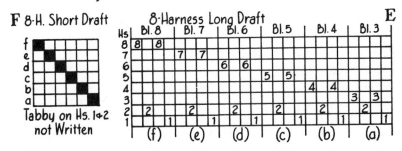

Thread: A to B; then B to C, then A to B.

Enlarge Units to: Hs. 1,3,2,3; Hs. 1,4,2,4; Hs.1,5,2,5.

F 8-H. Short Draft   8-Harness Long Draft   **E**

Tabby on Hs. 1&2
not Written

Fig. 104 — Tie-up and drafts for five- and eight-harness Summer and Winter patterns.

The tie-up and directions for this rug are given in *A, B, C,* and *D,* Figure 104. Thread *A* to *B; B* to *C;* then *A* to *B.* In weaving, use single treadles or combine any two treadles desired, to make such a design as that given in Figure 101.

A SUMMER AND WINTER PINE-TREE AND SNOWBALL RUG ON SIX HARNESSES (Fig. 105)

A rug of real beauty may be woven with Pine-Tree borders at the ends and a center repeat of the famous Colonial Snowball pattern; all this with only six harnesses in a Summer and Winter threading, and a fairly simple draft.

WARP PLAN

Warp: Carpet warp, 8/4 or equivalent
Weft: Pattern weft: rug wool or cotton rug yarn
   Tabby: Same as warp
Threads per Inch: 15 or 16
Width: For 15 per inch: 35 in.
   For 16 per inch: 33 in.
Total Threads: 528

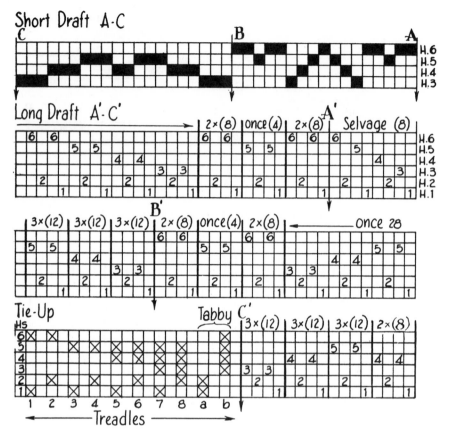

Fig. 105 — Summer and Winter Pine-Tree and Snowball rug draft for six harnesses.

TIE-UP

See Figure 105.

THREADING PLAN

The short draft at the top of Figure 105, *ABC,* is enlarged into the long draft below, *A'B'C'*. Thread the draft from right to left, repeating each unit as directed. Starting at the right of the short draft, the first unit on harness 6 is enlarged to harnesses 1, 6, 2, 6, on the long draft. This is repeated 2 times.

224

Next is a unit of harness 5, enlarged to harnesses 1, 5, 2, 5, on the long draft, threaded only once. Add harnesses 1 and 2 thus to each unit. For a complete explanation see Chapter 22 on Summer and Winter, and the foregoing explanation of multiharness Summer and Winter in this chapter. Refer to Figure 104.

WEAVING PLAN

For weaving, see tie-up, Figure 105, treadle 1, harnesses 1–6; treadle 2, harnesses 2–6, etc., two treadles for each block.

Each block unit is woven with 4 rows: first row pattern, such as treadle 1, followed by (a) tabby; second row pattern, treadle 2, followed by (b) tabby. In the following directions, read each row from left to right, completing four rows for each block. Then repeat these 4 rows as directed in furthest right column to form the Pine-Tree or Snowball parts of the pattern.

Pine-Tree Border

Pattern	Tabby	Pattern	Tabby	Number of Repeats
Treadle 1	(a)	Treadle 2	(b)	Once
Treadle 7	(a)	Treadle 8	(b)	Once
Treadle 5	(a)	Treadle 6	(b)	Once
Treadle 3	(a)	Treadle 4	(b)	Once

Repeat the above 16 rows, 2 or 3 times for base lines of tree.

Pattern	Tabby	Pattern	Tabby	Number of Repeats
Treadle 1	(a)	Treadle 2	(b)	Once
Treadle 7	(a)	Treadle 8	(b)	2 times
Treadle 5	(a)	Treadle 6	(b)	3 times
Treadle 3	(a)	Treadle 4	(b)	6 times
*Treadle 5	(a)	Treadle 6	(b)	Once
Treadle 7	(a)	Treadle 8	(b)	Once
Treadle 3	(a)	Treadle 4	(b)	Once

Repeat from *, 3 units or 12 rows, 4 or 5 times for tree branches.

Pattern	Tabby	Pattern	Tabby	Number of Repeats
Treadle 5	(a)	Treadle 6	(b)	Once
Treadle 3	(a)	Treadle 4	(b)	3 times (Top of tree)

Snowball Center: First Motif. Outlining blocks for snowballs.

Pattern	Tabby	Pattern	Tabby	Number of Repeats
Treadle 1	(a)	Treadle 2	(b)	4 times
Treadle 3	(a)	Treadle 4	(b)	Once
Treadle 5	(a)	Treadle 6	(b)	Once
Treadle 7	(a)	Treadle 8	(b)	Once
Treadle 1	(a)	Treadle 2	(b)	Once
Treadle 7	(a)	Treadle 8	(b)	Once
Treadle 5	(a)	Treadle 6	(b)	Once
Treadle 3	(a)	Treadle 4	(b)	Once
Treadle 1	(a)	Treadle 2	(b)	4 times

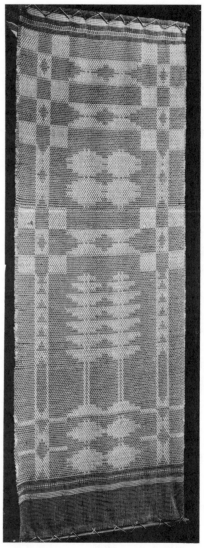

Fig. 106 — Handwoven panels of a screen in the Pine Tree and Snowball pattern, Summer and Winter technique. Both sides are shown.

Second Motif. Snowball.

Pattern	Tabby	Pattern	Tabby	Number of Repeats
Treadle 3	(a)	Treadle 4	(b)	2 times
Treadle 5	(a)	Treadle 6	(b)	2 times
Treadle 7	(a)	Treadle 8	(b)	2 times
Treadle 5	(a)	Treadle 6	(b)	Once only
Treadle 7	(a)	Treadle 8	(b)	2 times
Treadle 5	(a)	Treadle 6	(b)	2 times
Treadle 3	(a)	Treadle 4	(b)	2 times

Alternate the first and second motifs of the Snowball center as desired. End with the first motif. Then weave the Pine-Tree border backward, reading directions from left to right.

MODERN WEB, AN EIGHT-HARNESS RUG PATTERN (Fig. 107)

Modern Web is a stunning rug texture based on much the same principle as Log Cabin. However, while Log Cabin is usually threaded in two colors of the same weight thread, Modern Web is threaded in one color only but with two weights of thread, a heavy thread and a fine one.

If the heavy threads are lowered in the weaving, the weft shows clearly across the wide spaces; if the alternate fine threads are lowered, the weft shows less clearly. Thus blocks may be formed by providing for the tying down of the heavy warps in groups where desired, as shown in the sketch, Figure 107. The effect is still more pronounced when a heavy and a fine filler also alternate. In the draft of Figure 107, the notes to be threaded with the heavy warp are circled.

WARP PLAN

Warp: 8/4 or 8/3 carpet warp, or equivalent, and 4-strand cotton, or equivalent

Weft: Two weights of rug yarn: such as cotton rugro and rug-weave yarn: or wool rug yarn and Germantown, doubled. No tabby binder. Weaving also can be done with a heavyweight weft only. The resulting texture is not as interesting.

Threads per Inch: 15 or 16, two per dent in an 8-dent reed

Width in Reed: 29 to 30 in.; weaves to 27 to 28 in.

Total Number of Threads: 464 if heavy and fine

THREADING PLAN

Thread heavy warps through the even numbered harnesses, fine through the odd. If one weight of warp is used, we recommend threading with

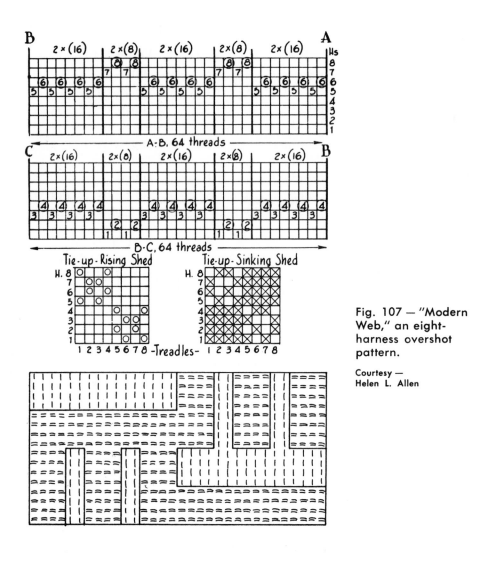

Fig. 107 — "Modern Web," an eight-harness overshot pattern.

Courtesy — Helen L. Allen

15 or 16 threads of carpet warp per inch. Use groups of three successive threads as triple warp; i.e., three successive threads through separate heddle eyes on same harness such as harness 6; follow with a single warp on next harness, harness 5; alternate thus, treating these three successive warp threads as one heavy warp. In sleying place the three consecutive and a single together through the same dent of the 8-dent reed; then skip a dent. This is really four threads to every two dents. Or if you do not have an 8-dent reed, sley the triple and single through a dent of a 15- or 16-dent reed, and skip 3 dents. This method is desirable if one already has a carpet warp on the loom at 15 or 16 per inch, and wishes to try this rug, without having to change warp.

Selvage: single strand carpet warp, harnesses 8, 7, 6, 5, 4, 3, 2, 1 .	8
Main Pattern: A–B (64 notes on draft, requires twice as many threads if using carpet warp triple then single) — 128 threads	
B–C (64 notes on draft, requires twice as many threads) — 128 threads	
Total ends of carpet warp necessary for *A–B–C* — 256	
Repeat *A–B,* then *B–C,* 3 times — Total threads	768
Add *A–B* only	128
Selvage: Harnesses 4, 3, 2, 1, 8, 7, 6, 5	8
Total Threads	912

THREADING PLAN FOR TWO DIFFERENT WEIGHTS OF WARP

Instead of grouping the carpet warp to make a heavy strand you may prefer to use a heavy warp such as 4-strand cotton alternating with a finer warp such as carpet warp. In this case, you will need only four heavy warps and four fine warps per inch, the heavy ones threaded on the even-numbered notes, 6, 8, 2, 4, and the fine on the odd-numbered notes, 5, 7, 1, 3. Thread singly through the heddle eyes but sley a heavy and a fine together through every other dent of an 8-dent reed. This requires only 8 threads per inch and the total number of threads is half as many as required for the carpet warp groups.

Selvage: Single strands of carpet warp sleyed 2 per dent in 8-dent reed — harnesses 8, 7, 6, 5, 4, 3, 2, 1	8
Main Pattern: A–B, 64 threads, plus *B–C,* 64 threads: total, 128	
Repeat *A–B,* then *B–C,* 128 threads, 3 times	384
Add *A–B* only	64
Selvage: Harnesses 4, 3, 2, 1, 8, 7, 6, 5	8
Total Threads	464

WEAVING PLAN

The numbers given for each block in the following refer to treadles in the tie-up. Each row of weaving requires two treadles to be depressed at the same time, i.e., four harnesses. For instance, block (a) below depresses treadles 4 and 7. This includes harnesses 6 and 8 and 2 and 3; four harnesses in all. This is the case for the treadling of all the blocks.

Eight blocks are given in the directions: a, b, c, d; and a′, b′, c′, d′. Combine these as follows: Weave sections of a, b, c, d; or a, b′, c, d′; or a′, b, c′, d; or a′, b′, c′, d′; or any succession of the eight blocks given below. These blocks are expanded into complete weaving directions.

229

Block (a)	Treadles 4–7, heavy; Treadles 3–8, fine
	Repeat 3 times Add 4–7, fine
Block (b)	Treadles 4–8, heavy Treadles 3–7, fine
	Repeat 3 times Add 4–8, fine
Block (c)	Treadles 1–5, heavy Treadles 2–6, fine
	Repeat 3 times Add 1–5, fine
Block (d)	Treadles 2–5, heavy Treadles 1–6, fine
	Repeat 3 times Add 2–5, fine
Block (a')	Treadles 3–8, heavy Treadles 4–7, fine
	Repeat 3 times Add 3–8, fine
Block (b')	Treadles 3–7, heavy Treadles 4–8, fine
	Repeat 3 times Add 3–7, fine
Block (c')	Treadles 2–6, heavy Treadles 1–5, fine
	Repeat 3 times Add 2–6, fine
Block (d')	Treadles 1–6, heavy Treadles 2–5, fine
	Repeat 3 times Add 1–6, fine

BRONSON ON EIGHT HARNESSES FOR TEXTURE MATS

The Bronson weave, not limited to its openwork effect only, may be interpreted in an attractive texture for rugs or runners. It is especially interesting if woven on more than four harnesses, for each added harness makes possible another block to increase the scope of the design. As openwork, Bronson is woven with one weft only; but if used for heavier textures, it is woven with both pattern and tabby, a heavy pattern yarn, and a finer tabby binder. A row of pattern is followed by the first tabby, and a second row of pattern by the alternate tabby. Following are the blocks possible on looms of various harnesses. The blocks of four-harness Bronson are given in Figure 96.

FOUR-HARNESS BRONSON

(a) *Block:* harnesses 1, 3, 1, 3, 1, 2
(b) *Block:* harnesses 1, 4, 1, 4, 1, 2
Tabby: harness 1 alone; harnesses 2, 3, 4 together

FIVE-HARNESS BRONSON

(a) *and* (b) *Blocks:* Same as in four-harness
(c) *Block:* harnesses 1, 5, 1, 5, 1, 2
Tabby: harness 1 alone; harnesses 2, 3, 4, 5 together

SIX-HARNESS BRONSON

(a), (b), *and* (c) *Blocks:* Same as in five-harness
(d) *Block:* harnesses 1, 6, 1, 6, 1, 2
Tabby: harness 1 alone; harnesses 2, 3, 4, 5, 6 together

SEVEN-HARNESS BRONSON

(a), (b), (c), *and* (d) *Blocks:* Same as in six-harness
(e) *Block:* harnesses 1, 7, 1, 7, 1, 2
Tabby: harness 1 alone; harnesses 2, 3, 4, 5, 6, 7 together

EIGHT-HARNESS BRONSON

(a), (b), (c), (d), *and* (e) *Blocks:* Same as in seven-harness
(f) *Block:* harnesses 1, 8, 1, 8, 1, 2
Tabby: harness 1 alone; harnesses 2, 3, 4, 5, 6, 7, 8 together

A BRONSON RUG WITH PLAIN WEAVE BORDER

WARP PLAN

Warp: Carpet warp 8/4 or equivalent set at 10 to 12 per inch
Weft: Pattern: Wool or cotton rug yarn; or evenly cut wool thrums
　　Tabby: Carpet warp or a yarn finer than pattern filler

THREADING PLAN

Thread right to left on your loom:
Right Border: Plain weave, harness 1 then harness 2. Repeat for 2 in.
Center: Develop the blocks given above for eight-harness Bronson in the following order: blocks (a), (b), (c), (d), (e), (f), (a), (f), (e), (d),

(c), (b). Repeat all. At the end of the entire threading add Block (a). A development consists of replacing each block with its six harnesses. For instance, Block (a) becomes harnesses 1, 3, 1, 3, 1, 2; Block (e) becomes harnesses 1, 7, 1, 7, 1, 2. Follow above detailed notations for each block.

Left Border: Plain weave — harness 1 then harness 2. Repeat for 2 in.

NOTE: One repeat of the center motif, 12 units of 6 threads each, covers about 6 in. Plan the rug design accordingly.

TIE-UP

Tie up the harnesses in the second column below to the treadles in the third column. The tie-up given is for a jack loom.

Pattern: Block		Harnesses	Treadles
	a	2–4	1
	b	2–3–5	2
	c	2, 3, 4, 6	3
	d	2–3–4–5–7	4
	e	2–3–4–5–6–8	5
	f	2–3–4–5–6–7	6
Tabby:	First tabby	1 alone	7
	Second tabby	2–3–4–5–6–7–8	8

In planning Bronson designs, use any or all of the above blocks. The design given here produces a point, and, when woven in reverse, a diamond.

WEAVING PLAN

Follow each row of pattern rug yarn with a row of tabby, using carpet warp. Read the following rows from left to right, each block or woven section consisting of four rows in all, two each pattern and tabby, thus: treadle 1, pattern; treadle 7, tabby; treadle 1, pattern; treadle 8, tabby. Then repeat these four rows to square the pattern, or as far as desired.

Pattern	Tabby	Pattern	Tabby
Treadle 1	Treadle 7	Treadle 1	Treadle 8
Treadle 2	Treadle 7	Treadle 2	Treadle 8
Treadle 3	Treadle 7	Treadle 3	Treadle 8
Treadle 4	Treadle 7	Treadle 4	Treadle 8
Treadle 5	Treadle 7	Treadle 5	Treadle 8
Treadle 6	Treadle 7	Treadle 6	Treadle 8
Treadle 1	Treadle 7	Treadle 1	Treadle 8

These last four rows, treadles 1, 7, 1, 8, form the center. Reverse from here, reading each line always from left to right, thus, treadles 6, 7, 6, 8, etc.

232

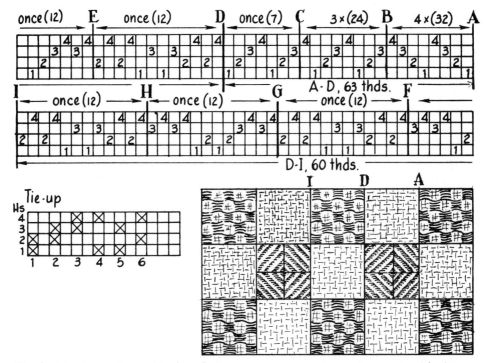

The finished rug shows blocks of plain weave separating alternating blocks of Herringbone and M's and O's.

Fig. 108 — Rug design combining herringbone and M's and O's.

RUG DESIGN COMBINING HERRINGBONE AND M'S AND O'S ON FOUR HARNESSES (Fig. 108)

Many attractive pattern textures may reveal new lights and shadows when arranged alongside other textures. Such an arrangement as that in Figure 108 creates a pleasing textural effect. While the three distinct textures of this design might seem to indicate a multiharness draft, only four harnesses are required. However, it seems suitable for placement in this chapter, since it produces much the same type of rug as that in Figure 103.

Both the herringbone and M's and O's techniques are one-shuttle weaves; hence this rug draft is an efficient and economical way to thread a loom. The diagonal texture of the herringbone is in good contrast to the units of the M's and O's blocks in which the texture lines are parallel to warp and weft. The blocks made by these two textures alternate with squares of a mottled weave not far removed from plain weave.

The draft gives one repeat each of the herringbone and M's and O's sections. In threading the warp, repeat these two in succession as desired. Begin and end with herringbone section for an odd number of units across the warp.

233

WARP PLAN

Warp: 8/4, 8/3, or 5/3 cotton; or 10/2 linen
Weft: Rug yarn, no tabby
Threads per Inch: 10 or 12
Width: 25 or 30 in.
Total Threads: 309

THREADING PLAN

Threads
A–D . . . . 63 (Herringbone)
D–I . . . . 60 (M's and O's)
A–D . . . . 63 (Herringbone)
D–I . . . . 60 (M's and O's)
A–D . . . . 63 (Herringbone)

	Total Threads	309

TIE-UP

Regular 6-treadle tie-up given in Figure 108.

WEAVING PLAN

Alternate the herringbone and M's and O's blocks below.

Herringbone

Harnesses	*Treadles*	*Repeats*	*Number of Rows*
1–2; 2–3; 3–4; 4–1; each once	1, 2, 3, 4	4 times	16
3–4; 2–3; 1–2; 4–1; each once	3, 2, 1, 4	3 times	12
Add 3–4; 2–3; 1–2 each once	3, 2, 1	once only	3
		Total Rows	31

M's and O's

1–3; then 2–4	5 then 6	3 times	6
1–2; then 3–4	1 then 3	3 times	6
1–3; then 2–4	5 then 6	3 times	6
1–2; then 3–4	1 then 3	3 times	6
1–3; then 2–4	5 then 6	3 times	6
		Total Rows	30

Heading at Rug Ends: Weave with carpet warp.
1–4; then 2–3   4 then 2   Repeat to desired width.

The alternation of these two harness combinations results in a weave very similar to plain weave, but not quite the same. It is the nearest texture to plain weave which can be secured on an M's and O's threading, and therefore serves as the rug heading in M's and O's rugs. In this case where there are both M's and O's and herringbone sections, it serves equally well.

234

CHAPTER 27

Two-Warp (Double-Beam) Rugs

THIS type of rug has two thicknesses bound together by its weave. It is double the thickness of the usual handwoven rug, with its heavy and firm texture lying flat on the floor. It lasts longer than many types, and not only sells better than others but brings a higher price because of its durable construction and the added amount of material used to make it. Its thick quality gives a satisfying feeling to the foot. Its design potentials are considerable. Because of its many advantages it is well worth the while of the rugmaker to investigate. However, to make this type of rug, the loom must have two warp beams since there are two warps coming forward at different tensions. We shall term these the "straight" warp and the "sewing" warp. Examples of rug designs suitable for two-beam looms are shown in Figures 53, 96, 109, and Nos. 1, 3, 4, Figure 94. A loom of four harnesses is used for two-block designs in this technique, and looms of more than four harnesses for designs with more blocks.

TEXTURE AND DECORATIVE USE

While each of the two surfaces of a two-warp beam rug resembles a flat rug in plain weave, their combined texture is soft, smooth, and cushiony. These rugs make wonderful floor coverings for living rooms. Long narrow double-beam rugs also are good for hallways. The rugs should not be too small; their feeling of weight suggests a rug measuring at least 30 by 42 in. or larger, and these can be made into sets of rugs for rooms if desired. The large block designs most often used make this type of rug excellent for modern decoration. Its simplicity makes it generally useful in any home.

DESIGN AND COLOR

A double-surface rug is made somewhat like a double weave except that the two fabrics are bound together by continuous warp threads that sew or tie them together throughout the texture. Two separate weft colors are used,

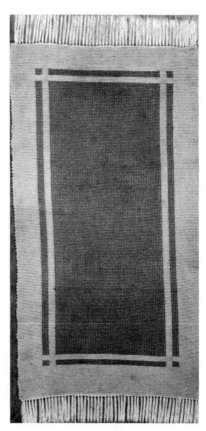

Fig. 109 — A two-warp beam rug of durability and beauty with reversible design.

and when one shows on the upper surface, the other shows on the lower surface. Designs are vertical and horizontal following the lines of warp and weft; but rectangular forms can be of any size, as shown in Figure 94. The colors selected for these adjacent forms should be carefully chosen either in contrasting tones or complimentary colors. Dark and light can be balanced to suggest borders and a center as in the rug of Figure 109.

DESIGN POSSIBILITIES

Two block designs are possible on a four-harness loom, and for each additional block an extra harness is required, as five harnesses for three blocks, six for four blocks, etc.

The two-warp beam method also provides a tool for weaving free designs into rugs of double thickness. As such, there is no technique in this book of greater use to the creative weaver in producing rugs of free forms keyed to contemporary decoration.

236

MATERIALS

Warp. In two-warp beam rugs with their two warps, regulation 8/3 or 8/4 carpet warp is used for both. One of these warps, called the "sewing" warp, stitches under and over the double thickness of the filler, passing up and down in the form of a figure eight, and in so doing crosses back and forth over the other warp, called the "straight" warp, which lies straight between the two surfaces of filler. There is therefore much more take-up to the sewing warp, and this should be twice the length of the straight warp. There is also more tension on the hidden straight warp than on the sewing warp. The latter is taken up rapidly as it passes back and forth from the under to the upper surface and around the filler appearing on both surfaces. Since the straight warp is hidden, it may be any color, and it is easier to thread these two warps if the two warps are different colors.

Filler. The filler can be wool or cotton; wool rug yarn makes very beautiful rugs of this type. Cotton rug yarn, 3- or 4-ply, can be used effectively. Chenille is excellent, and evenly cut rags also make good weft; a plain rag used for one of the wefts with a figured rag for the other makes a stunning rug design.

There is no tabby binder, of course, since two shuttles of filler in two contrasting colors weave alternately on the "on-opposites" principle. However, one should plan to weave a heading, and for this use carpet warp.

EQUIPMENT

How to Add an Extra Beam to the Loom, (Fig. 110). The loom, either jack or counterbalanced, must have two warp beams. It is not hard to make a loom into a double-beam type. It must be an extra strong floor loom. The extra beam is added at the back above the regular warp beam and should be more or less the same in size as that used on the loom. Reinforcing bars or braces will hold it in place. It must turn freely and must have a separate slip tension, and this should be adjustable to feed as necessary. Use an extra beam with brake drums at both ends, *A*, Figure 110. These may be supported by an extension beam, *B*, projecting at the back of the loom above the other beams, *C*, and fastened to the loom with strong bolts. The back beam of the loom is shown at *D*. Over the brake drums of the added beam, run rubber or web upholstery straps for tension, as at *E*. Tension is obtained by hanging a sack with sand in it at each side, *F*. To make more tension, add sand to both sacks, and to relieve tension, take out sand. The straps, *E*, should be so installed as to get as much traction or braking contact as possible. For this reason, attach the straps to the loom with a heavy screw, *G*, much lower than the center of the brake drum, *A*. Each strap, *E*, fastened to its screw, *G*, travels up and around the brake drum, and hangs down in back with its bag of sand, *F*.

237

The warp that comes from the regular beam, *C,* is marked *J,* arrow, and is shown traveling up and over the back beam, *D,* toward a heddle at the front of the loom, *L.* The extra beam and brake drums, *A,* must be so placed that the added warp threads traveling around them (see slanting thread just above *K,* arrow) will lie just a little lower than the level of the regular warp, *J.* This pulls the new warp down firmly, and keeps it traveling along on the same level as the regular warp while passing to the heddle eyes, *L.*

If at any time this arrangement does not give enough tension, tie a cord around the hanging strap, *E,* and pull it in toward the loom, as at arrow, *M.* In other words you need all the contact of the strap to the brake drum that you can get. See Figure 110. Half the warp threads are distributed on each beam. The regular warp beam, *C,* is called the "straight-warp" beam, with threads coming forward in pairs, *J,* and passing midway between the upper and lower rug surfaces. The added loom beam, *A,* is called the "sewing-warp" beam, with threads coming forward singly, from lowest point of *A* drum, as at *K,* to form the warps for the upper and lower surfaces. Warp

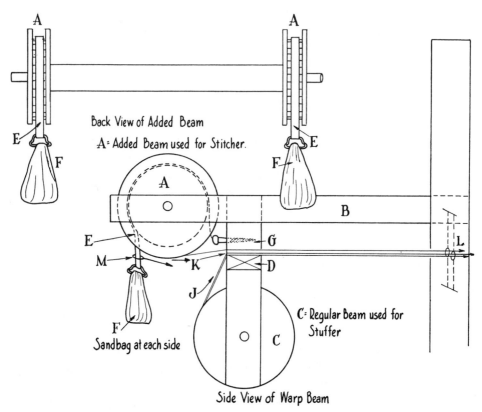

Fig. 110 — Method of adding extra warp beam for making two-warp rugs.

238

the thread in the usual way, 16 single threads per inch, 8 threads per inch on each beam; then combine the threading as directed here.

METHOD: TWO-WARP RUGS ON FOUR-HARNESS LOOMS (Figs. 109–111)

Warping Plan

Warp: 8/4 or 5/3 cotton
Weft: Pattern filler, cotton or wool rug yarn, or chenille
Threads per Inch: 16, 8 on each beam
Width: 28½ in.
Total Number of Threads: 456
Total Number of Sewing-Warp Threads: 228
Total Number of Straight-Warp Threads: 228
$$\text{Total Threads:} \quad \overline{456}$$

EXPLANATION OF THREADING DRAFT (Fig. 111)

Each Mark (:) represents a pair of threads on the regular or straight-warp beam.

Each Mark (x) represents a single thread on the extra beam for the tying warp, but note that two of the (x) warps always appear in succession, although on different harnesses. The threading calls for two (x) warps, then two (:) warps, etc.

Right Border: 50 sewing warps on harnesses 1–2	.	50
50 straight warps on harness 3	.	50
Center: 128 sewing warps on harnesses 1–2	.	128
128 straight warps on harness 4	.	128
Left Border: 50 sewing warps on harnesses 1–2	.	50
50 straight warps on harness 3	.	50
Total Warps:		$\overline{456}$

THREADING DRAFT IN DETAIL (Fig. 111)

Threads

First Part of Right Border 68

   A–B (34 straight warps on harness 3; 34 sewing warps on harnesses 1–2)

Second Part of Right Border

   B–C (8 straight warps on harness 4; 8 sewing warps on harnesses 1–2) 16

   C–D (8 straight warps on harness 3; 8 sewing warps on harnesses 1–2) 16

Total Border: $\overline{100}$ — 100

239

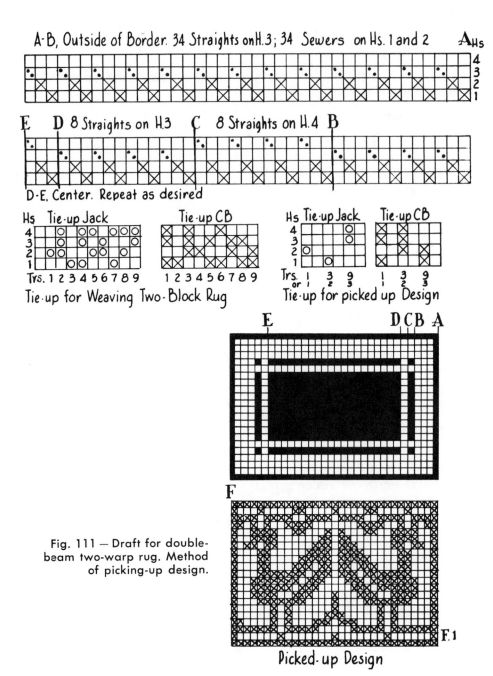

A-B, Outside of Border. 34 Straights on H.3; 34 Sewers on Hs. 1 and 2   A Hs

E   D 8 Straights on H.3   C   8 Straights on H.4 B

D-E, Center. Repeat as desired

Hs Tie-up Jack   Tie-up CB   Hs Tie-up Jack   Tie-up CB

Trs. 1 2 3 4 5 6 7 8 9   1 2 3 4 5 6 7 8 9   Trs. 1   3   9   1   3   9
                                                or 1 2   3   1   2   3
Tie-up for Weaving Two-Block Rug   Tie-up for picked up Design

E   D C B A

F

Fig. 111 — Draft for double-
beam two-warp rug. Method
of picking-up design.

F.1

Picked-up Design

Center: Consists of a continuous repeat of *D–E,* 4 threads
(2 straight warps on harness 4; 2 sewing warps on harnesses
1–2)
Repeat 64 times (128 sewing warps, 128 straight warps)
Total Center: 256 — 256

Left Border: Thread *C* to *D* just as above 16
Thread *B* to *C* just as above 16
Thread *A* to *B* just as above . . . . <u>68</u>
Border   100 — 100
Total: 456

Process of Threading. To carry out the foregoing threading plan, first thread all the way across with threads from the sewing-warp beam; i.e., thread harness 1, then harness 2, then skip a heddle on harness 3 and one on harness 4; thread harness 1, then harness 2, then skip one on harness 3 and one on harness 4. Repeat all the way across the warp. The skipped heddles are for the straight warps which go between the sewing warps. Leave one on each harness to provide the weaver with a choice of design. Shove the extra heddles along in between the others. When finished, lift these sewing warps up out of the way with a bar; then thread the straight-warp threads, as shown in the draft, a pair together through one heddle either on the third or fourth harness as designated in the draft or your own design, leaving the unused heddle empty.

Note that the draft calls for quite a section of harnesses: 1 and 2 (x), then harness 3 (:), before changing to harnesses 1 and 2 (x), then harness 4 (:). These sections on harnesses 3 and 4 represent the dark and light portions of the rug; see design, Figure 109. When harness 3 is used, the wefts will appear light on the right side and dark on the wrong side; and when harness 4 is used, they will appear dark on the right side and light on the wrong side. These sections on harnesses 3 and 4 act as the two blocks of this rug.

Knowing this, the threading may be altered at will, making a wide or narrower border, as at *A–B,* Figure 111, (harnesses 1–2 [x] and harness 3 [:]); then several light and dark bands between border and center, *B–C* (harnesses 1–2 [x] and harness 4 [:]); also *C–D* (harnesses 1–2 [x] and harness 3 [:]). Finally the center follows, composed on a continuous repeat, *D–E* (harnesses 1–2 and harness 4 [:]). Work out such a plan on graph paper. See *ABCDE* in both draft and rug plan of Figure 111.

WEAVING PLAN

In addition to tabby, harnesses 1–2 and 3–4, eight combinations are used in this treadling, with a ninth for pickup design if desired. Since most four-harness looms have only four or six treadles, it is best to make a direct tie-up of harness 1 to treadle 1; harness 2 to treadle 2; harness 3 to treadle 3; harness 4 to treadle 4. Use both feet to obtain the combinations given below. If, however, the loom has eight treadles, use the tie-up given in Figure 111. This technique works best on a jack loom although a counterbalanced (CB) may be used.

241

To start rug, weave plain weave with two threads up and two down, using carpet warp: harnesses 1–2 followed by harnesses 3–4. For the two color effects, prepare two fillers of rug yarn or smooth cut rags of blending or contrasting colors, light (L) and dark (D).

(a) Block. This is used for all light parts of sketch, Figure 111, top right.

Treadles	Counterbalanced	Jack	Direction and Color
1	1, 3, 4	2	Weave dark color from right to left
2	1 alone	2, 3, 4	Light, from right to left
3	2, 3, 4	1	Dark, from left to right
4	2 alone	1, 3, 4	Light, from left to right

(b) Block. This is used for all dark parts of sketch, Figure 111, Band B–C, and Center, D–E.

Treadles	Counter- balanced	Jack	Direction and Color
5	1–3	2–4	Weave dark, right to left
6	1–4	2–3	Light, right to left
7	2–3	4–1	Dark, left to right
8	2–4	1–3	Light, left to right

WEAVING PLAN—ENTIRE RUG (Fig. 111, right)

Heading. Weave plain weave with carpet warp over pairs of warp: harnesses 1–2, then 3–4.

First Border. Weave A–B, (a) block, 4 to 6 in.; B–C, (b) block, 1 in.; C–D, (a) block, 1 in.

Center, D–E. Repeat (b) block as far as desired.

Last Border. Same as first border reversed: C–D, (a) block, 1 in.; B–C, (b) block, 1 in.: and A–B, (a) block, 4 to 6 in.

Heading. Same as above.

MULTIHARNESS TWO-WARP DESIGNS

If a multiharness loom is used, there can be more blocks in the design than the two given here for four-harness. Each additional block of the design requires one more harness. Four-harness two-warp yields two blocks; five-harness, three; six-harness, four; etc. See the threading notation for each additional block given below.

Block 1: (3–harnesses) harness 1, one sewer, (x); harness 2, one sewer (x); harness 3, two straight warps (:). *Block 2:* (4-harnesses) harness 1, one sewer (x); harness 2, one sewer (x); harness 4, two straight warps (:). *Block 3:* (5–harnesses) harness 1, one sewer (x); harness 2, one sewer (x); harness 5, two straight warps (:). *Block 4:* (6-harnesses) harness 1, one sewer (x); harness 2, one sewer (x); harness 6, two straight warps (:).

In weaving, follow the method of first using the straight warps with harness 1, then with harness 2, alternating any combination of blocks thus:

TWO-WARP RUG ON FIVE HARNESSES: THREE-BLOCK EFFECTS

First Effect:

Counterbalanced Harnesses	Jack Harnesses	Direction and Color
1, 3, 4	2–5	Weave dark, right to left
1–5	2, 3, 4	Light, right to left
2, 3, 4	1, 5	Dark, left to right
2–5	1, 3, 4	Light, left to right

Second Effect:

1–3	2, 4, 5	Weave dark, right to left
1–5	2, 3, 4	Light, right to left
2–3	1, 4, 5	Dark, left to right
2–5	1, 3, 4	Light, left to right

Third Effect:

1–4	2, 3, 5	Weave dark, right to left
1–5	2, 3, 4	Light, right to left
2–4	1, 3, 5	Dark, left to right
2–5	1, 3, 4	Light, left to right

PICKED-UP FIGURES IN DOUBLE-BEAM RUG (F, Fig. 111)

Any simple figure designed on graph paper can be woven into this type of rug by the use of a pickup stick. The figures are woven as part of its smooth, even, unaltered structure. The parts of the design which are dark on one side with a light background become light on the other side with a dark background. The interplay of the warps takes care of the color reverses.

If a rug with figures is woven, the filler used should be somewhat lighter in weight than the coarse rug yarn used for 2-block rugs of similar straight-line designs of single thickness. Both wool rug yarn and cotton chenille are excellent. Bath-mat yarn, rug-weave yarn, or tufting cotton may all be used. Narrow rags, carefully cut, can be used.

Two colors are chosen, both the same thickness. Call the darker one the pattern, and the lighter the background. The dark filler corresponds to the dark squares of the design, the light to the background.

243

METHOD FOR FREE DESIGNS IN PICKUP
ON FOUR-HARNESS LOOM

The principle is to raise the straight-warp threads, use this shed for the pickup design, then use the two sheds of the sewing warp for the binding. Use the same threading as given here, Figure 111, or any threading based on this principle, since the pattern is always laid across a shed with all the straight-warp threads up. Thus the same double-weave threading can serve for a rug in which the pattern is set to certain width blocks as at *A–B, B–C,* etc., Figure 111, or one in which the weaver plans to create a free design.

WEAVING PLAN

See the regular tie-up, Figure 111, and the special tie-up for picked-up design. Here the former treadles 1, 3, 9 are grouped together and may be renumbered 1, 2, 3, if desired.

With two colors, weave several inches of dark background, then a short space of light weft, alternating (a) and (b) blocks, as described under the weaving plan above. You are now ready to weave your figure from the graph-paper plan, Figure 111. The first row of the design is dark; therefore weave one complete band of the (b) block. The next row is marked F. 1 and is the first row of pickup.

There are eight steps to follow for each row of squares on the graph paper, but they make only four rows. The succession is soon memorized. While the pickup figures take a little longer to weave than blocks, the resulting rug justifies the effort. Start laying in the first design row above dark bottom row, F. 1, Figure 111.

Step 1. Straight warps up, treadle 9 (jack, harnesses 3–4) (counterbalanced, harnesses 1–2).

Insert a pickup stick in front of the reed under the desired number of the straight warps, allowing each two pairs of straight warps, i.e., 4 actual threads, to correspond to a square of graph-paper design.

Pick up the dark squares of the design, and skip over the light squares. For instance, in *F,* Figure 111, row 1, pass the stick under the warps to correspond to one square (i.e., 2 pairs of straight warps, 4 threads); skip 6 squares (12 pairs of straight warps, 24 threads); pick up one square (2 pairs, 4 threads); skip 6 squares (12 pairs, 24 threads), etc., across the pattern.

Step 2. Treadle 1 (jack, harness 2) (counterbalanced, harnesses 1, 3, 4).

Let the pickup stick with its warps ride on top of the shed while you weave the background or light color under the stick through the shed just made. To make the shed wider push the pickup stick back against the reed.

Step 3. Treadle 9 (jack, harnesses 3–4) (counterbalanced, harnesses 1–2).

Pick up all straight warps not picked up before, or the warps which form the background of the design.

Step 4. Treadle 1 (jack, harness 2) (counterbalanced, harnesses 1, 3, 4). Let the pickup stick ride on the top of the shed while you weave with pattern color, dark.

Step 5. Treadle 9 (jack, harnesses 3-4) (counterbalanced, harnesses 1-2). Pick up the same pattern threads as under Step 1.

Step 6. Treadle 3 (jack, harness 1) (counterbalanced, harnesses 2, 3, 4). Weave the background color, light.

Step 7. Treadle 9 (jack, harnesses 3-4) (counterbalanced, harnesses 1-2). Pick up the same background threads as in Step 3.

Step 8. Treadle 3 (jack, harness 1) (counterbalanced, harnesses 2, 3, 4). Weave the pattern color, dark.

CHAPTER 28

Twice Woven and Double-Weave Rugs

TWICE-WOVEN RUGS

What can be done with worn-out or outmoded rugs? The modern hand-weaver can answer this, as well as commercial rug companies that reprocess old rugs. Cut the old rugs into strips and weave them again into rugs which have a semipile texture. Some of the most durable and attractive rugs are made by cutting up threadbare carpets, such as old Ingrain or Wilton, and weaving the strips into a heavy rug. These rugs make heavy, durable hall rugs or door mats. One of the authors used four of them in her living room for fifteen years, and they are still good. The strips must be cut from rugs not too loosely woven in the first place, or the new rug will have too shaggy an appearance, as the cut threads come up through the warps. A moderate amount of frayed edge is good and makes the soft, short pile surface. The rugs should be clean, of course, and when woven through bright colorful warps present a fresh new look.

TEXTURE AND DECORATIVE USE

Twice-woven rugs are among the heaviest and most satisfactory of hand-made rugs. They are always thick, heavy, and soft to the foot. The cut edges of the weft produce both unusual textures and colors; and, since the weft always turns slightly in the shed, lights and shadows are bound to appear. Mottled effects often come unexpectedly as a pleasant surprise. These rugs can be used in modern interiors. Their heavy texture makes them a welcome type for the more lived-in rooms of a home. A full-size-room rug of this type is shown in Figure 113.

DESIGN AND COLOR

The color and design of these rugs depend upon the character of the rug cut up for weft. Usually the rugs are hit-and-miss in effect, rather low in tone, but always interesting. The new warps give them a fresh appearance; they can be used to give the finished rugs bright, cheery fringes or they can be arranged in bands of alternating colors, in an intriguing alignment of black and white, or in one solid hue.

By keeping definite color sections of the old rug in separate piles, attractive borders can be placed at the rug ends. Two old rugs of different colors may also be combined to form new rugs with the background of one rug color and the border of the other.

EQUIPMENT

For these thick, twice-woven rugs with a rather unwieldy weft, a strong floor loom is required. The rugs are most often woven on a plain-weave shed, although twill may be used.

The loom should have a heavy beater, and the weaver should have large rug shuttles.

MATERIAL

Close-grained rugs or carpets may be used, as well as worn handwoven rugs which are not too coarse and are made on a closely set warp in a well-tied-down weave like Summer and Winter or Crackle. Rugs made of rug-weave yarn, 3-ply rug yarn, wool rug yarn, and fine silk strips or wool thrums may all be recut. Commercially woven rugs offer the best material if worn thin, and provide beautiful new rugs for the effort. Regular rag rugs in plain weave should not be used, as they are too coarse. However, most rag rugs can be unraveled if the warp wears out before the filler. A bright colored warp will freshen up the appearance of perfectly good rags; just un-ravel, cut the warp ends off as you go, roll rags into balls, and reweave.

WARP AND SETTING

When a rather heavy weft material is used, the warp must be strong. Use carpet warp, 8/4, set double at 6 pairs per inch; or 10/5 linen or 4/4 cotton warp set at 6 singles per inch. For very heavy strips, use heavy warp at 4 pairs per inch. In this case, the warp is too sparse for fringe tying, but a fringe of rug wool in the colors of the rug can be added as shown at *O,* Figure 129. An added fringe of wool is shown on a finished rug, Figure 24.

CUTTING THE RUGS INTO STRIPS (Fig. 112)

Cut the old rug in strips parallel to the warp, as shown at *A,* Figure 112. The old ends of weft will spring out in a fringelike edge. Some strips will curl. Use them in the new weaving way.

Each old rug texture has its own character. Do not cut the strips so narrow that they will fall apart. Experiment to find the best width for your strips.

247

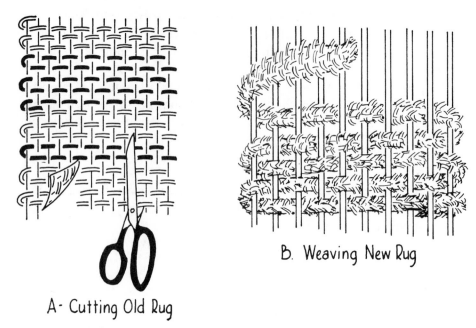

B. Weaving New Rug

A- Cutting Old Rug

Fig. 112 — Method of cutting and weaving twice-woven rugs.

WEAVING THE CUT STRIPS (B, Fig. 112)

The important thing in weaving rugs of this type is to beat the rows very tightly together. The threading can be plain weave or twill and the filler will add its own character to these textures. Use a large shuttle, and remove loose ends as you proceed. At *B,* Figure 112, see the nature of the weaving.

CHENILLE EFFECT (Fig. 113)

Rugs of this type look like chenille and often are given that name, although the term "twice-woven" is more descriptive. The word "chenille" should be left for rugs with a warp take-up described in Chapter 6, Figures 29 and 30. While the allover living-room rug in Figure 113 is woven with strands of heavy, rough chenille ready for the loom when purchased, the same restful allover effect is obtainable by planning a twice-woven rug from used, formerly woven rug fabrics.

DOUBLE-WEAVE MATS.
ENCLOSED SEAT CUSHIONS. CARPET BAGS

DOUBLE-WEAVE MATS

It is possible to weave a mat in double weave on two surfaces with color changes on a four-harness loom. While pattern figurations in double weave cannot be made on a four-harness loom, two-block designs, like those of

248

Figures 53; 93, right; 94, No. 4; and 96, can be worked out. Use rug-weave yarn in two colors; the resulting texture is double the thickness of an ordinary rug-weave yarn mat.

Here is the way to thread and weave designs in double weave with two colors. The colors change at the same points where the lines of the block change, becoming dark above and light below instead of light above and dark below. This shows the colors in the block squares. It differs from the two-warp, beam-rug product in that, in double-weave, the two surfaces are connected only at the points of change between blocks, whereas in the two-warp type, they are firmly fastened throughout.

Threading

Use a jack loom preferably; if a counterbalanced loom is used, even up the harness combinations where three harnesses are woven against one, by pulling the harnesses apart to give a better shed.

Unit (a): Thread harnesses 1, 2, white; harnesses 3, 4, red.

Unit (b): Thread harnesses 1, 2, red; harnesses 3, 4, white.

The warp must be set twice as close as is usually used.

To thread the designs in Figure 96 follow the draft from right to left (such as the draft, "M's and O's") Unit (a) first row, 3 units; Unit (b) second row, one unit; Unit (a), once; Unit (b), once; Unit (a), 5 times, center, etc. Replace each unit of M's and O's with the two-color units just given — for Unit (a): harnesses 1, 2, white; harnesses 3, 4, red; for Unit (b): harnesses 1, 2, red; harnesses 3, 4, white.

Courtesy — Dorothea Engleman

Fig. 113 — Allover living room rug woven with chenille filler similar to strips of twice-woven rugs.

Weaving

For plain weave, weave with carpet warp, harnesses 1–3; 2–4. For the blocks choose two colors similar to the two warp colors, in this case white and red rug-weave yarn.

First Block Effect:

Row 1: Counterbalanced: harnesses 1, 2, 3 together; then harnesses 1, 2, 4; jack: harness 4 then harness 3. Weave with red; makes upper fabric red.

Row 2: Counterbalanced: harness 1 alone; then harness 2 alone; jack: harnesses 2, 3, 4; then 1, 3, 4. Weave with white; makes lower fabric white beneath the red. If you now change to second block you will find that the colors reverse at point of change, but first repeat these two rows to square the block.

Second Block Effect:

Row 3: Counterbalanced: harnesses 2, 3, 4; then harnesses 1, 3, 4; jack: harness 1; then harness 2. Weave with white; makes upper fabric white.

Row 4: Counterbalanced: harness 3 alone; then harness 4 alone; jack: harnesses 1, 2, 4; then harnesses 1, 2, 3. Weave with red; makes lower fabric red beneath the white.

Repeat these two rows to square the block.

The (a) and (b) units are always of the opposite color to each other both above and below. Weave the successive blocks of your draft as-drawn-in, squaring each as it occurs along the diagonal. The blocks alternate, producing a plaid red and white surface, double thickness.

ENCLOSED SEAT CUSHIONS

A tubular fabric can be made on this same threading by weaving continuously with one weft only. The order of the treadles is changed, and one weaves first above on row 1, then below on row 2. The tube can be closed at the start with a section of plain weave after which the tubular part is woven, stuffed with kapok right on the loom, then woven closed at the end with plain weave again. This makes a pin cushion or a small pillow. If closed at the starting end only, the result is a seamless bag open at the top.

Set warp twice as close as usual. If the loom is threaded to the striped threading given in the preceding with units (a) and (b), the pattern will come up in colored stripes. If harnesses 1, 2, 3, 4 are threaded to one unit only, such as unit (a), harnesses 1, 2, white; harnesses 3, 4, red, and repeating continually, the result will be an upper surface throughout of red and a lower surface of white. This arrangement has been chosen for the tubular material in the following.

Threading

Repeat harnesses 1, 2, white; harnesses 3, 4, red; to desired width.

Weaving

Step 1. Weave 1-in. tabby, harnesses 1–3, 2–4.

Step 2. Tube: Weave with one color of rug-weave yarn, either red or white. Carry as directed below around the warp, from above to below, in a circular weaving motion. Start at the right side, upper fabric surface.

Row 1: Counterbalanced: harnesses 1, 2, 3; jack: harness 4. Weave above, right to left.

Row 2: Counterbalanced: harness 1 alone; jack: harnesses 2, 3, 4. Weave below, left to right. Bring weft around right selvage to upper surface again.

Row 3: Counterbalanced: harnesses 1, 2, 4; jack: harness 3. Weave above, right to left.

Row 4: Counterbalanced: harness 2 alone; jack: harnesses 1, 3, 4. Weave below, left to right.

Continue repeating these four rows.

Step 3. Stuff the cushion when weaving its desired size. Most looms will permit stuffing a 6-in. pillow before warp needs bringing forward.

Step 4. Weave 1 in. of tabby at the end to close the tube.

CARPET BAGS

If the tube is used as a bag, do not close the top but fold it over. If woven with sturdy yarn and set to a good width, the directions for threading and weaving a tube just given will make a splendid carpet bag in coarse, durable texture to hold rags or laundry.

DOOR MATS

In these days, when the price of fiber mats used for doorways often is high, and a good bit of protection is necessary at the front door for wet boots and shoes, it is practical to know how to make door mats at home. Rugs made in the same way are excellent in front of fireplaces or in front of sinks or stoves where the floors are cold.

The mats shown in Figure 114 are made of remnant twines or jute strips cut from burlap bags. Two methods are given. One is to cut the burlap bags in 1-in. strips and weave them as weft through coarse cotton warp, 8/5, 4/4, or 8/4 doubled. The other method is to unravel the jute strings originally used in weaving the bags, and group them in clumps to make weft loops in tufted technique, as shown in Figure 33, Chapter 7.

METHOD NO. 1

The door mat of strips (Fig. 114) is cut from burlap bags or coarse discarded clothes. Pieces of any coarse fabric may be cut in frayed strips to use as weft

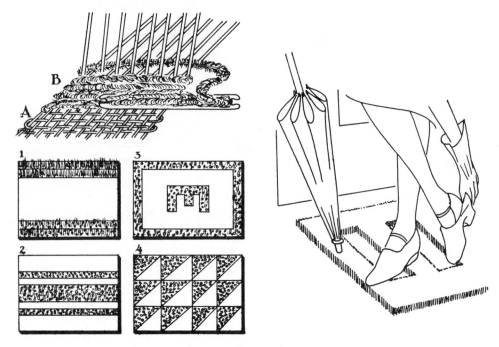

Fig. 114 — How to design and weave heavy doormats.

on a heavy warp. After weaving, the surface may be brushed up to form a rough pile surface.

For the warp, use 8/4 cotton set at 6 pairs per inch, or 8/5 or 4/4 cotton warp set at 8 singles per inch. Having the warp threads this far apart allows the frayed weft to come through to form the rough texture desired. A 10/5 linen warp also may be used. This is coarse and strong and should be set at 6 singles per inch. For very coarse wefts, set the warp at 4 pairs of 8/4 or 8/5 per inch.

For the weft strips, cut old burlap from bags, or coarse men's suiting or overcoat material, into strips from 1 to 1½ in. wide. Threadbare, commercially woven rugs also can be cut into strips ¾ to 1 in. wide, cutting parallel to the warp and across the weft. This makes a strip with shaggy sides as described for twice-woven rugs in this chapter. When used for weft again, these strips make a very fluffy texture, especially when brushed.

To make such a rug, follow the procedure in Figure 114. First weave a heading ½ in. wide if you wish a fringe, or 1½ in. wide if you want a hem. Use carpet warp double or 4-strand cotton for this heading. Now weave with the rough weft, as at *B*. Beat closely, and pack firmly.

Design. Door mats should be simple in design, or with a hit-and-miss or neutral mottled texture. Of course, dark borders can be woven at the ends or strips of darker weft where desired, as shown at 1 and 2, Figure 114.

252

METHOD NO. 2

Use the boutoné method of Figure 33, Chapter 7.

Unravel a burlap bag and save both the warp and weft strands of jute. Put them together in clumps of from 5 to 10 strands. Use this clump as a heavy weft for picking up loops where the design indicates.

Design. Several types of design, as shown in Figure 114, may be used. First of all, the burlap may be tied in bunches and dyed beautiful dark tones of red, green, and brown, with diamond dyes. Or use the natural burlap and one color to make a mat.

Design 1. Plan simple borders at the ends of the rug with dark tufts or loops, as shown at No. 1.

Design 2. Make stripes of dark loops across the center of the mat, as at No. 2.

Design 3. Make a continuous rectangular dark border all around a field of natural burlap in the center, No. 3. On graph paper, make a simple initial. Put this in with the tufts in the dark color across the center.

Design 4. Make 2-color blocks of any design planned on graph paper. Simple triangular forms are best to start with. Later, design diamonds and forms within borders can be added.

CHAPTER 29

Rugs of Unusual Design

THERE are some rugs that are difficult to classify, for they differ in their design or texture from the usual categories. The rugs grouped in this chapter are unique in some way, either as to textural structure, design, or technique. In several cases they combine various techniques.

For instance, the rug in Figure 119 cannot be classified as Flossa, because no knots are made but small bits of cotton are run into the weft sheds. It is similar to laid-in, but has a pile effect. The rug in Figure 121 combines several techniques, and a study of this rug will serve to show the modern weaver what can be done by applying a knowledge of rug techniques to a creative floor covering.

After mastering the techniques in this book, the ingenious weaver will not be long in grasping the infinite possibilities in the achieving of new effects in rug and carpet designs. He can play with both design and material, applying them to the method desired. Starting with any preferred design, he can go through the book choosing those techniques which seem most suited. Then he can lay out his materials in possible colorings and combine them most effectively. It is a good idea to lay out a plan on a large smooth piece of wrapping paper the desired size of the rug.

A great deal of variation can be gained by changing rug backgrounds. New ideas in pile rugs in Half-Flossa, Half-Rya, or tufted rugs, are given by experimenting with different kinds of rags, jute, or even the latest synthetic materials to get a background effect that is intriguing as well as pleasing.

TAPESTRY RUG IN PEACOCK DESIGN (Fig. 115)

The beauty of this rug lies in its design, and the relationship of the center to the border. Two pairs of peacocks face each other to form the center portion of bodies and heads with combs erect. The tail feathers extend outward to form the border.

254

Fig. 115 — A rug in Gobelin tapestry technique, Peacock design. By Marianne Richter, studio of Marta Maas, Fjetterstrom, Sweden.

A bit of clever designing is shown in the way the legs of the birds extend down into the border. They are nicely spaced and form pleasing breaks in an otherwise all-feather surface design. The colors are bright red and green, and well-spun wool was used for filler in the tapestry technique, Chapter 8. An inexperienced weaver should not attempt to make a rug of this type.

TUFTED RUG IN HALF-RYA (Fig. 116)

This tufted rug in Half-Rya shows the beauty of free designs possible for the handweaver to create in pile techniques. The highly stylized design, suggestive of Aztec or South American figurations, is beautifully executed with a background sprinkled with starry forms. It has a rare delicacy of conception and would make a lovely rug for an entrance hallway or open spot in a living room.

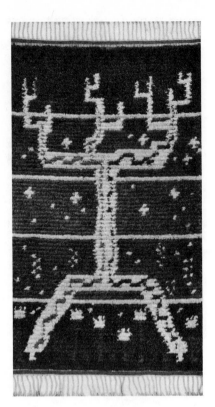

Courtesy — Nils Nessim Workshop

Fig, 116 — Tufted rug, "Celebration," designed by Sigvard Bernadotte.

BATH MAT IN TILE DESIGN WITH TUFTING ON A TEXTURED GROUND (Fig. 117)

This bath mat in tile design is one of the firmest, most satisfactory bath mats ever designed. The weaver used several of this type in her rich-looking and comfortable bathroom. The tufts of tan and white are woven into the rich ivory texture of the background. When finished, the edge is turned to wrong side and bound with tape.

DESIGN

Tile designs have been used for floors for hundreds of years. In Italy tile designs form one of the most interesting features of home and public life. Handmade tiles of exquisite designs and bright colors are used in the humblest of dwellings where it is a matter of pride to polish them into a glistening cleanliness, and we are all familiar with pictures of tiled court-yards in palaces and mosaic tiles of indescribably beautiful colorings.

A study of tile designs and their history could well fill a lifetime. For the handweaver, here is a field of great interest, and he can make good use of the carefully wrought tile figures found in pictures and museums, in the making of rugs and bath mats in pile techniques.

256

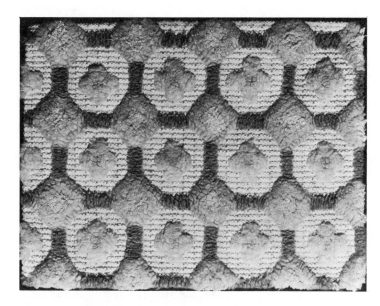

Fig. 117 — Bath mat in tile design with tufting on a textured ground.

Courtesy — Mrs. Leigh Hunt

In this mat, the soft inviting color effect is given by carefully sheared tufts of brown, beige, deep cream, and ivory.

WARP PLAN

Warp: Carpet warp used double or linen 10/5
Weft: Background weft: 4-strand natural cotton filler
Threads per Inch: 8 pairs of carpet warp, or 8 single strands linen
Threading: Twill

WEAVING OF BACKGROUND

2 rows tabby: harnesses 1 and 3, then 2 and 4
1 row tufting according to pattern; use wool ends as in Figure 119
2 rows tabby
2 rows on opposites using same 4-strand cotton filler: harnesses 1 and 2, then 3 and 4.

GREEN MARBLE, A MOTTLED RUG (Fig. 118)

This rug was designed for an entrance hall with a rubber-tile floor patterned in classical squares about half of which are solid beige, others olive-green, and the remainder marbleized in greens, chartreuse, and brown tones. The sturdiness of the rug is related to the long-wearing floor tile. The marbleized effect of the design adds grace to the severe floor pattern, as though one of the squares grew and grew until it became a large area of the floor.

257

The basic color of olive-green is a warm appealing shade sparked with a not-too-bold chartreuse, enhanced by a shadowy green intended to cast shadows from olive to chartreuse to give the eye a "neutral zone" as it travels from one color to another. The olive-brown adds depth in pulling the whole theme earthward in an earthy color. The areas of color in their particular forms give the impression of an aerial view of a countryside, further associating the design and its colors to nature, to the earth (viz., coming from out-of-doors into an entrance hall). A beige fringe (not shown) was meant almost to embed the rug into the floor, since it matches the beige squares.

All yarns in their various weights and colors were selected and mixed as are oils for a painting. The rug was first designed in water color. This sketch was then sectioned for proper placement of color and 84,000 yards of yarn were measured off into the proper lengths for each amount of color and knotted together in color sequence. After this the yarn was knitted into tubing and woven into the rug arranging each "throw" in its proper place to form the design. The weft ends were smoothly joined to avoid overlapping.

258

Warp: 8/4 carpet warp, color beige

Weft: Tubed yarn consisting of carpet warp, 10/2 and 20/2 cotton yarn, and crochet cotton

Threads per Inch: In a 10-dent reed, 3 ends per dent in every fourth dent, with 4 ends in the two end dents on right and left selvages to reinforce edges

Size of rug: 30 x 60 in.

Threading: Standard twill or tabby, woven as plain weave

RAG RUG WITH LAID-IN TUFTED DESIGN
(Fig. 119)

It would be hard to classify this rug, for it is half shaggy tufts and half rags, the entire background texture being woven with rags alternating with a jute cord. The tufts seem to resemble Rya loops but are made of bits of yarn slipped horizontally under two adjacent warps at a time, no knot being tied.

Fig. 119 — Rag rug with laid-in tufted design.

Courtesy — The Peasantcrafters

In this type of rug one can devise many interesting forms in both free and conventional design. It gives complete liberty for choice of color, since the tufts are arranged in a group of harmonizing tones set off by a soft colored rag background.

The rug is very economical to weave, for both the rags and the tufts can be salvaged materials. All the tufts must be of the same material such as all wool or all cotton rug-weave yarn; and the rags must be all the same kind of cloth such as old sheeting or finely cut silk stockings. The jute rows between the rag tabby give firmness to the rug.

WARP PLAN

Warp: 4-ply carpet warp
Threads per Inch: 10
Weft: Alternate rows of fine white rags and natural-colored jute
Tufts: Soft bits of wool or cotton
Colors of Tufts: Brown, yellow, green, henna

METHOD OF WEAVING

Heading: Weave ½-in. tabby with carpet warp same as warp.
Design: 4-in. alternate tabby of rag and jute (the size of a matchstick); 2-in. shag tufts in adjacent arrowlike formations. Tufts 1½ in. long. Insert under 2 adjacent warps on harnesses 1 and 3; then skip 2 warps. After inserting tufts according to your color plan across warp, weave one row tabby with no tufts, harnesses 2–4. Then repeat with tufts on harnesses 1–3. *7-in. Diamond Design* — colors reading from center: green, yellow, red, and dark brown diamond on outside; 3-in. tabby.
Center: A 1-in. strip of shag tufts with successive brown, yellow, green, and rust clumps. Reverse from here.

A PLAY ON DIAGONALS (Fig. 120)

This rug is one of simple elegance. The background is just a solid twill weave and the lines or bands were embroidered on afterward.

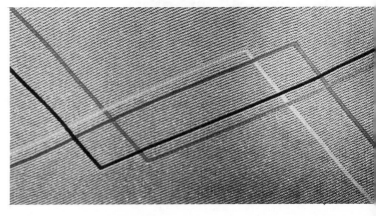

Fig. 120 — A play on diagonals, a rug made of knitted tubing.

Courtesy —
Elvira R. Ponkey

The colors and design of the rug were specifically arranged so that black would always show up as the dominant color (related to the warp), red next, dark green next, and chartreuse last. The reason for this arrangement is that the rug was designed with the intention of using it as a fireside rug before the hearth with burning logs. The design is so arranged that certain lines disappear and reappear depending on the angle at which it is viewed and the lighting effects, while the Lurex glitters, catching every dancing flame. This rug also gives striking effects under flooding sunlight and artificial light.

RUG PLAN

Warp: Black carpet warp set two per dent in a 15-dent reed

Weft: Knitted tubing consisting of 1-strand heavy crochet cotton, 1-strand fine crochet cotton, and 1-strand silver Lurex. The crochet cotton strands are both a silver-gray color.

Threading: Standard plain twill, standard tie-up

Weaving: Weave plain twill for the whole length of the rug, never reversing or changing the direction of the twill at any time.

Shaping: Pin the rug down on a very closely woven commercially made rug (pin to size), steam and block, let dry well.

Adding Design: The diagonal design is made by hand by entwining a very long double thread of carpet warp with the warp threads of the rug. This amounts to embroidering on the surface. Four zigzag columns were planned and four different colors were used: bright red, black, dark green, and chartreuse. To form the zigzag columns follow chosen pattern lines from the direction of the twill weaving and embroider two rows 1 in. apart and parallel for each column of the design, which amounts to boxing the design as one does when making block letters in printing. After the embroidery is finished, fill in the spaces by overcasting with finely cut chenille in the same colors as the outlines.

RUG DESIGN COMBINING SEVERAL TECHNIQUES: HALF-FLOSSA, RAG-RUG WEAVING AND TAPESTRY (Fig. 121)

In this heavy living-room rug the border effect is given by change of material. The warp is heavy cotton twine set at 6 per inch, and the weft is made of jute, rags, and chenille.

The main pebbly-looking filler is of jute, with ends left extending at the sides. Over this, the Half-Flossa bands of black are added to make the center columnar effect. Between the jute rows are light-colored bands of cut rags or chenille, and across these tufted strips of gray Flossa are spaced the same length as the black. Solid black bands travel nearly across the fabric, and these, as well as the white ones, lock with a crinkly filler like a border.

261

Fig. 121 — Rug design combining several techniques: Half-Flossa, rag weaving, and tapestry. Untrimmed ends form side borders. A braided fringe adds interest.

Courtesy — Robert D. Sailors

Note that this is a very flexible design and could be applied to several techniques — Half-Flossa, rag weaving, and tapestry.

MODERN RUG WITH LAID-IN SISAL DESIGN
(Fig. 122)

This idea in a rug has a chance for infinite variations. The rug of white sisal on a black warp is quite an innovation. It is simple, charming, and durable.

The technique is a laid-in method with the rows of white sisal coming between rows of black cotton. The occasional tufts of the sisal, a wirey jute fiber, are laid in for design and trimmed level after completion. The background of black cotton twine warp at 6 per inch is crossed with rag filler that goes all across the rug except where tufts are laid in; then the rags are woven up to the sisal, leaving the sisal area free. A black cotton weft alternates with the rag rows and this goes all across the entire rug even between the rows of white sisal tufts. The fringe is braided cotton warp.

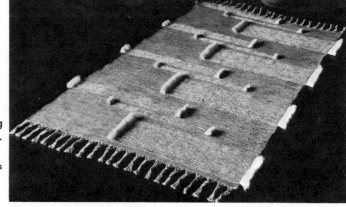

Fig. 122 — Modern rug with laid-in sisal design.

Courtesy — Robert D. Sailors

WARP PLAN

Warp: Black cotton twine
Weft: Black cotton twine, alternating with rags
Laid-In Material: Lengths of sisal, a wirey jutelike substance
Threads per Inch: 6

PILE RUG DEPICTING A NATURAL SCENE (Fig. 123)

It is possible to work out free rug designs on graph paper and weave them as pile by the Swedish Flossa Rug Technique, Chapter 4, or by the Embroidered Flossa Rug Technique, Chapter 5. It is wise to use subdued colors and subtle shades of color. This rug was so lovely when finished that the owner decided to use it as a wall hanging. The deeper tones of the foliage are brought out in the neck and legs of the deer, while many shades of tan, soft green, and brown were used for the grasses, and beige for the deer's body.

WARP PLAN

Warp: Use either 8 single heavy warps per inch, such as 4/4 cotton, or 8
    pairs of carpet warp. In each case there will be 4 knots per inch.
Weft: For rug knots, use rug wool filler or its equivalent in doubled yarns.
    Weave headings for wide hems at ends of 4-strand cotton or carpet warp
    double.

Fig. 123. — A pile rug depicting a natural scene.

CHAPTER 30

Rug Borders

IF WE could have at our tongue's end the many advantages of handwoven over factory-made rugs, we could easily convince our customers of their higher price value. The handweaver should take advantage of every sales point that makes his particular rug different — a quality product resulting from highly creative effort. The fact that a handwoven rug can have a border of any width or design proves one of its greatest assets, and every handweaver should know how to design borders. Horizontal borders across the width of a rug or at its ends are simple and easy enough to plan. Many interesting examples are scattered throughout this book. Borders on all four sides of a rug prove of still greater advantage to the handweaver.

In any art, the borders form both an approach and a protective frame to the main part of the design. Like preludes in music or frames in painting, they suggest a purpose in the complete concept and often give a hint of what is to follow. Setting the central design apart from its surroundings, they help to direct the eye to the design and add charm and accent to its outlined form. While some rug types do not need borders distinct from a main central part, others are definitely enhanced by the addition of a border. Border designing is a fine point in the perfection and completion of the fabric.

When it comes to rugs, borders help greatly in placing the woven unit within the decorative scheme, framing its design, defining its size, and often giving the keynote to what lies within. Some borders are nothing more or less than continuous repeats of a small part of the central motif, as shown in No. 4, Figure 126. Others are in marked contrast to it and accent its character, as in No. 2. Well-designed rug borders are shown in Figures 6, 48, 78, 81, 84, 85, etc.

Rug borders can be wide or narrow, and this, too, is determined by the design they frame. A simple wide border acts as a relief against a small

Fig. 125 — Corner of rug design with border formed by a table.

detailed design, and a simple repeated twill border serves as a satisfying frame when large figures form the main part of a rug.

SUGGESTIONS FOR RUG BORDERS

While all our rules come down to the basic fact that if a border looks right it is right, there are certain design suggestions that may help us combine pattern and border more effectively.

1. If a pattern has one or several large motifs, design a border with many close repeats of a small motif or use a twill or herringbone repeat for the border.

2. If the main pattern is composed of a section of small repeated motifs, plan a simple border of one large motif such as a table, diamond, wheel, or plain block.

3. The width of the border depends upon the preference of the weaver. It is advisable, however, not to make a border measure more than one fifth the width of the total rug. Borders from one sixth to one tenth of its width are good.

4. The border may suggest the main character of the design. If it is a field of circles, the border may be composed of closely repeated semicircles or curving lines as shown in Figure 127. If it is composed of alternate tables or stars and diamonds, the border may be a larger table or star as in No. 1, Figure 126, or an asymmetrical design like a winding vine may have an irregular border.

265

5. A part of any figure in the pattern may be repeated for the border as in No. 5, Figure 126. A border also can be planned in such sharp contrast to the center field that it will accent its character, as in the detailed border against the plain center in No. 3; or the block border against a center with circular motifs in No. 2. Sometimes just one of two alternating blocks is used as a border, Figures 96 and 109.

6. Very often both the border and the pattern are improved by separating them with a narrow section of twill, as shown in No. 2, Figure 94; with a diamond figure as in Figure 77; or with a small block, as in No. 1, Figure 126.

7. Borders on diamond rugs can be a succession of four blocks, harnesses 1–2, 2–3, 3–4, 4–1, written 1, 2, 1, 2, 3, 2, 3, 4, 3, 4, 1, 4, while the main pattern uses the same succession of blocks and their reverse, but with more harness notes in each block, such as a six- or eight-thread block. Start the main pattern on harness 1 and the 1–2 block. This harness 1 also finishes the border ending on harness 4 of the 4–1 block.

8. Twill or Rose Path makes an excellent close-grained border for a large-motif center. Repeat harnesses 1, 2, 3, 4; or harnesses 1, 2, 3, 4, 3, 2; or, for a larger herringbone border, harnesses 1, 2, 3, 4, 1, 2, 3, 4, 3, 2, 1, 4, 3, 2, as in No. 4, Figure 126.

9. Some techniques lend themselves naturally to borders. A series of these is shown in Figures 95 and 96. Two-block designs are among the easiest to handle. Alternating single units always can be used to form a closely set border, or just one large block at a corner.

10. Reversing the colors in the rug motifs will produce a most satisfying border. A beautiful example is the rug in the Sunset pattern, Figure 78. Note that the design of the border is the same as the center but in opposite colors.

11. Sometimes it is enough to outline a rug design with a narrow accenting margin, as in lower left, Figure 39, where a Navajo rug in gray and white and black is bordered with 2 in. of black margin. Note that this is further accented by a pure white line next to the black. In Figure 111, lower right, the outline is dark against a light center.

12. A Modern treatment is to alter the rug texture near the margins, thus suggesting a border effect, as in Figure 121.

13. One senses that a border would be accessory to many rug designs which are quite complete in themselves, such as the lovely modern rugs, Figure 5 and 10, the allover key pattern in Figure 22, the Green Marble Rug in Figure 118, and of course a great many patterns with repeated motifs, Figures 16, 18, 19, 79, and 92.

14. In many techniques, where designs are created against a background, such as in Flossa, tapestry, and laid-in, the background itself is sufficient for the border. This is true of Figures 57, 106, and 120; note the clever way in

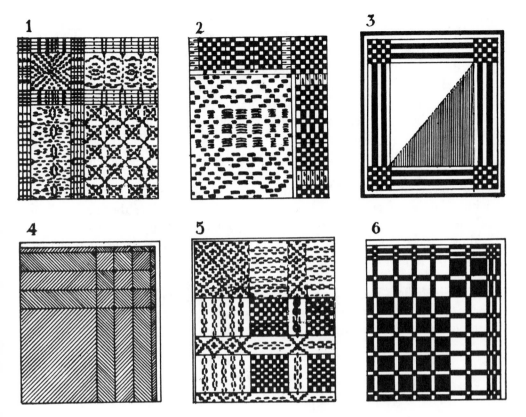

Fig 126 — Six border variations for rugs.

which the background is extended to form a border around repeated motifs in Figure 17.

SIX BORDER VARIATIONS FOR RUGS

The rug borders in Figure 126 are described in the following. Only one corner of each is shown, except for No. 3.

1. Here the border becomes the main feature of the rug, with a radiating pattern at the corner separated from the main ground by a small table which forms a column along the sides. The main pattern shows a ground of crosses and stars, the latter in keeping with the radiating corner motif. It can be worked out in Overshot technique, Chapter 21.

2. A large circle repeated throughout for the center pattern is sharply defined by a border composed of a large table of two alternating small blocks. This is an example of a border setting off the main pattern by contrast. It can be worked out in Overshot, Chapter 21.

3. A Summer and Winter rug presents one repeated block for its large uniform center which is light on one side and dark on the other, while the

267

two alternating Summer and Winter blocks are used in small size for the border. Use either a light or a dark center. See the diagonal line. This rug may also be designed in any of the two-block techniques of Chapters 23 and 24.

4. Beautiful rugs and coverlets are made with borders of twill and reverse twill. Here the twill reverses three times to form the border with a small reverse for an outside margin. The center of the rug may be twill only, or there may be one reverse at the center, dividing the rug into four quarters. Find directions in Chapter 20.

5. This is a good example of a rug in which one of the smaller pattern motifs is repeated to form the border. The main pattern consists of a small cross and a large table. This is made into an attractive rug by framing it with a border of crosses. This rug also can be finished at the outside edge of one of the center tables, enlarging it to one and a half its regular size and adding a selvage of harnesses 1, 2, 3, 4. Enlarge the corner table, as shown in Figure 125. This is a four-harness Overshot pattern; plan it from information in Chapter 21.

6. Here again a two-block rug is attractively outlined by a border repeating the large blocks twice and adding four smaller blocks at the edge. This rug can be made in any of the textures of Chapters 23 and 24, Figures 94 and 96.

Fig. 127 — Wheel of Fortune rug with undulating wave borders, called also "Cup and Saucer." The draft is shown in Figure 86.

CHAPTER 31

Finishes for Rugs

THE finishing of a rug and the treatment of its ends can add greatly to its appearance. Examples of rug finishes are shown in Figures 129 and 131. To determine the type of finish suitable for a rug, consider its style, shape, and design. If it is tailored with square or oblong designs, or just plain borders, a hem is good, as shown in *A* or *B*, Figure 129; also in Figures 5 and 6. If the rug is of the Indian Navajo or tapestry type, it is correct to have a fringe, as in *C* or *D*, Figure 129. If the warp is sparsely set, make a double fringe to fill in or add interest, *E*, or add more strands to make the fringe fuller, as in *H* and *O*. If the warp is closely set, use the soft fringe shown in *F*. The decorative fringes, *G* to *N*, show how to add material for extra fringe bulk. See braided rug fringe with extra ends of yarn added in Figure 24; also heavy added wool fringe, Figure 128.

RUGS WITH HEMMED ENDS (A and B, Fig. 129)

In planning a rug with a hem, allow 1 in. of tabby weaving at the ends, using weft like the warp. If the rug has a right and a wrong side, turn the hem entirely under, as shown at *A*. To make the hem inconspicuous even on the wrong side, weave the section of tabby heading in the color of the rug material.

If there is no right or wrong side, plan 1½ to 2 in. of tabby weaving at both rug ends. Make the hem only up to the last row of rug material, as at *B*. The same amount of tabby weaving will show on both sides. This may be made a definite part of the rug design, if planned in appropriate colors, and will form an attractive finish at the end. This method makes the rug reversible, since both sides show a hem designed to be an integral part of the rug.

PLAIN FRINGES FOR RUGS (C, Fig. 129)

If the warp is of wool, a closely beat section of tabby at the ends will hold without tying a fringe, as at *C*. Use fine material, and beat it as firmly as

Fig. 128 — Tufted rug with uncut loops and wool yarn added to make a heavy fringe.

Designed and woven by Elmer Guy.

possible. Weave from ¼ to ½ in. of this. It is most effective when this fine weft covers the warp. The hairy fibers of the wool warp will keep the weft from unraveling.

REGULAR FRINGE (D, Fig. 129)

For the regular tied fringe at *D*, weave a heading of ½-in. tabby to tie against. Then leave 4 in. of warp unwoven to have plenty of fringe for tying easily. Let the last row of tabby weaving act as a safety row so the others will not fray out, as shown by the dotted line and arrow in *D*. Unravel this as you come to each knot, but not before.

A tied fringe must be made with the same count of warps for each group, and all knots must be tied evenly and close against the tabby section or heading. Choose the number of threads to go into the knots, the same for all knots, such as four, five, six, etc. Make an overhand knot of the group as shown in *D*. Keep the knot loose until pushed up close to the tabby heading; then tighten it. If it seems difficult to push the knot up close, insert a crochet hook into the center of the knot, and shove up against the heading with this.

DOUBLE FRINGE (E, Fig. 129)

If a decorative fringe is desired, tie several rows of knots, as in *E*, but allow greater length to the fringe to make room for these knots. After tying one row across, take half of the strands from the first knot and let them hang unused for this row, as shown by the dotted lines, 2, in *E*. Take the rest of this group, 1, *E*, and tie it to half of the threads from the second knot. Split each knot of the former row in half, and tie it to half of the threads from the next knot all the way across. The last half of the knot at the selvage always waits over for the third row and is then tied to half of what became the end knot of the previous row. A double fringe is shown in the modernistic rug, Figure 10.

270

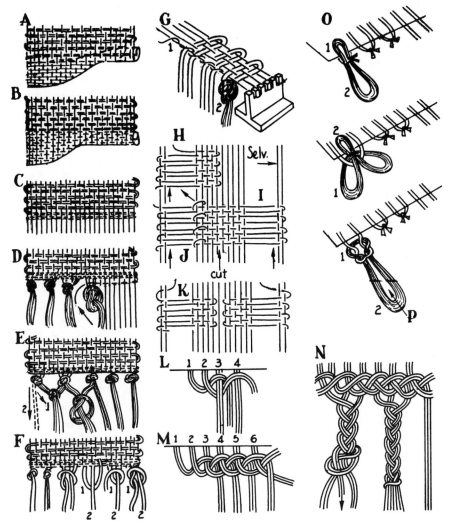

Fig. 129 — Ways to finish rugs.

SMOOTH FRINGE FOR HEAVY WARP THREADS
(F, Fig. 129)

If the warp threads are heavy, take half of the threads in each group to tie over the other half, as shown in *F*. This fringe will prove most attractive. To tie a knot, take half of the threads in group 1, carry them under group 2, then up and to the left over this same group 2 to form a loop. Now bring down the threads of group 1 through the opening of the loop, as shown. Pull on group 1, and shove the knot up close to the heading.

ADDED FRINGE MADE ON A BELT LOOM
(G, Fig. 129)

Fringes may be woven separately on an Inkle loom or narrow belt loom. Stretch a few warps across, and for the fringe cut yarns 8 to 12 in. long. Weave them in as tabby, as shown at G, making a selvage on one side only. Either overcast the fringe side as at 1, or tie the ends into regular rug knots as at 2. Sew this woven selvage to the end of the rug.

WOVEN FRINGE ON ANY LOOM   (H, Fig. 129)

Either wide or narrow fringes can be woven on any warp. Use the regular rug warp, but add extra selvage threads, as at H, with a 3-in. space between them and the rest of the warp. Weave the fringe yarn back and forth allowing ½ to 1 in. for solid weaving or a fringe heading. Either weave one strip only, as at H, or weave all the way across the warp and make fringes at each side, as shown at I. Even if the center part of a wide warp is wasted, it is often a good plan to do this rather than to set up a new warp. While many rugs have sufficient warp for their own fringes, added fringes are excellent for weft-surface rugs in which warps are set far apart.

Overcast the lower portion of the fringe next to the open space, as at curving stitches, J; then cut as shown at the vertical arrows. The fringe at I makes two strips, with cut cloth at the upper part of the heading at the center arrow. This can be turned under when attaching the fringe to the rug. For two separate fringes, each having selvages, weave two strips side by side as at K. Use two wefts, weaving first a row with one, then the other. Reverse at the center warp thread. When finished, pull out the extra guide warp threads at outer selvages, and the two fringes will come apart ready to use. While this method takes longer to weave, it makes it easy to attach the resulting uncut edges to a rug.

PLAITED AND BRAIDED FRINGES
(L, M, N, Fig. 129; Fig. 122; and Fig. 130)

Decorative braided borders may be made in the manner shown here. These finishes have been found on the fabrics of civilizations older than ours, where the hand was master of intricate twining methods. One of these is shown in L and M, Figure 129. With a group of warps, L, 1, weave under the next group 2, and over 3. Weave group 2 under 3 and over the next group, 4. Continue thus, "under one, over one, and down" throughout the warp, looping last group around the adjacent group with an overhand knot to fasten at the finish. The finished edge resembles the sketch at M. Draw all groups up snugly. Either let the warps hang loose as at M, or braid them as at N.

To braid the ends, assemble 3 or 4 adjacent groups, and make a 3- or 4-strand braid of them. When it is the desired length, take one of the groups, and tie in an overhand knot around the others, as at N, arrow.

Courtesy — **Handweaver and Craftsman**

Fig. 130 — Pile rugs against tapestry
background, showing Oriental fringes.

More decorative fringes can be made by leaving very long ends for braiding, then braiding or interlacing the braids themselves in about the same manner as shown for the tied fringes at *E*. The beautiful Oriental braided rug fringe is shown in Figure 131, bottom right. In Figure 24 the strands are braided directly downward without the decorative top braid.

HOW TO MAKE TASSELS (O, Fig. 129)

Added tassels are used for rugs, runners, pillows, the corners of mats or seat cushions, bag cords, and saddle bags.

A clever tasseled fringe may be added where the warp threads of a rug are scarce. First tie the thin cut ends of warp into loops, using a regular number for each loop at planned intervals, as shown in *O*, Figure 129. Wrap several rounds of the colored warp to be added around a book, and insert this circle of threads into the loop made by the tied warp ends as shown in

273

the top sketch at *O*. Call the top loop 1, the bottom one, 2; draw 2 up through 1, as shown in the center sketch. Pull on 2 until 1 has been fastened tight about the warp loop; 2 is now down at the bottom of the tassel again. Cut 2 through the center as shown in the bottom sketch at *P*. Put a tassel in each warp loop. When the added fringe or tassel has been completed, comb it out carefully with a coarse-toothed comb.

Courtesy — **Handweaver and Craftsman**

Fig. 131 — Examples of rug fringes.

CHAPTER 32

Preservation and Care of Rugs

IF WE like rugs well enough to design them, plan their colors, and weave them, we surely do not wish to shorten their life by lack of care. The beauty of a rug is enhanced by its cleanliness and the preservation of its colors and texture. There are various suggestions which will help the owner of rugs to make them last for a longer period of enjoyment.

HANGING RUGS

When rugs are used as tapestries or wall panels, they should not be hung for too long a time. One month a year they should be kept rolled or lying flat.

In hanging rugs, try to distribute the strain of the rug weight evenly. The best way is to sew a tape all across the end of the rug. If this is a wide tape or piece of cloth 1 to 2 in. wide, sew one side of the tape to the rug, let the other roll over a dowel or metal rod; then attach it to the rug. Tie cords at the ends of the rod and hang the rug as shown in *A*, Figure 133.

If the rug is heavy, sew rings to the tape in the back of the rug at intervals across the top. Then get a strong board to hang on the wall horizontally; and across this, at the same intervals as the rings, place hooks and slip the rings over the hooks. Neither the board, rings, nor hooks need show, because they are fastened to the rug just under the top.

Another method is to bring the end of the rug over in a hem at the top, and run an enameled dowel or regular tapestry rod through the hem. Attach a silk cord at both sides and hang it from a point at the center above the panel, as shown at *A*, Figure 133. Attach tassels at the sides if desired. See Figure 129 for making tassels.

Regular drapery rings of metal or wood may be attached at the top of the hem, as at *B*, Figure 133. Cords to match the rug may go directly upward from points along the rod, as shown. To carry out the handwrought idea,

Fig. 133 — How to mount rugs for use as wall hangings.

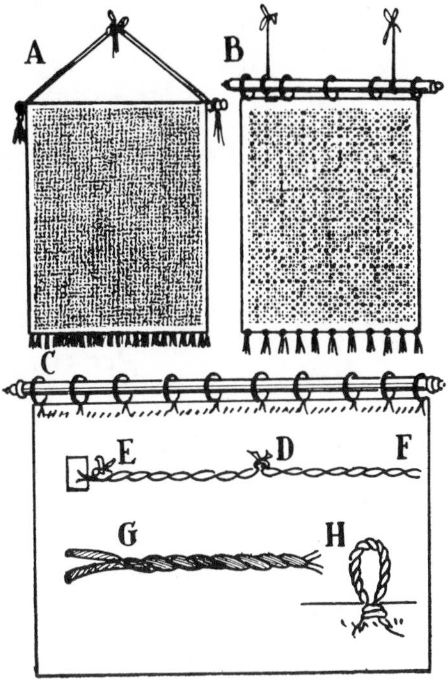

Fig. 132 — An excellent type of rug rack for displaying rugs.

make your own twisted cords using the same yarn as that of the rug. Make the cords as shown at *D–H*. Attach two strands, possibly of two different colors, together in a knot, as at *D*. Fasten the end of one to a hook, *E*. Twist the other end, *F*, until the yarn is tight and kinks. Then hold *D* taut, bring end *F* back to end *E*, and twist in the opposite direction. This forms a rope, *G*. Out of this handmade cord, make loops for the top of the rug, as at *H*, instead of commercial metal rings.

STORING RUGS

In storing rugs, always roll them with the right side inward, that is, the tufted side of Flossa, the looped side of laid-in, etc. Never fold a rug. Roll it on poles 3 in. or more in diameter, of lightweight wood, well seasoned so no sap will exude. Firm cardboard rolls or cylinders also can be used. The bamboo poles used by rug dealers are excellent.

Rugs should be stored in dry, cool places with moth spray or crystals in some form used as a protective measure.

CLEANING RUGS

Once a year all rugs should have a good vacuum cleaning, with both right and wrong sides cleaned.

Before rolling for storing again, sprinkle moth flakes all over the right side. Never shake rugs as this causes undue strain and weak spots may appear. Woven and braided rugs will last much longer if swept or cleaned with a vacuum cleaner. If you prefer to shake out your rugs, be sure to shake any woven rugs from the sides, holding them by the selvage. This prevents shaking out the fringe and loosening the rug in general.

A very fine way to clean rugs is to take them out on the grass on a snowy day, cover them with clean snow, then sweep this off. The dirt goes along with the snow, and leaves the rugs fresh and clean. Another excellent method is to scatter bits of newspaper, soaked in water, all over the rug, then sweep them off. The damp newspaper bits carry the dust with them, and help to clean the rug. This is a good method for cleaning large rugs. The newspapers are torn into small 2- or 3-in. squares, dropped into a pail of water, then excess moisture is squeezed out before scattering. Any large wood or tile floor also can be cleaned well in this way, the advantage being that the dust is taken up by the moist paper as the floor is being swept.

Flossa rugs, or any tufted type, should not be cleaned with a vacuum, for the suction of the machine may pull out the tufts or loops, or pull apart the ends of the knots. Various pastes can be used on the backs of such rugs to render the tufts secure. It is more advisable, however, to clean this type of rug by sweeping with moistened papers, or by shaking gently or just sweeping carefully. The old-fashioned method of hanging rugs over a clothesline and whacking with a flat wire rug beater is not such a bad idea after all. If this is done carefully, it is a good way to clean handwoven pile rugs.

WASHING RUGS

Before washing a rug, be sure the colors are fast. Darn any weak or torn places carefully to prevent still greater damage while cleaning. In mending, always match with the same kind of material, if possible — either the rug yarn in the main part of the rug or the fringe.

In general, the best way to wash rugs, whether of cotton or wool rug yarn, is to prepare a tub of warm sudsy water, and slush the rugs up and down until the dirt comes out. Try two washings if necessary. Rinse in the same temperature in the same way. To dry, hang the rugs evenly on a line in a shady place as the sun might fade them; or roll them between large bath towels.

A good way to wash heavy rugs that are somewhat awkward to handle is to lay them flat over newspapers, then scrub over their surface with a brush and sudsy warm water until they are clean. Then scrub them again with fresh water until the soap has been removed.

Some sturdy rugs can be washed in a washing machine. It is best to run

277

one rug through at a time. Also soak well in suds, then cut the washing time in half for less wear. Rugs with fringes should never be washed in a machine, for the fringes might fray. Washing machines also are hard on choice handwoven rugs. Really good rugs should go to a dry cleaner.

Producers of commercial rug yarns issue directions for their washing. Some advise adding a teaspoon of lye to a tub of water to insure fast colors.

PACKING RUGS FOR SHIPPING

Commercial weavers should roll their rugs when packing them. If many rugs are placed in a box side by side, they are easily handled and counted.

Rag rugs may be folded four to eight times, parallel to the weft only, placed singly or in piles in strong wrapping paper, and shipped thus. If tied several times, their firmness will hold the package flat.

CHAPTER 33

Short Cuts

IN ANY craft, time and dollars are saved by knowing the right way of doing little things. Working efficiency comes not only from long experience, but from being watchful of ways to improve one's skill. The following suggestions will prove helpful to rug weavers. Figure 136 consists of short cuts and helpful hints as follows:

LOCKING ALTERNATING WEFTS AT SELVAGES

To secure a good selvage when using two wefts, the rule is: If the last weft passes *under* the last warp, put the other weft *under* it before weaving through. If it passes *over* the last warp, put the other weft *over* it. This method takes care of locking the wefts around each other (follow diagram *A,* Fig. 136).

TO MAKE UNIFORM EDGES FOR LAID-IN MOTIFS

When turning laid-in yarn around at the reverse point of the design, carry the yarn around a hairpin or thin wire. This will produce an even outline, *B,* Figure 136.

HOW TO KEEP TRACK OF SEVERAL SHUTTLES

When using two or three shuttles in succession, always place them in the same order on the cloth. Weave the shuttles in the order 1, 2, 3, until all emerge at the same side, *C.*

TO MAKE AN EVEN FRINGE

The quickest and most accurate way to cut a straight edge across a fringe is to lay it at the edge of a table; comb it out with a coarse comb; then trim off the uneven lengths by running sharp shears close to the edge of the table.

TO MAKE A NEAT SPLICE

When piecing a heavy rug filler at selvage, cut out half of it, *D;* turn the other half into the next shed; lay the new end through; cut off flush, *E.*

279

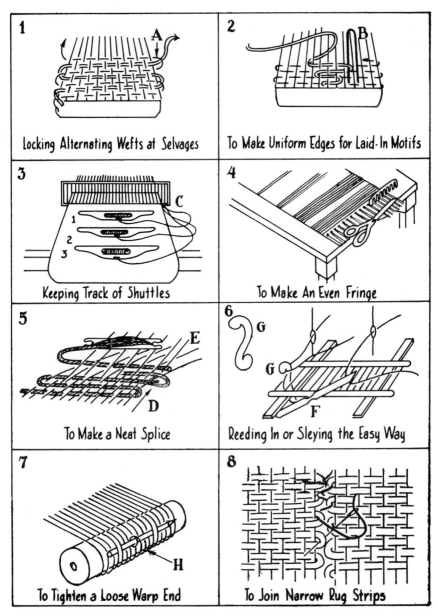

1 Locking Alternating Wefts at Selvages	**2** To Make Uniform Edges for Laid-In Motifs
3 Keeping Track of Shuttles	**4** To Make An Even Fringe
5 To Make a Neat Splice	**6** Reeding In or Sleying the Easy Way
7 To Tighten a Loose Warp End	**8** To Join Narrow Rug Strips

Fig. 136 — Short cuts and helpful hints for rugweavers.

SLEYING WARP THE EASY WAY

A very convenient tool for sleying the warp in the reed is a kitchen knife, shown at *F*. The hilt of the knife prevents it from sliding through the reed dents. A Swedish S hook is also excellent, shown at *G*. This is made of a thin piece of hardwood in the shape shown, carefully sandpapered and shellacked or waxed.

HOW TO TIGHTEN A LOOSE WARP END

When a warp thread loosens, slip a wire, match, pencil, or dowel under the thread. Twist this device around once or twice to tighten it, and then slip the ends of tightening device under the warp as shown at *H*. The looser the warp thread, the more twists necessary in tightening.

TO JOIN NARROW RUG STRIPS

To join rug lengths for a room-size rug, sew the adjacent edges together using the "figure-of-eight" or "in-and-out" stitch. The sewing thread should be in a neutral or blending color so as not to show, and it should be either a ply cotton, doubled and waxed to add strength, or a strong linen, such as 10/5 or 20/2. After the strips for the entire rug have been sewed together, the seams should be pounded down flat with a wooden mallet.

RUG SHRINKAGE OR TAKE-UP

All handwoven fabrics shrink both warp-ways and weft-ways when taken from the loom. This is especially true of rugs, where the heavy materials cause a greater take-up.

TAKE-UP IN WIDTH

Rugs shrink or pull in across their width about 1 in. for each 2 ft. of width. A large rug will shrink from 1 to 2 in., and a width of 40 in. on the loom becomes 38 in. off the loom.

TAKE-UP IN LENGTH

Take-up along the length is very important for determining how many rugs can be made out of a warp. Shrinkage runs from 10 to 12 per cent. This means that for every yard woven, about 3 in. of warp will be lost. The take-up is caused by the thickness of the weft, and the passing of the warp threads above and below the weft. This up-and-down movement of the warps can be seen by looking at the rug sideways.

TO SECURE A GOOD RUG SELVAGE

The selvages of a rug are a problem, for the weft is generally heavy and, as it reverses, causes quite a nub or projection. The best way to keep the edge even is to pull each row of filler taut at the selvage, then leave the yarn on a considerable upward slant until at the other edge it is 3 or 4 in. away from the last row. This slanting trend allows for the take-up all across the weft without drawing in the edge. If you do this with the same tension each time, and leave the same upward slant, the edge will be even. Heavy pattern yarns, rugro, rags, thrums, etc., protrude from the selvage about ¼ in., and this is taken for granted when weaving rugs. The projections, however, must be even.

A good way to test the straightness of the edge is to keep a ruler near at hand and lay it along the looped projections occasionally. The loops that have been pulled too taut are readily seen, as they form an indenture at one side of the ruler. If the loops are even, they will all touch the ruler's edge in about the same way.

DOUBLING THE SELVAGE THREADS

Some weavers prefer to thread their selvages with single warps, for in weaving there is enough pull-in at the edges to draw the edge threads close together.

Others sley the outside or selvage threads of the warp closer than the rest of the warp. In rugs this is recommended, since it strengthens the edge against the pull of heavy reversing wefts, and may help the weaver to keep a straight edge. The edge can be strengthened in two ways:

1. Sley double threads through the last two dents on each side.

2. If the warp threads have skipped every other dent of the reed for a wide setting, sley the four last threads on each side through each dent singly.

STRONG CARPET WARP RECOMMENDED

The difference between reliable handwoven rugs and the cheaper commercial variety sometimes found for sale in chain stores is their construction. We use or should preferably use a 4-strand carpet warp known as cotton 8/4. Note in comparison the sleazy warp of the commercial variety set too far apart for permanence. These rugs soon fall apart or wear out.

For rugs of any worth use cotton 8/3 or 8/4 set at 10, 12, or 15 per inch. Cotton 9/3 set at 12 to 15 per inch is all right. The stronger warps, cotton 5/3, 4/4, and linen 10/5, should be used for very heavy rugs and especially for Indian Saddle Blanket and bound weaves and twice-woven rugs, as well as for door mats. In double-beam rugs there are two warps, so the combined weight of these makes a doubly strong warp. If you do not have the stronger warps and are weaving heavy rugs, set carpet warp at 6 to 8 pairs per inch, and note the difference in strength and quality. One can simply draw two threads off their spools and let them twist together to make a pair, but for the best way to warp pairs, thread each two warps through two successive heddles of the same harness, such as: harness 2, harness 2, harness 3, harness 3, etc. They weave up as parallel threads in pairs.

The regular warp setting of 12 per inch can be adapted to very heavy rugs by threading the warp in pairs or groups of three warps, as described. Sley the entire group of two or three through a dent of the reed, then skip one dent if it is a pair, or two dents if a group of three. Four groups per inch of three warps each makes the strongest warp. This is excellent for twice-woven rugs or any rug of extremely heavy filler.

MATS VERSUS RUGS ON TABLE LOOMS

Rugs should be firmly woven and heavy enough to lie flat on the floor. While it is possible to weave ruglike textures on table looms, it is impossible to beat successive rows close enough to make a firm durable floor rug. However, lighter-weight ruglets and mats are useful in bedrooms and bathrooms or for seat covers and chair backs. Some folks, especially those living in apartments, prefer a bath mat of light structure, more or less like a heavy towel, that can be washed easily and will dry overnight.

For those who enjoy weaving rug textures, and yet who do not own a floor loom, it is possible to make an "imitation" heavy rug, by weaving two small rugs of the same texture and size on a table loom, and joining them together at fringed edges and sides, as well as in several places across the center, somewhat like a tufted quilt. The double weight gives the firm feeling of a heavier rug.

PIECING RUG FILLER

Wool and cotton rug yarn and also rag-rug filler with which rugs are woven may all be spliced in the middle of a row or at the selvage. The filler does not show if the ends of the two joined pieces are tapered carefully. The weaver can always stop a moment to trim down a bulky end, or to twist together two tapered ends, so that their joining will not show. It has been found conducive to neat joinings to untwist the rug filler and part the separate strands used in its "ply" at different distances. This tapers the ends of the rug filler perfectly and makes a very neat splice.

At the selvage, in turning the old end of a heavy rug filler around preparatory to its overlapping with the new end, half of it should be cut out underneath the turning angle, as in sketch 5, Figure 136. This gives only half the bulk to be concealed along with the new end which can also be tapered somewhat. The beauty of the finished rug depends upon the care exercised in such details.

283

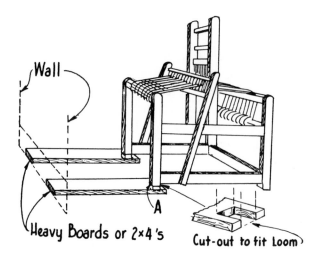

Fig. 137 — How to keep
the loom from slipping.

Wall

Heavy Boards or 2×4's

Cut-out to fit Loom

A

HOW TO KEEP A LOOM FROM SLIPPING
(Fig. 137)

Since the strength of the beat is quite important to assure a firmly beat rug, a strong compact beat should be given to every row of filler. This may cause the loom to slip forward gradually. There are several ways in which to offset this.

1. Some weavers place small squares of sponge rubber or rubber knee pads under the legs of the loom to keep it from slipping. This is helpful in ordinary weather, but in extreme heat the rubber may stick to the floor and leave a black residue. Hard rubber is not affected but is not so slip-proof. Any substance having some friction will help if placed under the legs of the loom. "Loom anchors" also can be obtained from supply companies.

2. The warp or back beam of the loom may be tied with a strong rope to a solid fixture in the wall. This method keeps the front of the loom out in the room, easy of access.

3. If the weaver does not mind having the front of the loom facing a side wall, with the warp beam projecting out into the room, the best way to keep the loom from slipping is to place two heavy wood boards or 2 by 4's against the front legs, with their other ends butting against the side wall, as shown in Figure 137. Make cuts into one end of the boards the size of the legs, so that the boards will fit snugly around the legs, as shown. The stronger the beating, the firmer the loom will stand.

4. If the weaver does not wish to make some such provision for this problem, his best solution is to obtain a very heavy loom to begin with, then practice a sharp, short, firm beat, which is not so likely to make the loom crawl forward.

ADDING WEIGHT TO THE BEATER

If the floor loom is only medium weight, additional weight can be given to the beater. This will be found to help greatly in the production of a firmly bound rug. The simplest way is to add a long bar of flat iron at the base of the beater in the back, placed horizontally and parallel to the length of the reed. This bar of iron should be ¼ x 2 in. in size and almost as long as the beater. Screw it to the bottom of the shuttle race with plenty of screws, countersunk.

DIFFERENT WAYS TO WEAVE RUGS

New effects are worth trying and sometimes give rise to very interesting and worthwhile textures. Try the following methods of weaving Overshot pattern rugs.

USING TWO ROWS OF TABBY

Instead of following each pattern row with a row of tabby, follow each pattern combination with two rows of tabby, both harnesses 1–3 and harnesses 2–4. This changes the character of the underlying texture, and offers a chance for more color in the binder. However, the rug may not be quite as heavy as with one tabby unless one uses a thicker tabby.

ALTERNATING HEAVY AND FINE FILLER IN PLAIN WEAVE

In weaving two-harness rugs in plain weave, try putting the heavy filler through on the first shed, and a tabby binder on the second shed, and keep repeating. All the rug yarns will show in a column on the first shed. This makes a lighter-weight rug than one in which every row is of heavy rug yarn, but it has its purpose in producing lightweight bath mats or cottage rugs.

WEAVING ON OPPOSITES

Weaving on opposites is an interesting way of making a heavy rug. It consists in following each pattern row of a four-harness threading with the opposite pattern row, using much the same weight of filler, instead of using a tabby of lightweight cotton. The opposite rows may be the same kind of filler but a different color, to set off the regular rows. Sometimes the weaver uses a filler of lighter weight for the opposites, although not as fine as a regular tabby binder. The difference in color sets off the pattern, so that it forms its true figuration, and the added weight of a heavier-than-tabby filler after each pattern row makes a rug of firm structure and durability. For a complete description of this method, see Chapter 21. Here are the opposite harness combinations: follow harnesses 1–2 with harnesses

285

3–4; harnesses 2–3 with harnesses 4–1; harnesses 3–4 with harnesses 1–2; harnesses 4–1 with harnesses 2–3.

WEAVING AS TWILL

Almost any Overshot pattern may be woven in the twill succession without any tabby binder, i.e., harnesses 1–2, 2–3, 3–4, and 4–1. Continue repeating these 4 rows. Most patterns will produce an attractive series of diagonal and curving lines in parallel formation. This texture can be used as a border against plain weave for the rest of the rug; or sections of the twill may be interspersed with sections of plain weave; or the entire rug may be twill-woven, possibly with change of colorings. Observe this precaution, however, if the pattern has long overshots, the successive long loops of twill woven without tabby may cause too much loop on the surface of the rug, a condition always to be avoided for the sake of practicality. However, rugs are planned with short overshot for this reason, no matter how they are to be woven. Usually, if a rug is woven as pattern with tabby, it may also be woven as twill without tabby, each successive twill row binding the previous row down.

HOW TO GET THE MOST FROM A PATTERN THREADING

Although there is an authentic way to weave every type of pattern, for truly creative weaving and to satisfy a market which demands the unusual and modern as well as the conservative and traditional type of fabric, the weaver should try many variations of his pattern, and experiment with different harness successions. A four-harness loom usually is thought of as having six harness combinations, but it really has fourteen. All of these should be tried and their succession altered in as many ways as possible until a pleasing texture has been discovered. The fourteen possible combinations are:

The two combinations usually employed for tabby: harnesses 1–3 and harnesses 2–4.

The four evenly balanced harness combinations, with two harnesses up and two down: harnesses 1–2, harnesses 2–3, harnesses 3–4, and harnesses 4–1.

The four combinations using three harnesses down at one time known as "three against one": harnesses 1–2–3 together, harnesses 2–3–4, harnesses 3–4–1, and harnesses 4–1–2.

The four treadlings using only one harness down at a time, known as "one against three": harness 1 alone; harness 2 alone; harness 3 alone; and harness 4 alone.

On a jack loom, all of these combinations are treadled with equal ease; but on a counterbalanced loom, the last four fail to give a good shed. However, if the palm of the hand is placed across the top of all the harnesses directly after treadling, the three that should rise together will all be brought to a common level, and although the shed is narrow, it will be an even shed and possible to use.

In the traditional 6-treadle tie-up, one can secure only six of these combinations at any one time. For this reason looms with a direct tie-up are successfully used for rug-weaving variations. This means that harness 1 is tied to treadle 1; harness 2 to treadle 2; harness 3 to treadle 3; and harness 4 to treadle 4. No lams are used, and one can get any of the fourteen combinations listed readily by the use of balanced foot action on convenient wide pedals.

TESTING OUT THE COMBINATIONS

It is an adventure to tread a new pattern on a loom and to test out the various harness combinations to see what each looks like. When these combinations are all laid out on the cloth, study them at leisure, note their possibilities, and then make a plan for the succession you think is suitable to the purpose at hand. The combinations should, of course, be separated from each other by a little plain weave. For instance, weave harnesses 1–2 (tabby after each row) several times, enough to see this particular formation; add several rows of plain weave only; then weave harnesses 2–3 several times, followed by a section of plain weave, etc. Continue to weave each combination — those with one or three as well as two harnesses — until you are completely familiar with the layout of all of them as they will appear when woven on the cloth. Then combine them to form designs of your own creation.

ACCENTING RUG PATTERNS WITH PLAIN-WEAVE SECTIONS

Charm and variety can be added to pattern rugs by setting off sections which show their figurations with background sections which are quite plain. This also saves material. Such a rug is shown in Figure 6, the Whig Rose rug woven star-fashion. For this particular rug, a better quality rug filler was used for the Whig Rose borders. In between them, sections of tabby were woven using cheap natural cotton rug filler, known as "mop yarn." The rug proved even more interesting than if woven with a repeated pattern throughout. Rugs that can be woven in this way are Indian Saddle-Blanket rugs, Chapter 17; twill and herringbone rugs, Chapter 20; Overshot pattern rugs, Chapter 21; the Summer and Winter weave, Chapter 22; and Crackle-weave rugs, Chapter 25.

HOW TO USE WARP AND WEFT WASTE

Every rug weaver knows that there is often a small amount of warp or weft left after weaving up a loom full of rugs. This can be used in many ways. If there is a short length of warp still left on the loom, weave this up into a strip to be folded over to make a purse or bag. These small lengths can also be used for table mats or seat covers. If the ends are cut off they are called "thrums" and sometimes used as filler.

The weaver can save odds and ends of warp in a box and later put them all together in a mottled warp of many colors — often found productive of interesting rug effects. The same is true of the filler — stunning rugs have been made by simply laying short lengths of filler in through the shed, hit-and-miss fashion. Provided tapering ends of the pieces overlap, this kind of a rug proves as durable as any other.

Colorful bits of filler can also be used for accents bordering the edges of stripes. Just one row of flame, skipper blue, or gold, or even black or white between border sections serves to set off the stripes at both sides.

Waste warps and wefts can be woven up into practical and good-looking laundry bags, hot pads, pot holders, sturdy seat mats for porch chairs, sofa protectors, and many other useful household items.

HANDWOVEN STAIR TREADS

In Figure 138 is shown a special use for small amounts of leftover warps and wefts. To protect nicely finished or painted stairs in period homes, the handwoven stair tread has many advantages over the modern rubber or synthetic type. Into it one can weave both cheery color and design interest, and thus transform a dark colorless stairway into a place of unexpected charm. The smart handweaver, developing such an idea for his own use, might find a ready market for such little stair rugs, and become skilled in weaving miniatures of surprising beauty. The same idea can be applied still further to seat mats and footstool covers.

There are many ways in which to weave them. Tiny rag rugs can be woven on an 8/4 carpet warp set at 12 per inch and woven with fairly narrow rags well packed, with close tabby at the ends or sides for a hem. Into these one can weave a gay mottled array of colors, or simply use one interesting stripe. The warp is very effective if planned with two side stripes after the manner of the early Colonial stair carpets, Figures 66 and 67. In other words, what we are really doing is making a modern version of this charming type of traditional stair carpet with its gaily striped warp.

The two-block Log-Cabin technique was used to weave the treads in Figure 138. Other practical and closely woven textures good to use are: Summer and Winter, Crackle, twill, or herringbone, and for a very thick

Fig. 138 — Little rugs make lively stair treads.

and durable stair mat, the double-beam method of Chapter 27. From the Soumak technique the weaver can also design lovely examples using simple conventional motifs. Soumak also offers a durable way of binding left-over lengths of filler into a useful article. Try successive rows of shades of color, or simply a series of gay colors in any desired order for a colorful modern expression. For Soumak technique, see Chapter 10.

The stair treads can be woven the long way on a warp 10 in. wide or less, which gives firm selvage edges along the sides of the strip that lie parallel to the stair edge. In this case the narrow ends are woven as tabby and close to the woven portion. Stair treads can also be woven in the other direction across a regular rug width of from 30 to 42 in., beginning with 1 in. of closely packed plain weave for a hem, the center section woven in a design for the stair width of from 8 to 10 in., then the hem at other side. In either case, the important thing is to use good strong warp and weft, to select a technique that will produce a firm, durable rug surface, and to weave the ruglets on a loom that enables the weaver to beat them firmly. These three requisites might be said to form the basic essentials for the weaving of all our handwoven rugs, large or small — strong warp and weft, a well-integrated texture, and a reliable loom and weaver.

Index

293

A CATALOGUE OF SELECTED DOVER BOOKS
IN ALL FIELDS OF INTEREST

A CATALOGUE OF SELECTED DOVER
BOOKS IN ALL FIELDS OF INTEREST

CONDITIONED REFLEXES, Ivan P. Pavlov. Full translation of most complete statement of Pavlov's work; cerebral damage, conditioned reflex, experiments with dogs, sleep, similar topics of great importance. 430pp. 5⅜ x 8½.   60614-7 Pa. $4.50

NOTES ON NURSING: WHAT IT IS, AND WHAT IT IS NOT, Florence Nightingale. Outspoken writings by founder of modern nursing. When first published (1860) it played an important role in much needed revolution in nursing. Still stimulating. 140pp. 5⅜ x 8½.   22340-X Pa. $3.00

HARTER'S PICTURE ARCHIVE FOR COLLAGE AND ILLUSTRATION, Jim Harter. Over 300 authentic, rare 19th-century engravings selected by noted collagist for artists, designers, decoupeurs, etc. Machines, people, animals, etc., printed one side of page. 25 scene plates for backgrounds. 6 collages by Harter, Satty, Singer, Evans. Introduction. 192pp. 8⅞ x 11¾.   23659-5 Pa. $5.00

MANUAL OF TRADITIONAL WOOD CARVING, edited by Paul N. Hasluck. Possibly the best book in English on the craft of wood carving. Practical instructions, along with 1,146 working drawings and photographic illustrations. Formerly titled *Cassell's Wood Carving*. 576pp. 6½ x 9¼.
23489-4 Pa. $7.95

THE PRINCIPLES AND PRACTICE OF HAND OR SIMPLE TURNING, John Jacob Holtzapffel. Full coverage of basic lathe techniques—history and development, special apparatus, softwood turning, hardwood turning, metal turning. Many projects—billiard ball, works formed within a sphere, egg cups, ash trays, vases, jardiniers, others—included. 1881 edition. 800 illustrations. 592pp. 6⅛ x 9¼.   23365-0 Clothbd. $15.00

THE JOY OF HANDWEAVING, Osma Tod. Only book you need for hand weaving. Fundamentals, threads, weaves, plus numerous projects for small board-loom, two-harness, tapestry, laid-in, four-harness weaving and more. Over 160 illustrations. 2nd revised edition. 352pp. 6½ x 9¼.
23458-4 Pa. $6.00

THE BOOK OF WOOD CARVING, Charles Marshall Sayers. Still finest book for beginning student in wood sculpture. Noted teacher, craftsman discusses fundamentals, technique; gives 34 designs, over 34 projects for panels, bookends, mirrors, etc. "Absolutely first-rate"—E. J. Tangerman. 33 photos. 118pp. 7¾ x 10⅝.   23654-4 Pa. $3.50

CATALOGUE OF DOVER BOOKS

DRAWINGS OF WILLIAM BLAKE, William Blake. 92 plates from Book of Job, *Divine Comedy, Paradise Lost,* visionary heads, mythological figures, Laocoon, etc. Selection, introduction, commentary by Sir Geoffrey Keynes. 178pp. 8⅛ x 11. 22303-5 Pa. $4.00

ENGRAVINGS OF HOGARTH, William Hogarth. 101 of Hogarth's greatest works: *Rake's Progress, Harlot's Progress, Illustrations for Hudibras, Before and After, Beer Street and Gin Lane,* many more. Full commentary. 256pp. 11 x 13¾. 22479-1 Pa. $12.95

DAUMIER: 120 GREAT LITHOGRAPHS, Honore Daumier. Wide-ranging collection of lithographs by the greatest caricaturist of the 19th century. Concentrates on eternally popular series on lawyers, on married life, on liberated women, etc. Selection, introduction, and notes on plates by Charles F. Ramus. Total of 158pp. 9⅜ x 12¼. 23512-2 Pa. $6.00

DRAWINGS OF MUCHA, Alphonse Maria Mucha. Work reveals draftsman of highest caliber: studies for famous posters and paintings, renderings for book illustrations and ads, etc. 70 works, 9 in color; including 6 items not drawings. Introduction. List of illustrations. 72pp. 9⅜ x 12¼. (Available in U.S. only) 23672-2 Pa. $4.00

GIOVANNI BATTISTA PIRANESI: DRAWINGS IN THE PIERPONT MORGAN LIBRARY, Giovanni Battista Piranesi. For first time ever all of Morgan Library's collection, world's largest. 167 illustrations of rare Piranesi drawings—archeological, architectural, decorative and visionary. Essay, detailed list of drawings, chronology, captions. Edited by Felice Stampfle. 144pp. 9⅜ x 12¼. 23714-1 Pa. $7.50

NEW YORK ETCHINGS (1905-1949), John Sloan. All of important American artist's N.Y. life etchings. 67 works include some of his best art; also lively historical record—Greenwich Village, tenement scenes. Edited by Sloan's widow. Introduction and captions. 79pp. 8⅜ x 11¼. 23651-X Pa. $4.00

CHINESE PAINTING AND CALLIGRAPHY: A PICTORIAL SURVEY, Wan-go Weng. 69 fine examples from John M. Crawford's matchless private collection: landscapes, birds, flowers, human figures, etc., plus calligraphy. Every basic form included: hanging scrolls, handscrolls, album leaves, fans, etc. 109 illustrations. Introduction. Captions. 192pp. 8⅞ x 11¾. 23707-9 Pa. $7.95

DRAWINGS OF REMBRANDT, edited by Seymour Slive. Updated Lippmann, Hofstede de Groot edition, with definitive scholarly apparatus. All portraits, biblical sketches, landscapes, nudes, Oriental figures, classical studies, together with selection of work by followers. 550 illustrations. Total of 630pp. 9⅛ x 12¼. 21485-0, 21486-9 Pa., Two-vol. set $15.00

THE DISASTERS OF WAR, Francisco Goya. 83 etchings record horrors of Napoleonic wars in Spain and war in general. Reprint of 1st edition, plus 3 additional plates. Introduction by Philip Hofer. 97pp. 9⅜ x 8¼. 21872-4 Pa. $4.00

THE PHILOSOPHY OF HISTORY, Georg W. Hegel. Great classic of Western thought develops concept that history is not chance but a rational process, the evolution of freedom. 457pp. 5⅜ x 8½.   20112-0 Pa. $4.50

LANGUAGE, TRUTH AND LOGIC, Alfred J. Ayer. Famous, clear introduction to Vienna, Cambridge schools of Logical Positivism. Role of philosophy, elimination of metaphysics, nature of analysis, etc. 160pp. 5⅜ x 8½. (Available in U.S. only)   20010-8 Pa. $2.00

A PREFACE TO LOGIC, Morris R. Cohen. Great City College teacher in renowned, easily followed exposition of formal logic, probability, values, logic and world order and similar topics; no previous background needed. 209pp. 5⅜ x 8½.   23517-3 Pa. $3.50

REASON AND NATURE, Morris R. Cohen. Brilliant analysis of reason and its multitudinous ramifications by charismatic teacher. Interdisciplinary, synthesizing work widely praised when it first appeared in 1931. Second (1953) edition. Indexes. 496pp. 5⅜ x 8½.   23633-1 Pa. $6.50

AN ESSAY CONCERNING HUMAN UNDERSTANDING, John Locke. The only complete edition of enormously important classic, with authoritative editorial material by A. C. Fraser. Total of 1176pp. 5⅜ x 8½.
20530-4, 20531-2 Pa., Two-vol. set $16.00

HANDBOOK OF MATHEMATICAL FUNCTIONS WITH FORMULAS, GRAPHS, AND MATHEMATICAL TABLES, edited by Milton Abramowitz and Irene A. Stegun. Vast compendium: 29 sets of tables, some to as high as 20 places. 1,046pp. 8 x 10½.   61272-4 Pa. $14.95

MATHEMATICS FOR THE PHYSICAL SCIENCES, Herbert S. Wilf. Highly acclaimed work offers clear presentations of vector spaces and matrices, orthogonal functions, roots of polynomial equations, conformal mapping, calculus of variations, etc. Knowledge of theory of functions of real and complex variables is assumed. Exercises and solutions. Index. 284pp. 5⅝ x 8¼.   63635-6 Pa. $5.00

THE PRINCIPLE OF RELATIVITY, Albert Einstein et al. Eleven most important original papers on special and general theories. Seven by Einstein, two by Lorentz, one each by Minkowski and Weyl. All translated, unabridged. 216pp. 5⅜ x 8½.   60081-5 Pa. $3.50

THERMODYNAMICS, Enrico Fermi. A classic of modern science. Clear, organized treatment of systems, first and second laws, entropy, thermodynamic potentials, gaseous reactions, dilute solutions, entropy constant. No math beyond calculus required. Problems. 160pp. 5⅜ x 8½.
60361-X Pa. $3.00

ELEMENTARY MECHANICS OF FLUIDS, Hunter Rouse. Classic undergraduate text widely considered to be far better than many later books. Ranges from fluid velocity and acceleration to role of compressibility in fluid motion. Numerous examples, questions, problems. 224 illustrations. 376pp. 5⅝ x 8¼.   63699-2 Pa. $5.00

THE COMPLETE BOOK OF DOLL MAKING AND COLLECTING, Catherine Christopher. Instructions, patterns for dozens of dolls, from rag doll on up to elaborate, historically accurate figures. Mould faces, sew clothing, make doll houses, etc. Also collecting information. Many illustrations. 288pp. 6 x 9. 22066-4 Pa. $4.50

THE DAGUERREOTYPE IN AMERICA, Beaumont Newhall. Wonderful portraits, 1850's townscapes, landscapes; full text plus 104 photographs. The basic book. Enlarged 1976 edition. 272pp. 8¼ x 11¼.
23322-7 Pa. $7.95

CRAFTSMAN HOMES, Gustav Stickley. 296 architectural drawings, floor plans, and photographs illustrate 40 different kinds of "Mission-style" homes from *The Craftsman* (1901-16), voice of American style of simplicity and organic harmony. Thorough coverage of Craftsman idea in text and picture, now collector's item. 224pp. 8⅛ x 11. 23791-5 Pa. $6.00

PEWTER-WORKING: INSTRUCTIONS AND PROJECTS, Burl N. Osborn. & Gordon O. Wilber. Introduction to pewter-working for amateur craftsman. History and characteristics of pewter; tools, materials, step-by-step instructions. Photos, line drawings, diagrams. Total of 160pp. 7⅞ x 10¾. 23786-9 Pa. $3.50

THE GREAT CHICAGO FIRE, edited by David Lowe. 10 dramatic, eyewitness accounts of the 1871 disaster, including one of the aftermath and rebuilding, plus 70 contemporary photographs and illustrations of the ruins—courthouse, Palmer House, Great Central Depot, etc. Introduction by David Lowe. 87pp. 8¼ x 11. 23771-0 Pa. $4.00

SILHOUETTES: A PICTORIAL ARCHIVE OF VARIED ILLUSTRATIONS, edited by Carol Belanger Grafton. Over 600 silhouettes from the 18th to 20th centuries include profiles and full figures of men and women, children, birds and animals, groups and scenes, nature, ships, an alphabet. Dozens of uses for commercial artists and craftspeople. 144pp. 8⅜ x 11¼.
23781-8 Pa. $4.50

ANIMALS: 1,419 COPYRIGHT-FREE ILLUSTRATIONS OF MAMMALS, BIRDS, FISH, INSECTS, ETC., edited by Jim Harter. Clear wood engravings present, in extremely lifelike poses, over 1,000 species of animals. One of the most extensive copyright-free pictorial sourcebooks of its kind. Captions. Index. 284pp. 9 x 12. 23766-4 Pa. $8.95

INDIAN DESIGNS FROM ANCIENT ECUADOR, Frederick W. Shaffer. 282 original designs by pre-Columbian Indians of Ecuador (500-1500 A.D.). Designs include people, mammals, birds, reptiles, fish, plants, heads, geometric designs. Use as is or alter for advertising, textiles, leathercraft, etc. Introduction. 95pp. 8¾ x 11¼. 23764-8 Pa. $3.50

SZIGETI ON THE VIOLIN, Joseph Szigeti. Genial, loosely structured tour by premier violinist, featuring a pleasant mixture of reminiscenes, insights into great music and musicians, innumerable tips for practicing violinists. 385 musical passages. 256pp. 5⅝ x 8¼. 23763-X Pa. $4.00

HISTORY OF BACTERIOLOGY, William Bulloch. The only comprehensive history of bacteriology from the beginnings through the 19th century. Special emphasis is given to biography-Leeuwenhoek, etc. Brief accounts of 350 bacteriologists form a separate section. No clearer, fuller study, suitable to scientists and general readers, has yet been written. 52 illustrations. 448pp. 5⅝ x 8¼.   23761-3 Pa. $6.50

THE COMPLETE NONSENSE OF EDWARD LEAR, Edward Lear. All nonsense limericks, zany alphabets, Owl and Pussycat, songs, nonsense botany, etc., illustrated by Lear. Total of 321pp. 5⅜ x 8½. (Available in U.S. only)   20167-8 Pa. $3.95

INGENIOUS MATHEMATICAL PROBLEMS AND METHODS, Louis A. Graham. Sophisticated material from Graham *Dial*, applied and pure; stresses solution methods. Logic, number theory, networks, inversions, etc. 237pp. 5⅜ x 8½.   20545-2 Pa. $4.50

BEST MATHEMATICAL PUZZLES OF SAM LOYD, edited by Martin Gardner. Bizarre, original, whimsical puzzles by America's greatest puzzler. From fabulously rare *Cyclopedia,* including famous 14-15 puzzles, the Horse of a Different Color, 115 more. Elementary math. 150 illustrations. 167pp. 5⅜ x 8½.   20498-7 Pa. $2.75

THE BASIS OF COMBINATION IN CHESS, J. du Mont. Easy-to-follow, instructive book on elements of combination play, with chapters on each piece and every powerful combination team—two knights, bishop and knight, rook and bishop, etc. 250 diagrams. 218pp. 5⅜ x 8½. (Available in U.S. only)   23644-7 Pa. $3.50

MODERN CHESS STRATEGY, Ludek Pachman. The use of the queen, the active king, exchanges, pawn play, the center, weak squares, etc. Section on rook alone worth price of the book. Stress on the moderns. Often considered the most important book on strategy. 314pp. 5⅜ x 8½.   20290-9 Pa. $4.50

LASKER'S MANUAL OF CHESS, Dr. Emanuel Lasker. Great world champion offers very thorough coverage of all aspects of chess. Combinations, position play, openings, end game, aesthetics of chess, philosophy of struggle, much more. Filled with analyzed games. 390pp. 5⅜ x 8½.   20640-8 Pa. $5.00

500 MASTER GAMES OF CHESS, S. Tartakower, J. du Mont. Vast collection of great chess games from 1798-1938, with much material nowhere else readily available. Fully annotated, arranged by opening for easier study. 664pp. 5⅜ x 8½.   23208-5 Pa. $7.50

A GUIDE TO CHESS ENDINGS, Dr. Max Euwe, David Hooper. One of the finest modern works on chess endings. Thorough analysis of the most frequently encountered endings by former world champion. 331 examples, each with diagram. 248pp. 5⅜ x 8½.   23332-4 Pa. $3.75

THE EARLY WORK OF AUBREY BEARDSLEY, Aubrey Beardsley. 157 plates, 2 in color: *Manon Lescaut, Madame Bovary, Morte Darthur, Salome,* other. Introduction by H. Marillier. 182pp. 8⅛ x 11. 21816-3 Pa. $4.50

THE LATER WORK OF AUBREY BEARDSLEY, Aubrey Beardsley. Exotic masterpieces of full maturity: *Venus and Tannhauser, Lysistrata, Rape of the Lock, Volpone,* Savoy material, etc. 174 plates, 2 in color. 186pp. 8⅛ x 11. 21817-1 Pa. $5.95

THOMAS NAST'S CHRISTMAS DRAWINGS, Thomas Nast. Almost all Christmas drawings by creator of image of Santa Claus as we know it, and one of America's foremost illustrators and political cartoonists. 66 illustrations. 3 illustrations in color on covers. 96pp. 8⅜ x 11¼. 23660-9 Pa. $3.50

THE DORÉ ILLUSTRATIONS FOR DANTE'S DIVINE COMEDY, Gustave Doré. All 135 plates from Inferno, Purgatory, Paradise; fantastic tortures, infernal landscapes, celestial wonders. Each plate with appropriate (translated) verses. 141pp. 9 x 12. 23231-X Pa. $4.50

DORÉ'S ILLUSTRATIONS FOR RABELAIS, Gustave Doré. 252 striking illustrations of *Gargantua and Pantagruel* books by foremost 19th-century illustrator. Including 60 plates, 192 delightful smaller illustrations. 153pp. 9 x 12. 23656-0 Pa. $5.00

LONDON: A PILGRIMAGE, Gustave Doré, Blanchard Jerrold. Squalor, riches, misery, beauty of mid-Victorian metropolis; 55 wonderful plates, 125 other illustrations, full social, cultural text by Jerrold. 191pp. of text. 9⅜ x 12¼. 22306-X Pa. $7.00

THE RIME OF THE ANCIENT MARINER, Gustave Doré, S. T. Coleridge. Dore's finest work, 34 plates capture moods, subtleties of poem. Full text. Introduction by Millicent Rose. 77pp. 9¼ x 12. 22305-1 Pa. $3.50

THE DORE BIBLE ILLUSTRATIONS, Gustave Doré. All wonderful, detailed plates: Adam and Eve, Flood, Babylon, Life of Jesus, etc. Brief King James text with each plate. Introduction by Millicent Rose. 241 plates. 241pp. 9 x 12. 23004-X Pa. $6.00

THE COMPLETE ENGRAVINGS, ETCHINGS AND DRYPOINTS OF ALBRECHT DURER. "Knight, Death and Devil"; "Melencolia," and more—all Dürer's known works in all three media, including 6 works formerly attributed to him. 120 plates. 235pp. 8⅜ x 11¼. 22851-7 Pa. $6.50

MECHANICK EXERCISES ON THE WHOLE ART OF PRINTING, Joseph Moxon. First complete book (1683-4) ever written about typography, a compendium of everything known about printing at the latter part of 17th century. Reprint of 2nd (1962) Oxford Univ. Press edition. 74 illustrations. Total of 550pp. 6⅛ x 9¼. 23617-X Pa. $7.95

THE COMPLETE WOODCUTS OF ALBRECHT DURER, edited by Dr. W. Kurth. 346 in all: "Old Testament," "St. Jerome," "Passion," "Life of Virgin," Apocalypse," many others. Introduction by Campbell Dodgson. 285pp. 8½ x 12¼.   21097-9 Pa. $7.50

DRAWINGS OF ALBRECHT DURER, edited by Heinrich Wolfflin. 81 plates show development from youth to full style. Many favorites; many new. Introduction by Alfred Werner. 96pp. 8⅛ x 11. 22352-3 Pa. $5.00

THE HUMAN FIGURE, Albrecht Dürer. Experiments in various techniques—stereometric, progressive proportional, and others. Also life studies that rank among finest ever done. Complete reprinting of *Dresden Sketchbook*. 170 plates. 355pp. 8⅜ x 11¼.   21042-1 Pa. $7.95

OF THE JUST SHAPING OF LETTERS, Albrecht Dürer. Renaissance artist explains design of Roman majuscules by geometry, also Gothic lower and capitals. Grolier Club edition. 43pp. 7⅞ x 10¾   21306-4 Pa. $3.00

TEN BOOKS ON ARCHITECTURE, Vitruvius. The most important book ever written on architecture. Early Roman aesthetics, technology, classical orders, site selection, all other aspects. Stands behind everything since. Morgan translation. 331pp. 5⅜ x 8½.   20645-9 Pa. $4.50

THE FOUR BOOKS OF ARCHITECTURE, Andrea Palladio. 16th-century classic responsible for Palladian movement and style. Covers classical architectural remains, Renaissance revivals, classical orders, etc. 1738 Ware English edition. Introduction by A. Placzek. 216 plates. 110pp. of text. 9½ x 12¾.   21308-0 Pa. $10.00

HORIZONS, Norman Bel Geddes. Great industrialist stage designer, "father of streamlining," on application of aesthetics to transportation, amusement, architecture, etc. 1932 prophetic account; function, theory, specific projects. 222 illustrations. 312pp. 7⅞ x 10¾.   23514-9 Pa. $6.95

FRANK LLOYD WRIGHT'S FALLINGWATER, Donald Hoffmann. Full, illustrated story of conception and building of Wright's masterwork at Bear Run, Pa. 100 photographs of site, construction, and details of completed structure. 112pp. 9¼ x 10.   23671-4 Pa. $5.50

THE ELEMENTS OF DRAWING, John Ruskin. Timeless classic by great Viltorian; starts with basic ideas, works through more difficult. Many practical exercises. 48 illustrations. Introduction by Lawrence Campbell. 228pp. 5⅜ x 8½.   22730-8 Pa. $3.75

GIST OF ART, John Sloan. Greatest modern American teacher, Art Students League, offers innumerable hints, instructions, guided comments to help you in painting. Not a formal course. 46 illustrations. Introduction by Helen Sloan. 200pp. 5⅜ x 8½.   23435-5 Pa. $4.00

HOLLYWOOD GLAMOUR PORTRAITS, edited by John Kobal. 145 photos capture the stars from 1926-49, the high point in portrait photography. Gable, Harlow, Bogart, Bacall, Hedy Lamarr, Marlene Dietrich, Robert Montgomery, Marlon Brando, Veronica Lake; 94 stars in all. Full background on photographers, technical aspects, much more. Total of 160pp. 8⅜ x 11¼.   23352-9 Pa. $6.00

THE NEW YORK STAGE: FAMOUS PRODUCTIONS IN PHOTO-GRAPHS, edited by Stanley Appelbaum. 148 photographs from Museum of City of New York show 142 plays, 1883-1939. *Peter Pan, The Front Page, Dead End, Our Town,* O'Neill, hundreds of actors and actresses, etc. Full indexes. 154pp. 9½ x 10.   23241-7 Pa. $6.00

DIALOGUES CONCERNING TWO NEW SCIENCES, Galileo Galilei. Encompassing 30 years of experiment and thought, these dialogues deal with geometric demonstrations of fracture of solid bodies, cohesion, leverage, speed of light and sound, pendulums, falling bodies, accelerated motion, etc. 300pp. 5⅜ x 8½.   60099-8 Pa. $4.00

THE GREAT OPERA STARS IN HISTORIC PHOTOGRAPHS, edited by James Camner. 343 portraits from the 1850s to the 1940s: Tamburini, Mario, Caliapin, Jeritza, Melchior, Melba, Patti, Pinza, Schipa, Caruso, Farrar, Steber, Gobbi, and many more—270 performers in all. Index. 199pp. 8⅜ x 11¼.   23575-0 Pa. $7.50

J. S. BACH, Albert Schweitzer. Great full-length study of Bach, life, background to music, music, by foremost modern scholar. Ernest Newman translation. 650 musical examples. Total of 928pp. 5⅜ x 8½. (Available in U.S. only)   21631-4, 21632-2 Pa., Two-vol. set $11.00

COMPLETE PIANO SONATAS, Ludwig van Beethoven. All sonatas in the fine Schenker edition, with fingering, analytical material. One of best modern editions. Total of 615pp. 9 x 12. (Available in U.S. only)
                          23134-8, 23135-6 Pa., Two-vol. set $15.50

KEYBOARD MUSIC, J. S. Bach. Bach-Gesellschaft edition. For harpsichord, piano, other keyboard instruments. English Suites, French Suites, Six Partitas, Goldberg Variations, Two-Part Inventions, Three-Part Sinfonias. 312pp. 8⅛ x 11. (Available in U.S. only)   22360-4 Pa. $6.95

FOUR SYMPHONIES IN FULL SCORE, Franz Schubert. Schubert's four most popular symphonies: No. 4 in C Minor ("Tragic"); No. 5 in B-flat Major; No. 8 in B Minor ("Unfinished"); No. 9 in C Major ("Great"). Breitkopf & Hartel edition. Study score. 261pp. 9⅜ x 12¼.
                          23681-1 Pa. $6.50

THE AUTHENTIC GILBERT & SULLIVAN SONGBOOK, W. S. Gilbert, A. S. Sullivan. Largest selection available; 92 songs, uncut, original keys, in piano rendering approved by Sullivan. Favorites and lesser-known fine numbers. Edited with plot synopses by James Spero. 3 illustrations. 399pp. 9 x 12.   23482-7 Pa. $9.95

PRINCIPLES OF ORCHESTRATION, Nikolay Rimsky-Korsakov. Great classical orchestrator provides fundamentals of tonal resonance, progression of parts, voice and orchestra, tutti effects, much else in major document. 330pp. of musical excerpts. 489pp. 6½ x 9¼. 21266-1 Pa. $7.50

TRISTAN UND ISOLDE, Richard Wagner. Full orchestral score with complete instrumentation. Do not confuse with piano reduction. Commentary by Felix Mottl, great Wagnerian conductor and scholar. Study score. 655pp. 8⅛ x 11. 22915-7 Pa. $13.95

REQUIEM IN FULL SCORE, Giuseppe Verdi. Immensely popular with choral groups and music lovers. Republication of edition published by C. F. Peters, Leipzig, n. d. German frontmaker in English translation. Glossary. Text in Latin. Study score. 204pp. 9⅜ x 12¼.
23682-X Pa. $6.00

COMPLETE CHAMBER MUSIC FOR STRINGS, Felix Mendelssohn. All of Mendelssohn's chamber music: Octet, 2 Quintets, 6 Quartets, and Four Pieces for String Quartet. (Nothing with piano is included). Complete works edition (1874-7). Study score. 283 pp. 9⅜ x 12¼.
23679-X Pa. $7.50

POPULAR SONGS OF NINETEENTH-CENTURY AMERICA, edited by Richard Jackson. 64 most important songs: "Old Oaken Bucket," "Arkansas Traveler," "Yellow Rose of Texas," etc. Authentic original sheet music, full introduction and commentaries. 290pp. 9 x 12. 23270-0 Pa. $7.95

COLLECTED PIANO WORKS, Scott Joplin. Edited by Vera Brodsky Lawrence. Practically all of Joplin's piano works—rags, two-steps, marches, waltzes, etc., 51 works in all. Extensive introduction by Rudi Blesh. Total of 345pp. 9 x 12. 23106-2 Pa. $14.95

BASIC PRINCIPLES OF CLASSICAL BALLET, Agrippina Vaganova. Great Russian theoretician, teacher explains methods for teaching classical ballet; incorporates best from French, Italian, Russian schools. 118 illustrations. 175pp. 5⅜ x 8½. 22036-2 Pa. $2.50

CHINESE CHARACTERS, L. Wieger. Rich analysis of 2300 characters according to traditional systems into primitives. Historical-semantic analysis to phonetics (Classical Mandarin) and radicals. 820pp. 6⅛ x 9¼.
21321-8 Pa. $10.00

EGYPTIAN LANGUAGE: EASY LESSONS IN EGYPTIAN HIERO-GLYPHICS, E. A. Wallis Budge. Foremost Egyptologist offers Egyptian grammar, explanation of hieroglyphics, many reading texts, dictionary of symbols. 246pp. 5 x 7½. (Available in U.S. only)
21394-3 Clothbd. $7.50

AN ETYMOLOGICAL DICTIONARY OF MODERN ENGLISH, Ernest Weekley. Richest, fullest work, by foremost British lexicographer. Detailed word histories. Inexhaustible. Do not confuse this with Concise Etymological Dictionary, which is abridged. Total of 856pp. 6½ x 9¼.
21873-2, 21874-0 Pa., Two-vol. set $12.00

HOUSEHOLD STORIES BY THE BROTHERS GRIMM. All the great Grimm stories: "Rumpelstiltskin," "Snow White," "Hansel and Gretel," etc., with 114 illustrations by Walter Crane. 269pp. 5⅜ x 8½.
21080-4 Pa. $3.50

SLEEPING BEAUTY, illustrated by Arthur Rackham. Perhaps the fullest, most delightful version ever, told by C. S. Evans. Rackham's best work. 49 illustrations. 110pp. 7⅞ x 10¾. 22756-1 Pa. $2.50

AMERICAN FAIRY TALES, L. Frank Baum. Young cowboy lassoes Father Time; dummy in Mr. Floman's department store window comes to life; and 10 other fairy tales. 41 illustrations by N. P. Hall, Harry Kennedy, Ike Morgan, and Ralph Gardner. 209pp. 5⅜ x 8½. 23643-9 Pa. $3.00

THE WONDERFUL WIZARD OF OZ, L. Frank Baum. Facsimile in full color of America's finest children's classic. Introduction by Martin Gardner. 143 illustrations by W. W. Denslow. 267pp. 5⅜ x 8½.
20691-2 Pa. $3.50

THE TALE OF PETER RABBIT, Beatrix Potter. The inimitable Peter's terrifying adventure in Mr. McGregor's garden, with all 27 wonderful, full-color Potter illustrations. 55pp. 4¼ x 5½. (Available in U.S. only)
22827-4 Pa. $1.25

THE STORY OF KING ARTHUR AND HIS KNIGHTS, Howard Pyle. Finest children's version of life of King Arthur. 48 illustrations by Pyle. 131pp. 6⅛ x 9¼. 21445-1 Pa. $4.95

CARUSO'S CARICATURES, Enrico Caruso. Great tenor's remarkable caricatures of self, fellow musicians, composers, others. Toscanini, Puccini, Farrar, etc. Impish, cutting, insightful. 473 illustrations. Preface by M. Sisca. 217pp. 8⅜ x 11¼. 23528-9 Pa. $6.95

PERSONAL NARRATIVE OF A PILGRIMAGE TO ALMADINAH AND MECCAH, Richard Burton. Great travel classic by remarkably colorful personality. Burton, disguised as a Moroccan, visited sacred shrines of Islam, narrowly escaping death. Wonderful observations of Islamic life, customs, personalities. 47 illustrations. Total of 959pp. 5⅜ x 8½.
21217-3, 21218-1 Pa., Two-vol. set $12.00

INCIDENTS OF TRAVEL IN YUCATAN, John L. Stephens. Classic (1843) exploration of jungles of Yucatan, looking for evidences of Maya civilization. Travel adventures, Mexican and Indian culture, etc. Total of 669pp. 5⅜ x 8½. 20926-1, 20927-X Pa., Two-vol. set $7.90

AMERICAN LITERARY AUTOGRAPHS FROM WASHINGTON IRVING TO HENRY JAMES, Herbert Cahoon, et al. Letters, poems, manuscripts of Hawthorne, Thoreau, Twain, Alcott, Whitman, 67 other prominent American authors. Reproductions, full transcripts and commentary. Plus checklist of all American Literary Autographs in The Pierpont Morgan Library. Printed on exceptionally high-quality paper. 136 illustrations. 212pp. 9⅛ x 12¼. 23548-3 Pa. $12.50

UNCLE SILAS, J. Sheridan LeFanu. Victorian Gothic mystery novel, considered by many best of period, even better than Collins or Dickens. Wonderful psychological terror. Introduction by Frederick Shroyer. 436pp. 5⅜ x 8½. 21715-9 Pa. $6.00

JURGEN, James Branch Cabell. The great erotic fantasy of the 1920's that delighted thousands, shocked thousands more. Full final text, Lane edition with 13 plates by Frank Pape. 346pp. 5⅜ x 8½. 23507-6 Pa. $4.50

THE CLAVERINGS, Anthony Trollope. Major novel, chronicling aspects of British Victorian society, personalities. Reprint of Cornhill serialization, 16 plates by M. Edwards; first reprint of full text. Introduction by Norman Donaldson. 412pp. 5⅜ x 8½. 23464-9 Pa. $5.00

KEPT IN THE DARK, Anthony Trollope. Unusual short novel about Victorian morality and abnormal psychology by the great English author. Probably the first American publication. Frontispiece by Sir John Millais. 92pp. 6½ x 9¼. 23609-9 Pa. $2.50

RALPH THE HEIR, Anthony Trollope. Forgotten tale of illegitimacy, inheritance. Master novel of Trollope's later years. Victorian country estates, clubs, Parliament, fox hunting, world of fully realized characters. Reprint of 1871 edition. 12 illustrations by F. A. Faser. 434pp. of text. 5⅜ x 8½. 23642-0 Pa. $5.00

YEKL and THE IMPORTED BRIDEGROOM AND OTHER STORIES OF THE NEW YORK GHETTO, Abraham Cahan. Film *Hester Street* based on *Yekl* (1896). Novel, other stories among first about Jewish immigrants of N.Y.'s East Side. Highly praised by W. D. Howells—Cahan "a new star of realism." New introduction by Bernard G. Richards. 240pp. 5⅜ x 8½. 22427-9 Pa. $3.50

THE HIGH PLACE, James Branch Cabell. Great fantasy writer's enchanting comedy of disenchantment set in 18th-century France. Considered by some critics to be even better than his famous *Jurgen*. 10 illustrations and numerous vignettes by noted fantasy artist Frank C. Pape. 320pp. 5⅜ x 8½. 23670-6 Pa. $4.00

ALICE'S ADVENTURES UNDER GROUND, Lewis Carroll. Facsimile of ms. Carroll gave Alice Liddell in 1864. Different in many ways from final Alice. Handlettered, illustrated by Carroll. Introduction by Martin Gardner. 128pp. 5⅜ x 8½. 21482-6 Pa. $2.50

FAVORITE ANDREW LANG FAIRY TALE BOOKS IN MANY COLORS, Andrew Lang. The four Lang favorites in a boxed set—the complete *Red, Green, Yellow* and *Blue* Fairy Books. 164 stories; 439 illustrations by Lancelot Speed, Henry Ford and G. P. Jacomb Hood. Total of about 1500pp. 5⅜ x 8½. 23407-X Boxed set, Pa. $15.95

AMERICAN ANTIQUE FURNITURE, Edgar G. Miller, Jr. The basic coverage of all American furniture before 1840: chapters per item chronologically cover all types of furniture, with more than 2100 photos. Total of 1106pp. 7⅞ x 10¾.   21599-7, 21600-4 Pa., Two-vol. set $17.90

ILLUSTRATED GUIDE TO SHAKER FURNITURE, Robert Meader. Director, Shaker Museum, Old Chatham, presents up-to-date coverage of all furniture and appurtenances, with much on local styles not available elsewhere. 235 photos. 146pp. 9 x 12.   22819-3 Pa. $6.00

ORIENTAL RUGS, ANTIQUE AND MODERN, Walter A. Hawley. Persia, Turkey, Caucasus, Central Asia, China, other traditions. Best general survey of all aspects: styles and periods, manufacture, uses, symbols and their interpretation, and identification. 96 illustrations, 11 in color. 320pp. 6⅛ x 9¼.   22366-3 Pa. $6.95

CHINESE POTTERY AND PORCELAIN, R. L. Hobson. Detailed descriptions and analyses by former Keeper of the Department of Oriental Antiquities and Ethnography at the British Museum. Covers hundreds of pieces from primitive times to 1915. Still the standard text for most periods. 136 plates, 40 in full color. Total of 750pp. 5⅝ x 8½.
     23253-0 Pa. $10.00

THE WARES OF THE MING DYNASTY, R. L. Hobson. Foremost scholar examines and illustrates many varieties of Ming (1368-1644). Famous blue and white, polychrome, lesser-known styles and shapes. 117 illustrations, 9 full color, of outstanding pieces. Total of 263pp. 6⅛ x 9¼. (Available in U.S. only)   23652-8 Pa. $6.00

Prices subject to change without notice.

Available at your book dealer or write for free catalogue to Dept. GI, Dover Publications, Inc., 31 East Second Street, Mineola, N.Y. 11501. Dover publishes more than 175 books each year on science, elementary and advanced mathematics, biology, music, art, literary history, social sciences and other areas.